LEGAC

Gardner Thompson is a historian of British colonialism and a fellow of the Royal Historical Society. He earned a BA in History from Cambridge University, an MA in East African History and Politics from the School of Oriental and African Studies, University of London, and a PhD on British Colonial Rule in Uganda from London University. Thompson taught History in Uganda, and then in London where he was Head of the History Department and the Academic Vice-Principal at Dulwich College. His other publications include *Governing Uganda: British Colonial Rule and its Legacy* and *African Democracy: Its Origins and Development in Uganda, Kenya and Tanzania*.

'Gardner Thompson throws a cool light on a very hot topic ... This illuminating book is an essential primer on the historical roots of the Israel/Palestine conflict.'
Nicholas Rankin, author of *Churchill's Wizards: The British Genius for Deception*

'An excellent, well-researched and timely book.'
Nur Masalha, author of *Palestine: A Four Thousand Year History*

'An illuminating account of both the emergence of Israel and of British policy during the three decades of the British Mandate in Palestine. It is a sobering and engrossing story of Britain's betrayal of the Palestinians from the Balfour Declaration to the present day.'
Avi Shlaim, author of *The Iron Wall: Israel and the Arab World*

GARDNER THOMPSON

LEGACY
OF
EMPIRE

Britain, Zionism
and the Creation of Israel

SAQI

To Elizabeth and Ed

Saqi Books
26 Westbourne Grove
London W2 5RH
www.saqibooks.com

First published in hardback 2019 by Saqi Books
This paperback edition published 2021

ISBN 978 0 86356 482 6
eISBN 978 0 86356 386 7

A full CIP record for this book is available from the British Library.

Printed and bound by Clays Ltd, Elcograf S.p.A

CONTENTS

MAPS

ILLUSTRATIONS

SELECTIVE TIMELINE

INTRODUCTION

'The two great evils which menace society in general and a society of nations in particular ... are hatred and ignorance.' Chaim Herzog[1]

'Boy shot during Gaza border protest dies'; 'Israeli sniper shot in border violence dies'.[1] The Arab-Israeli conflict continues, if only under 'Other News'. President Trump's 'Deal of the Century', revealed in January 2020, proved no such thing. It had been concocted by his son-in-law, Jared Kushner, who told the Israelis and the Palestinians not to talk to him about history.

A far wider ignorance remains: of the intercommunal antagonism that pre-dated and marked Israel's birth in 1948; of modern political Zionism; of the British Empire's historic responsibility for Palestine and its dismemberment; and – in consequence – of the continuing legacy of British rule for Israel, into the twenty-first century. Confusion persists, too, with few capable of distinguishing anti-Zionism from anti-Semitism. For many activists, passion surpasses knowledge.

◆

The modern state of Israel was proclaimed in May 1948, just three years after the end of the Second World War. Many assume a direct link between the two events, and of course there was one. Jewish survivors of the horror of Nazi-occupied Europe wanted to start new lives 'in the only place likely to welcome them', and Palestine presented itself as just that.[2] Tens of thousands of Jews made their way there. But Israel's origins are properly sought in the period of the First World War, not the Second.

It is sometimes argued that it is impossible to consider the political affairs of the Jewish people before the Second World War, except in the shadow of our knowledge of what occurred then. But the reverse is also true. We cannot properly consider post-war developments without a secure grasp of what went before: above all, the worsening conflict between indigenous Palestinians and the increasingly militant Zionist movement. This eventually led the British – who from 1922 had administered Palestine under a League of Nations mandate – to admit failure: provisionally before the war, in 1937; formally after it, in 1947.

It was the British who in 1917 committed themselves, owing to wartime exigency, to the Zionist project. In the 1920s and 1930s, despite evidence, argument and warnings, they oversaw the colonisation of Arab Palestine by Jewish immigrants: a trickle in the 1920s, a flood in the 1930s. There arose, as a result of Britain's policy, outright hostility between the peoples, which its administration could not reverse. The British abdicated in 1947 – but the conflict was inherited by Israel, after the United Nations awarded 55 per cent of the land of Palestine to a Jewish state in 1947 (to this extent fulfilling the Zionist dream). At heart it is this dispute that continues.

This is not a story of the inevitable. The British might not have done what they did in 1917 and the 1920s, especially under a prime minister other than David Lloyd George. A solution to the Jewish Question – how should Jews respond to anti-Semitism generally, though especially in Poland and Russia? – might have been found in a continuing welcome for Jewish refugees in Britain and the USA, for example, rather than in the colonisation of an Arab territory of the former Ottoman Empire in the Middle East. The initial British endorsement of Zionism was not inevitable; but its consequences flowed with 'a certainty like fate'.[3]

◆

Britain's critical role began with the Balfour Declaration. In November 1917, the British government of Lloyd George pledged to 'facilitate' the establishment in Palestine of a 'national home for the Jewish people', while stressing that 'nothing shall be done' to prejudice the rights of existing communities living there. In making these two contradictory promises, the Declaration – enshrined in a League of Nations mandate in 1922 – committed the British administration to a policy that was seen to fail before the Second World War and led to the ignominy of abdication shortly after it.

Balfour's Declaration was not the pure expression of sympathy with the aspirations of persecuted Jews that it is still widely held to have been. Far from it. In fact, the only Jewish member of the British Cabinet, Edwin Montagu, condemned his government's attitude to Palestine and Zionism in 1917 as anti-Semitic. The fantastic assumption that lay behind this commitment to Zionism – that 'world Jewry' was an agency so powerful that it could not be ignored – was itself indicative of an anti-Semitism well established in Central Europe. And this was the same Arthur Balfour who, as Prime Minister, had introduced the Aliens Act in 1905: primarily to prevent Jews who were fleeing persecution in Eastern Europe from entering Britain.

In the period 1917–1922, sympathy among British decision-makers for the persecuted Jews of Central and Eastern Europe was constrained within geographical limits. They conceded that the Jews had a problem, but they insisted that the location for its solution lay ... somewhere else. Zionists, who helped to formulate the Declaration in 1917, conveniently insisted that faraway Palestine should be the location for a Jewish National Home – even though its resident population was overwhelmingly Arab and Muslim (or, as the Declaration put it, 'non-Jewish') and known to be anti-Zionist (though not anti-Semitic). The Balfour Declaration was a landmark expression of nimbyism. Though Palestine, for most Jews, remained a far less attractive prospect than Britain or America, the Declaration became a template for other countries to adopt. As we shall see later, they too – including, crucially, the USA from 1924 – welcomed Zionism as an alternative to keeping their own doors open for any Jews fleeing persecution. They could go to Palestine instead. This approach did something to protect Britain and other states from politically unpopular Jewish immigration; it did nothing to recognise the rights of Palestinians in their homeland.

British Prime Minister from 1908–1916 Herbert Asquith had scant interest in Palestine, and none in Zionism. If Palestine was of little or no strategic value, the case for adopting Zionism was, from the British imperial point of view, thin indeed. However, Lloyd George made his commitments, not only to Palestine but also to Zionism, many years before the rise to power in Germany of Adolf Hitler and the Nazis. There was already a Jewish Question but there were, at that time, other answers to the worsening plight of Jews in Central and Eastern Europe. And Zionists conceded that a Jewish national home in Palestine could not accommodate all the world's Jews. For the time being, the USA, the choice of so many Jewish emigrants from Europe around the turn of the century, remained open.

Especially remarkable is the uncharacteristic ineptitude of decision-makers in the British government in the aftermath of the First World War: in respect to Palestine (their knowledge of which was largely biblical), and in respect to Zionism, too (their knowledge of which was minimal). Policy initiatives were not thought through. In some respects, the imperial attitude to Palestine was unexceptional. Here, as for other overseas British possessions at the time, it was claimed that colonies (repackaged now as mandates) benefited from imperial governance; that strategic purposes further justified them; that they were valuable as potential markets and sources of raw materials; that they must be developed as far as was practicable (to keep down metropolitan costs); that settlers, as in Kenya and Southern Rhodesia, would contribute, by making better use of land than natives could; and, lastly, that there was plenty of time available in which to bestow the blessings of Western civilisation. For the most part, previous British imperial decision-making along such lines had been shrewd and realistic: pragmatic, even at times reluctant. And not all colonialism caused trauma among the colonised.

But there was caprice in Lloyd George's adoption of Zionism, along with a dogged refusal to grasp that it could not work. Zionists were a tiny minority among the world's Jews before the period of the First World War. Zionism – an ideology and movement committed to the colonisation of Palestine – was only one, eccentric, answer to the Jewish Question of the late nineteenth century. In sponsoring the Zionist project for its own ends, Lloyd George's British imperial government adopted a unique, hybrid colonialism in Palestine: they 'administered', while Jewish immigrants 'settled'. They were thus responsible for creating, as prophesied, a problem in Palestine that before long grew to be beyond their capacity to solve.

◆

By the late 1930s, 'Israel' was not only conceptualised but already had an embryonic existence. The events of the following decade are horribly familiar. Less widely known is the fact that the Peel Commission's proposal in 1937 of a 'two-state solution' – *before* the Second World War and the genocide – closely foreshadowed that of the United Nations in 1947, which led to the birth of Israel the following year.

The legacy of thirty years of controversy and crisis in mandated Palestine was to be ineradicable. The new Israel was – and remains – scarred by an inter-communal conflict provoked by Zionist colonisation fostered by the British during an ill-judged administration of Palestine tied to the Balfour Declaration. The two-state solution advocated in response, first by the British and later by the UN, has so far produced neither two states nor a solution.

◆

The Balfour Declaration and its consequences continue to be widely seen in a far rosier light than they merit. The centenary of the issuing of the Declaration was marked in July 2017 by a debate in the British House of Lords in which more than two dozen members chose to speak.[4] The prevailing tone (there was a discordant minority of just two or three) was one of uncritical pride, and prejudice. There were many expressions of loyalty to, and praise of, Israel. There was an understated anti-Arab sentiment (though for the most part the Palestinians' experience was ignored). There was a good sprinkling of muddled thinking, too. The following extracts, each from a different contributor, give a representative indication of what was said.

Pride and prejudice: 'Let us choose this centenary to rededicate ourselves to the aspiration of this document.' 'Britain can rightly be proud of the Balfour Declaration, which well deserves a happy and dignified celebration of its 100th anniversary.' 'It is important that we, as Britons, feel immense pride in the Balfour Declaration and its consequences.' 'It was a hopelessly optimistic idea, and, at the time, little thought was given to how one group, the Jews, were supposed to protect the rights of another group, the Arabs, who were immediately trying to kill them off.'

Muddle: 'We are inspired by the pioneering spirit of those who wrote those sixty-seven words into history and in doing so saved the lives of millions.' 'We regret that Israel was not established ten years earlier, which would have largely prevented the Holocaust.' 'The Balfour Declaration ... was a momentous reversal of imperialism.' 'There had to be somewhere in the world where Jews would always be welcome and feel safe.' (Though another lord observed that 'suicide bombings, knifings and missiles are daily occurrences for the citizens of Israel who live in a constant state of siege'.)

One speaker asked – albeit a century after its attempted implementation began – 'How does she [the Minister Chair] think that the second part of the Balfour Declaration can be brought about, so that the rights of both Jewish and non-Jewish communities are on a truly equal footing?'

An all-but solitary critic stated: 'The Balfour Declaration has created endless misery for generations of Palestinians ... The Declaration and its aftermath are among the most shameful in our history.'

In her summing up, the Minister, Baroness Goldie, unconvincingly described what she had heard as 'powerful, eloquent, informed and helpful'.

◆

The level of ignorance, partiality and confusion revealed in the Lords debate of 2017 is disturbing as well as astonishing. As long as members of the British political establishment do not know or understand the turbulent history of Palestine (and Britain's leading role in it) before the Second World War – yet speak and act as if they do – they remain ill-equipped to pursue Arab-Israeli reconciliation now.

There could be no more eloquent illustration than this lop-sided debate of the need for a fresh, evidence-based corrective review of what happened when the British were responsible for Palestine.

EUROPE AND THE EASTERN MEDITERRANEAN IN 1914

1

THE BIRTH AND
EMERGENCE OF ZIONISM,
1897–1914

'Will those who are dispossessed remain silent and accept what is being done to them?' Yitzhak Epstein[1]

The beginning

Modern political Zionism was born in Basel. On 29 August 1897, around two hundred people gathered to discuss the predicament of the Jews in Europe. They had intended to meet in Munich, but the Jewish community there, fearing an anti-Semitic reaction, did not welcome them. The congress opened instead across the border in Switzerland. Proceedings began with a celebratory prayer: 'Blessed art thou, O Lord our God, King of the Universe, who has kept us alive and brought us to witness this day.' The assembly agreed that the oppressed Jews of Europe needed a homeland of their own. But at least one prominent contemporary Jewish intellectual wondered if this occasion might represent the last sigh of a dying people.[2]

The man behind the meeting was Theodor Herzl, a thirty-seven-year-old, Hungarian-born playwright and journalist. Eighteen months earlier, a booklet of his had been published by a Viennese bookseller. It was called *Judenstaat* ('The Jewish State'). Herzl wrote: 'Let sovereignty be granted us over a portion of the globe large enough to satisfy the rightful requirements of a nation.' This, he argued, was the solution to

Theodor Herzl (1860–1904)
Founder of modern political Zionism.

the Jewish Question, 'after eighteen centuries of Jewish suffering'.[3] There
was no alternative: this was a matter, he later wrote in his diary, 'which
only blockheads cannot find crystal clear'.[4] But the book's reception was
not encouraging. Herzl had expected to be ridiculed as a mad visionary,
and his expectations were fulfilled. The Basel Programme did not elicit
widespread approval among the Jews of Europe. Zionism did not have a
promising start.[5]

How different it looks in retrospect. These two somewhat obscure
events – in Vienna and in Basel – marked the emergence of modern
Zionism: unwavering ideological and practical commitment to the
creation, for the Jews, of a homeland of their own. In his publication
and at his congress, and by his exceptionally energetic advocacy
thereafter, Herzl shaped and inspired an extraordinary political
movement which not only endured but flourished.[6] In time, Zionism
was to have a profound impact on world history in the twentieth
century and beyond.

In this light, the Basel Programme deserves to be as widely known as the Balfour Declaration from twenty years later.[7] Here is the full text:

The aim of Zionism is to create for the Jewish people a home in Palestine secured by public law.

The Congress contemplates the following means to the attainment of this end:

1. The promotion, on suitable lines, of the colonisation of Palestine by Jewish agricultural and industrial workers
2. The organisation and binding together of the whole of Jewry by means of appropriate institutions, local and international in accordance with the laws of each country
3. The strengthening and fostering of Jewish national sentiment and consciousness
4. Preparatory steps towards obtaining government consent, where necessary, to the attainment of the aim of Zionism.

The Jewish Question

Zionism was one late-nineteenth century response, among many, to the Jewish Question in Europe.[8] Wherever Jews lived in perceptible numbers, Herzl wrote, 'they are more or less persecuted', and 'the nations in whose midst Jews live are all either covertly or openly anti-Semitic'. Hence the Jewish Question:

Are we to get out now, and where to; or may we yet remain, and [for] how long?[9]

Herzl's generalisation – that throughout Europe Jewish lives were becoming 'daily more intolerable' – blurred, deliberately, significant differences of Jewish experience across the continent. Jews in Western, even Central, Europe had benefited from the legacy of the Enlightenment and the French Revolution. Emancipated now, they might assume that they were secure, in the modern, relatively liberal, state. In Eastern Europe, however, the situation was quite different. Jewish communities, especially in Russia, suffered acute hardship. What was to become of them?

In two senses, this was the largest question of all. First, Jews in Russia suffered increasingly from punitive imperial edicts and, especially following the assassination in 1881 of Tsar Alexander II, violent pogroms. Second, there were far more Jews in Russia than anywhere else – that is, in the Pale of Settlement, designated by Catherine the Great of Russia, after the partitions of Poland, as a vast area where Jews were permitted to live. It included the cities of Warsaw, Minsk and Kiev and much of today's Latvia, Lithuania, Belarus, Poland and Ukraine.

It is estimated that, towards the end of the nineteenth century, nearly 7 million of the 11 million-or-so Jews in the world lived in Eastern Europe, with only 2 million elsewhere on the continent.[10] For the most part, Russian Jews stayed and lived wherever they were born, through force of inertia or fear of change. Some, however, saw emigration as a solution to their own 'Jewish Question'; and some of these went to Palestine. By 1885, Hovevei Zion (Lovers of Zion) societies in Russia had settled between two and three thousand emigrants there. In the Russian context – and for Palestine at this time, too – these were tiny numbers; but Hovevei Zion was a forerunner of the modern Zionist movement.

For Jewish observers such as Herzl, the case of Russian Jews was exemplary rather than exceptional: their experience was different from that of the Jews of Western Europe in degree only. European Jewry as a whole was deemed to have reached a critical point. To the West there was more to this crisis than the prevalence and occasional intensity of anti-Semitism – though it was the Dreyfus Affair which convinced Herzl, already himself a victim of anti-Semitism in Vienna, that Jews even in France would never be fully free.[11] There were, also, existential 'Jewish questions', two in particular. The first concerned identity: in the wake of major shifts within Judaism itself, what did it mean, now, to be a Jew? The second was about assimilation: was it possible; was it even desirable?

In an increasingly secular age, the faith itself was threatened. The Jewish Reform Movement and the *Haskalah* (Jewish Enlightenment) were responses, within Judaism, to 'the sad truth ... that it had become meaningless for many people'.[12] In the context of post-Enlightenment Europe there could be only one outcome in the clash between secularism on the one hand, and on the other hidebound religion-based prohibitions and customs dating from the distant past. The Jewish Reform Movement brought radical changes to Judaism, shedding much of its inherited religious content. The movement re-defined the *religion* of the Jews as an *ethical* creed. Henceforth it was the Jews' mission to steer all mankind towards justice and righteousness. At the same time, *Haskalah* led many Jews away from Judaism. While it saw a revival of Hebrew literature, it advocated secular education for personal fulfilment. This Jewish adaptation of the Enlightenment, arising in the age of Kant and Hegel, Goethe and Beethoven, was an exercise in rationalism. These two movements within Judaism overlapped, in both content and significance. Alongside the external force of anti-Semitism, they contributed to the assimilation of innumerable Jews into gentile society.

Notwithstanding these internal shifts towards secularism, in the latter half of the nineteenth century the contextual questions for Europe's Jews were real and urgent. What did they have to do to be fully accepted into gentile societies? If Jews adopted external conformity, 'accepting' at least the public aspects of the dominant gentile culture (or if they went further, and steeped themselves in it), would gentile society in turn 'accept' these erstwhile strangers? Would they be safe from discrimination and persecution? Would Jews be allowed *to remain Jewish* – in culture and community, if not in religious commitment? In short what, if any, was the price for being left alone in peace?

For some, the answer lay in intermarriage and/or conversion. The 'melting-pot' metaphor was first adopted in late-nineteenth-century

America, to which a great number of Jews, among other millions, migrated from Europe. For many in the USA, the full melting into homogeneity – the shedding of all sense of separate identity, and the reduction in due course of physical traces of distinct ethnicity – was to follow, then and later, through intermarriage. Conversion was comparably significant in its implications for Jewry and Judaism. There are no reliable statistics, but it is recognised that large numbers of Jews remaining in Europe converted to Christianity, from early in the nineteenth century. They may have been predominantly from among the intellectual elite and social establishment, but cases were numerous in Russia as well as in England and in Germany. In some communities, almost all the leading families converted; where parents hesitated, they had their children baptised.

Karl Marx's father provides an interesting example of recourse to conversion. Heinrich Marx had benefited from the emancipation of the Jews after the French entered the Rhineland in 1792. He was able to study law and to qualify as an attorney. But when the Prussians replaced the French in 1814, they prevented him from practising. So he chose to be baptised (opting, it is said, for Lutheranism rather than Roman Catholicism on the grounds that it required less attendance at church). Shortly afterwards, Karl, born in 1818, was duly baptised, not circumcised – 'and brought up with nothing of an authentically Jewish nature being taught to him'. David Vital, author and former member of the Israeli government, concludes that Heinrich's case illustrates 'ambition in its gross form'.[13] But this seems a harsh and unsympathetic judgement on a man who, having little respect for religion of any kind, merely wanted the best for himself and his family. His story paints a persuasive picture of a faith in crisis.

In sum, alongside the external pressure of ubiquitous anti-Semitism in all its forms, there was an internal stimulus, too, in what was happening to the religion itself. In the event, countless Jews across Europe chose some kind of assimilation positively, to pursue their own personal wishes and ambitions. It has been said of Jews even in 1930s Germany that 'for a majority, their Judaism was an innocent hobby that bordered and shaped their identity'.[14] Meanwhile, countless others sought to assimilate for more negative reasons: to merge, to shed what made them recognisable and vulnerable as strangers and become invisible.

Zionism and assimilation

But assimilation was anathema to Zionists. They passionately rejected assimilation in all its forms, from the mild to the extreme. For them, the aspiration to be accepted by gentile society was unrealistic; a readiness to melt into it was both degrading for the individual and unacceptable to the community. Their answer to the Jewish Question was a homeland which the Jews could migrate to, settle, and call their own.

Zionists believed that assimilation could never be relied upon. Their starting point was a conviction that anti-Semitism would always exist and would always present a threat. So, for example, in reaction to the Russian pogroms of 1881, Leo Pinsker, founder of Hovevei Zion, gloomily observed that anti-Semitism was no mere hangover from the medieval past, but a thoroughly modern phenomenon. It was thus a delusion to hope for better days in Russia, or wherever else Jews were under serious attack. There was only one workable solution, he wrote, fifteen years before Herzl's pamphlet was published: the Jews must find a country of their own. For Pinsker, writing in Odessa in the midst of pogroms, the priority was to remove Jews from a nightmare that was not only immediate but recurring and inevitable.[15] While the majority of Jews in Western Europe at this time might be inclined towards assimilation, for Jews in Eastern Europe assimilation did not appear to be an option.

Herzl, albeit from a Central/Western European perspective, was as trenchant a critic as Pinsker of assimilation, attacking it as delusory. In his introduction to *The Jewish State*, he wrote: 'We have honestly endeavoured everywhere to merge ourselves in the social life of surrounding communities' but 'we are not permitted to do so... In vain are we loyal patriots... In countries where we have lived for centuries, we are still cried down as strangers.' Jews did not ask for much: 'If we could only be left in peace,' he added despairingly. But there was no escape from anti-Semitism. 'We naturally move to those places where we are not persecuted, and there our presence produces persecution. This is the case in every country and will remain so.'[16]

For Chaim Weizmann too, seeking to assimilate was futile. He argued that the emancipated and assimilated Jew 'is felt by the outside world still to be something different, still an alien'. In fact, he went on, 'the phenomena of assimilation and of anti-Semitism go on side by side – and the position of the emancipated Jew, though he does not realise it himself, is even more tragic than that of his oppressed brother'.[17] Zionists did not deny the possibility of assimilation itself, for some Jews in some places and at some times. The evidence was too strong to the contrary, especially among better-educated and more prosperous Jews in Western Europe. Rather, Zionists stressed that, whatever they did to be accepted, and however apparently complete the mutual acceptance, Jews continued to be perceived as aliens and therefore to be at risk. So assimilation was possible; but it could not be the answer to the Jewish Question.

Second, Zionists believed that assimilation was degrading for the individual. Their opposition to it was both reasoned and passionate. Assimilation required Jews to abandon their heritage and identity. The French Revolution had brought emancipation, but for Jews this could be a trap. To be sure, there was the promise of freedom and equality for all – but how were Jews to safeguard their distinct and separate existence? Weizmann posed the question in 1918: 'The Jew sets the modern world the problem of finding for him a place in its social structure which shall enable him to live as a human being *without demanding that he cease to be a Jew*'.[18]

When Weizmann first left Russia and came across assimilated German Jews, he described their condition as 'demeaning, degrading, humiliating'. Weizmann preferred the world he had left, with all its persecution and poverty. Though confined within ghettoes, or the Pale,

Jews had been left alone, and so could continue to be Jewish. In July 1904, Weizmann wrote: 'There arises in me a terrible hatred towards "Jews" who turn away from Jewry. I perceive them as animals, unworthy of the name *homo sapiens.*' These chilling words were written to his wife Vera, who was herself an object of Weizmann's uncompromising ambition: 'I always wanted ... to cleanse you, my joy, of all assimilation, to lead you into the movement.'[19]

Third, Zionists believed that assimilation was disastrous for the Jews as a people. The individual might choose assimilation as a free agent, but for preservers of the community this was quite unacceptable. There was something ruthless in this standpoint. In their attitude to, for example, full assimilation through intermarriage and miscegenation, Zionists did not acknowledge the right of individual Jews, in all their diversity, to do whatever they wanted; instead, they stressed that assimilation (insofar as it was possible) led to the eclipse of the community. From this perspective, the grovelling required of Jews to be accepted in gentile society was more than repulsive: it amounted to a kind of treason. A degree of ruthlessness was to be seen, also, in the great controversy over whether to accept the British government's offer in 1903 of a refuge in East Africa for Russian Jewish victims of renewed pogroms. In rejecting the offer, the Zionist leadership showed that it was committed more to the cause of Jewry/Judaism as a whole than to the immediate rescue of individual, persecuted, Jews.

The fate of Jewry hung in the balance. In a period of increasingly assertive secular nationalisms, a number of Jews saw themselves as a people with no space and nowhere to go. This is colourfully recalled by the Israeli novelist and academic Amos Oz, describing his mid-1940s childhood in Jerusalem. 'In those days all the Poles were drunk on Polishness, the Ukrainians were drunk on Ukrainianness, not to mention the Germans, the Czechs, all of them, even the Slovaks, the Lithuanians and the Latvians: and there was no place for us in that carnival... Small wonder that we too wanted to be a nation, like the rest of them.'[20] Zionists could not be indifferent towards Jews who chose to be integrated into gentile society. Here they would lose their identity as Jews, and thereby undermine Jewry as a whole. Ari Shavit offers another sympathetic insight into the Jews' predicament and the uncompromising logic of the Zionist response. At stake, he writes, was nothing less than survival. In the hundred years before 1897, 'God drifted away and the ghetto walls collapsed. Secularisation and emancipation ... eroded the old formula of Jewish *survival*. There was nothing to maintain the Jewish people as a people living among others... If it was to *survive*, the Jewish people had to be transformed from a people of the Diaspora to a people of sovereignty.'[21]

A homeland: Palestine

It took a while before Palestine was adopted as the sole location for a Jewish national home. It is perhaps an indication of the perceived urgency of the situation that Herzl did not begin by insisting on Palestine. As noted above he specified no place, writing in *The Jewish State*: 'Let the sovereignty be granted us over a portion of the globe large enough to satisfy the rightful requirements of a nation.'

This concise appeal was loaded with significance. Let 'sovereignty' be granted: this was to be more than a homeland, it was to be an independent state. Yet sovereignty must be 'granted' and recognised by one or more contemporary Great Power. Therefore, focused diplomacy would have to be undertaken, alongside emigration and settlement. In seeking recognition of 'the rightful requirements of a nation', Herzl was presenting the Jews no longer as a religious community but as a nation comparable with other, also emergent, nations of his time.[22] He argued that, as in other cases, nationhood and homeland were inseparable. There was some ambiguity regarding 'large enough'. Was the homeland to accommodate *all* Jews? Probably not. Rather, it had to be large *enough* to allow a regenerated Jewish community to emerge. This – undiluted, unhindered and unthreatened – would foster Jewishness and inspire Jews throughout the diaspora.

Some years elapsed before the Zionist movement finally ruled out any alternative to Palestine. 'Shall we choose Palestine or Argentina?', Herzl was asking in 1896. And, later in his celebrated pamphlet, he again acknowledged that for him 'the Jewish state is conceived as a peculiarly modern structure *on unspecified territory*'.[23]

Approached by Herzl at the turn of the twentieth century, the British government responded with two alternatives to Palestine. The first was close to the Holy Land: El Arish, in Sinai. This, however, was effectively withdrawn when the British authorities in Egypt opposed it. They were worried that a Jewish colony in the region would have to draw off too much Nile water for irrigation. Then, in late August 1903, Herzl announced to the 600 delegates of the Sixth World Zionist Congress meeting in Basel a second British offer: of part of their recently acquired colonial territory in East Africa. To his dismay, Herzl's recommendation that the movement accept this offer provoked Zionism's gravest internal discord to date.

Zionists of Herzl's generation regarded Jews as the latter-day successors of an ancient people who, according to the Hebrew Bible, were descended from a common ancestor, Jacob (renamed 'Israel': Genesis 32: 28). With God's blessing they had settled in the land of Canaan, roughly 'Palestine', between the Eastern Mediterranean shore and the river Jordan. Herzl was certainly not questioning Palestine as the preferred long-term goal. Rather, he was arguing that a refuge had to be found at once for victims of anti-Semitism in Russia. The Kishinev pogrom of April that year had left around fifty dead, hundreds injured and Jewish property looted or destroyed. Nonetheless, his proposal caused uproar and deep division. Herzl himself was denounced as a traitor – by delegates from Russia. In the event, however, it was again British rather than Jewish resistance that killed off the notional scheme. Both a former high commissioner for Uganda and the first white settlers in Kenya expressed opposition that proved decisive.

Even after the formal rejection of the East Africa scheme, by the Seventh Zionist Congress in 1905, there remained within the movement some eminent figures who did not recognise any essential link between

Zionism and Palestine. Israel Zangwill, teacher, writer and playwright, was one. Born in London in 1864 of Russian Jewish immigrant parents, and subsequently a graduate of London University, he supported the idea of a national home in Palestine until he learned that, far from being a land without a people, Palestine had a sizeable indigenous population. He favoured 'territorialism', the project for repopulating Jews in a territory better suited to the purpose and without the prospect of local resistance. His preference was for the United States. America, he wrote, 'has ample room for all the six millions of the Pale; any one of her fifty states could absorb them'; and the American Constitution 'would practically guarantee them against future persecution.'[24]

Zangwill defies simple categorisation as a Zionist. His inferences from the persecution of Jews in Russia at that time were given literary form in his play *The Melting Pot*, first staged in 1908. The central character, David, who loses all his family in the Kishinev pogrom, chooses to emigrate not to Palestine but to America. He rejects exclusiveness and celebrates assimilation.

Meanwhile, in London in 1905, Zangwill and some Anglo-Jewish friends had founded the Jewish Territorial Organisation (JTO). Denying the by-now official Zionist line – that the vital interests of the Jewish people lay in Palestine – they continued to look at possibilities elsewhere. It was thought sensible to search, once more, for land within the British Empire. So, regions of Australia and Canada were considered (as well as locations as diverse as Cyrenaica, Mesopotamia and even Angola). But nothing came of any of these enquiries. Foreshadowing a commonplace of later times, no country was disposed to offer any of its own territory for a Jewish homeland. The JTO remained in existence until 1925, a year before Zangwill's death. In the previous year, 1924, the USA introduced such strict controls over immigration that his vision of America as a realistic alternative to the creation of a Jewish national home in Palestine – hitherto so attractive to so many Jews leaving Europe – was effectively destroyed.

Long before Weizmann wrote his *What is Zionism?* in 1918, the matter was closed. Zionists agreed that nowhere but Palestine offered the Jews an acceptable location for a homeland. Weizmann put the case so clearly and strongly in this pamphlet that it is worth quoting at some length.

> As to the land that is to be the Jewish land, there can be no question. Palestine alone, of all the countries in which the Jew has set foot throughout his long history, has an abiding place in his national tradition... The memory and the hope of Palestine have been bound up with the national consciousness of the Jewish people through all the centuries of exile and have been among the most powerful forces making for the preservation of Jewry and Judaism. The task of Zionism, then, is to create a home for the Jewish people in Palestine, to make it possible for large numbers of Jews to settle there and live under conditions in which they can produce a type of life corresponding to the character and ideals of the Jewish people.

This is Zionism at a glance. Most of the main themes are encapsulated here: Palestine; the nation; the exile; Jewry and Judaism; settlement; regeneration. Meanwhile, the sickness and possible collapse of the Ottoman Empire was widely discussed by the Great Powers of Europe. And 'one sign of disintegration was that the Zionists took an interest in Palestine'.[25] Moses Hess, mid-century advocate of a Jewish state in Palestine, contemplated bribery as a tool, asking: 'What European power would oppose a plan for the Jews ... to buy back their ancient fatherland? Who would object if they flung a handful of gold to decrepit old Turkey and said, "Give us back our old home and use this money to consolidate the other parts of your tottering old empire"?'[26]

Many Zionisms

Zionism was, for Jews of turn-of-the-century Europe, a broad church. Emigration – or 'return' – to Palestine, or *Eretz Yisrael* (The Land of Israel), would answer the Jewish Question, once and for all time. This would be a homeland of their own, where Jews would be free from the anti-Semitism that would forever haunt all attempts at assimilation; where they would be free, too, to nurture their distinctive culture, and flourish as never before as a people. On so much, Zionists agreed. But there was plenty of scope for disagreement too, regarding not only the means of achieving this goal but also the character of the newly established Jewish state itself. We will look shortly at the views, alongside Herzl's, of Asher Ginsberg (Ahad Ha'am), and Yitzhak Epstein.

First, in order better to understand Zionism as intellectual history, rather than as a practical project of colonisation, we turn to Arthur Hertzberg. Rabbi, scholar, and editor of the 1959 classic *The Zionist Idea*, Hertzberg observes, perhaps surprisingly, that 'from the Jewish perspective, messianism, and not nationalism, is the primary element in Zionism'; that 'Zionism is Jewish messianism in process of realising itself through this-worldly means'; and that 'the great virtue of this estimate of Zionism is that it seems to succeed in providing the modern movement with a long history of which it is the heir'.[27]

The inherited view of Jewish destiny was (to approximate) that of a religious community, chosen by God, looking towards His grace for redemption, and awaiting the Messiah who would gather the Jews in the Holy Land and usher in an era of peace in God's Kingdom. As Hertzberg puts it, 'the Jew conceived of himself as part of a holy community, a divine priesthood and the elected of God, in an attitude of waiting for the Messiah'.[28] But in the nineteenth century this perception came to be challenged; the era of Emancipation brought a radical break. Both the ghetto and inherited tradition evaporated. It was against this background that Zionists adapted the religious Jewish narrative to one they presented as something secular.

For Zionists, the Jews were a nation, bound by history and experience, culture and principle; and a nation in pursuit of self-determination and regeneration. In defiance of general and long-established religious assumptions within Judaism, their Jewish Kingdom was to be a kingdom of *this* world: man-made, and as soon as possible. Convinced of the rightness of their cause, Jews were now to step out of the past, abandon the defensiveness of an inward-turning spirituality, and adopt a radical, new, modern role among the (other) nations of the world. In short, Zionists sought a redefinition of Jewish identity and purpose. Theirs was a unique mission: to re-establish themselves in their historic homeland, Palestine; bring civilisation to the Middle East, the crossroads of continents; and act as a moral beacon for the world. This was Zionism as new messianism: one distinctive and extraordinary product of profound mid-nineteenth-century Jewish soul-searching.

However, stresses were concealed in this composite picture of Zionism. From the early days, there was tension between evolutionary and revolutionary ingredients (and perhaps personal temperaments). This is well illustrated by contrasting the positions of Herzl and of the essayist and activist Ahad Ha'am.

The two men were contemporaries – the one born in Hungary in 1860, the other near Kiev in 1856 – who after the First Zionist Congress of 1897 became locked in debate about the proper purposes of Zionism. Herzl's views, expressed at that meeting and in his publication of the previous year, have been rehearsed above. He may be seen as representing Political Zionism – optimistic and revolutionary. He preached, like Leo Pinsker before him, 'the total evacuation of the land of the gentiles'. This required intervention not from God but from a sympathetic gentile Great Power. This was messianism, in the sense that Herzl proclaimed 'the *historical inevitability* of a Jewish state in a world of peaceful nations'.[29]

If Herzl's focus was the Jews, by contrast Ahad Ha'am's was Judaism. He represented Spiritual (or Cultural) Zionism; and his approach was cautious and evolutionary. For Zionists like Ahad Ha'am, the 'chosen-ness' of the Jews lay in the uniqueness of their values and moral authority. Unlike Herzl, he did not detect any historical inevitability; rather defensively, he advocated careful, step-by-step, colonisation in Palestine, and he was unenthusiastic towards statehood. Being cautious, he was wary of that core political aspiration. He warned that it would be both wrong and dangerous for incoming Jewish settlers to treat the

Arabs with contempt. He warned, too, that even a total concentration of Jewry in Palestine (to which he was opposed) could not answer the Jewish Question. He feared that the geographical position of Palestine, and its global religious importance, would deny it for ever the status of a normal, small state; it would always be a football in the game of interests played by the others. He believed that only a small-scale community, of no political importance, could hope to be left alone by the Great Powers of the world.

Ahad Ha'am's vision was in fact quite different from Herzl's. He advocated settlement, not by as many Jews as possible but by a select group. He looked forward not so much to a Jewish state as to a time when a Jewish community in Palestine would represent a moral priesthood for all mankind. For him, as for Herzl, the Jews were a nation; but they were quite unlike all other nations. He rejected, as impracticable, 'the return' or the 'ingathering' of the Jewish people as a whole to Palestine. Nor did Ahad Ha'am trust gentiles to assist, as Herzl did: having grown up in a ghetto, he regarded the surrounding world as the enemy.

Here were two quite distinct visions, among many. Each was close to the heart of the Zionist movement. Such disagreements hint at the multi-layered complexity of an emergent ideology. They were of no interest and little significance for the Palestinians among whom early Zionists settled. But it was of great significance that a trenchant form of Herzl's Zionism – rather than Ahad Ha'am's – eventually triumphed. Most immigrants of the second *aliyah* (wave of immigration) adhered to Herzl's line.[30] Thereafter, Zionism in Palestine was clearly a political, not a spiritual, movement.

Rabbi and scholar Yitzhak Epstein offered a third vision. He favoured the Zionist project; but he raised so many objections, albeit ethical and practical rather than spiritual or religious, that he might have been criticising from the outside rather than from within. His misgivings regarding the project were humane. He chose, strikingly, to focus the attention of the Seventh Zionist Congress in 1905 on the impact of Zionist colonisation on the colonised.[31]

He began his address: 'Among the difficult issues regarding the rebirth of our people in its homeland, one issue outweighs them all: our relations with the Arabs.' He emphasised not only the ignorance of Zionists regarding Palestine's existing population, but also their blindness (which in part explained it). The issue had gone 'completely unnoticed'. The resident people had been 'overlooked'. Epstein here could have been describing Herbert Bentwich, who arrived in Palestine in 1897. His great grandson Ari Shavit later wrote: 'Bentwich sees ... the promise [but] he does not see the land as it really is.' Shavit goes on to ask, 'How is it possible that my great-grandfather does not see ... that the land is taken ... that there is another people now occupying the land of his ancestors?' Shavit's answer is persuasive: 'My great grandfather does not see, because he is motivated by the need not to see. He does not see because if he does see, he will have to turn back.'[32] Zionists preferred the fiction of a land without a people.

Epstein's primary concern was that none of the competing visions for a Jewish homeland in Palestine took account of reality on the ground: 'We are absolutely ignorant of everything regarding Arabs... There exists an entire people who have held [Palestine] for centuries and to whom it would never occur to leave... We are forgetting that the people who live there now also have a sensitive heart and a loving soul. The Arab, like any man, has a strong bond with his homeland.'

This, he continues, is 'the irresponsibility of our movement'; and 'it would be folly not to consider with whom we are dealing'. Dangerous, too. He went on to ask 'the hidden question': 'Will those who are dispossessed remain silent and accept what is being done to them?'

'In the end,' he answered, 'they will wake up... Powerful is the passion of those who have been uprooted from their land... Let us not tease a sleeping lion.' In retrospect, Epstein's words seem remarkably prophetic. Palestinian Arab resistance to Zionism was evident before the First World War, and it was to be a perennial reality of the British mandate years thereafter.

The answer, he advised his fellow Zionists, lay in Jewish values:

the Jewish commitment to 'justice and the law, egalitarianism and the brotherhood of man'. So 'we sin against our nation and our future if we facilely cast aside our choicest weapon: the justice and purity of our cause'. Epstein's prescription may appear to us now as naïve, though he insisted at the time that it was not a dream. He maintained that Jewish settlement 'requires the agreement of the other side'. If this were cultivated, the future could lie in consent and partnership: in cooperation, that is, between settlers and settled. There was, he argued, a possibility that the Arabs 'will not curse the day the Jews came to settle their land but will remember it as a day of redemption and salvation'. As if he needed to dispel doubts among his listeners, he concluded his address with a passionate commitment to Zionism: 'Heaven forbid that we should digress even momentarily from our act of creation.'

In this way, and a dozen years before Arthur Balfour's Declaration, Epstein stood up and confronted the culture clash and the contradiction; but contradiction it remained. In the eyes of the Palestinian Arabs, there was to be no recognition of the 'purity' of the Zionist cause, no sense of Zionist 'justice', and not much 'brotherhood of man'. Reading his speech now, it is not certain that Epstein had actually convinced himself. The response to Epstein's address was part scepticism – the Jews simply did not have the resources to build the new Zionist-Arab society that Epstein envisaged – and part scorn. Narrower-minded Zionists than Epstein were driven by a competing priority: settlement, not justice. For them it was time at last for the Jews to concern themselves with their own existence, survival and destiny. The debate provoked by Epstein contained, in essence, the main on-going argument among Zionists on the Arab question: on the one hand, Epstein's demand that Jewish settlement should be based on the highest moral principles, and proceed only in agreement with the Arabs; on the other, the self-centred nationalism urged by the Zionist vanguard.

Zionists tended to underestimate the problem of a resident Arab population in Palestine. After Epstein, they had no excuse to do so.

Jewish alternatives and opposition to Zionism

From the outset, there was considerable Jewish opposition to Zionism. Far from uniting Jewry in a nationalist mission, Zionism divided it. It was a small, minority movement among late-nineteenth-century Jews. In the literal sense of movement, few emigrated to (and remained in) Palestine. In the ideological sense, few subscribed to the project of a nation state acquired by human endeavour. On the contrary, Zionism provoked a range of opposition and alternative analyses wider than can be marshalled here. There was, first, the wholehearted opposition of Orthodox (or Ultra-Orthodox) Jews. Representing the traditional religious case – and in doing so lending some credibility to Zionism's claim to be secular – they 'resolutely opposed any manifestation of Jewish nationalism as sacrilege, an unnatural tampering with the work of God... Jewish redemption would come with the Messiah or not at all.'[33] Of Zionism's numerous other contemporary critics, we will look at one scholar, and two communities.

Contemporary Jewish critics of political Zionism could be fierce. A good example is Isaac Breuer. Hungarian-born, and still a teenager when Herzl published *The Jewish State*, in adulthood he was an assimilated German, having studied in German universities and then entered the legal profession. A neo-Orthodox rabbi, he fended off both the Reform Movement and *Haskalah*, insisting that the Jews remain a religious community, inspired by a unique divine mission. But his real enemy was Zionism, in both its 'political' and 'spiritual' forms. He accepted that the Jews were a nation; he approved of the Zionists' arousal of national consciousness. He went further and acknowledged the crippling effect of separation from the ancient homeland. But, he insisted, the Jews were *exceptional* as a nation, not merely one among many. Others might shape their own laws, but the Jews were shaped by the Torah. It was this God-given law that defined them and served as their constitution. It was inappropriate for Jews to be working out their own ideas; they should be seeking not a secular political state but redemption. Regarding the Zionist emphasis on the colonisation of Palestine, Breuer did not hold back. The Zionist movement, Breuer judged, was 'the most terrible enemy that has ever risen against the Jewish nation'.[34]

'Our hardest struggle everywhere is against the Bund,' wrote Weizmann in 1903.[35] The origins of the Bund – that is, the All-Jewish Workers' Union in Lithuania, Poland and Russia – lay in the Pale. In the course of the nineteenth century, the population of Jews in Russia multiplied. For the most part they were employed in industry and crafts, or they were merchants, shopkeepers and petty traders. Most Jews lived in small towns and villages, where segregation, and the prevalence of local anti-Semitism, meant that assimilation was not a realistic option. The political context became threatening. The Jews were increasingly demonised, and they became a convenient scapegoat for an increasingly authoritarian and incompetent regime.

The Bund sought to meet the needs of what became a sizeable Jewish urban industrial working class. Though it had origins in the 1880s, this labour union had its founding congress in Vilna (Vilnius), in September 1897 – just a month after Herzl's First Zionist Congress in Basel. The Bund demanded nationality status for the Jews (to this extent, imitating Zionism); but they sought national-cultural autonomy, with a protected Yiddish-based secular Jewish culture, not in an imagined ancient home, but within a federated Russian state.[36] In the meantime, the Bund engaged in class struggle, boasting the largest mass following of any social-democratic grouping in Russia at that time. The radical views of the Bund alarmed Western European Jewish assimilationists, who did not want to be associated with revolutionaries. Among Zionists, Weizmann considered the Bund's revolutionary doctrine 'facile'; and he belittled it further by branding it 'assimilationist'.[37] For their part, the Bund leadership labelled Zionism 'a counter-revolutionary fantasy'. The situation changed after 1917. It was the Zionists now, and no longer the Bund, who had the most potent ideology among the Jews of the empire. But their achievements were limited. As the distinguished scholar of Jewish history John D. Klier somewhat scathingly concludes, 'what the Zionist movement did not produce was widespread emigration to Palestine'.[38]

The opposition of another, less sizeable but still substantial, group of Jews is revealing and poignant: the Jews who were already living in Palestine, before the onset of Zionism. These were Jews for whom Palestine provided homes – not a homeland. Most of the Jews living in Palestine before the first Zionist settlers arrived were Mizrahim or Sephardi: Jews from the Islamic world of North Africa (and in an earlier age, Spain). They had been drawn to the Holy Land for a combination of religious, economic and personal reasons, before the emergence of Zionism. They wanted to live in it as Jews. This, however, did not preclude degrees of assimilation. Indeed, in some cases, so marked was their identification with local communities (they were especially numerous in Jaffa, for example) that they were termed 'Arab Jews'. They lived in mixed neighbourhoods and spoke Arabic; and their women dressed modestly. They enjoyed relations of mutual respect with the Arabs. These were Jews who, like innumerable fellow Jews across Europe, wanted to be left in peace. But their tranquillity was to be disturbed – not by gentile anti-Semitism, but by the arrival of second *aliyah* Zionists, predominantly Ashkenazi from Russia.

The newcomers, unlike the Jews already established, posed a threat to the Arabs. This was on a number of levels, not just land acquisition. In places like Jaffa, disputes could arise, for example, over the behaviour of women. When Ashkenazi Jewish women and girls dressed immodestly, their appearance provoked and angered the Arabs. Jaffa's resident Jews were also shocked: the flouting of moral customs that had been accepted for generations was jarring for both resident communities. Fights broke out between Arab and Jewish youths over the honour of immigrant Jewish women. Meanwhile, new arrivals from Russia provoked Arab fears that the Jews in general were trying to take over the country and marginalise them. In short, Zionism was destroying the trust that had existed in Palestine between Jews and their Arab neighbours. Another area of disagreement between resident Sephardi and immigrant Ashkenazi was the economy. The former chose to employ Arab – that is, relatively cheap – labour. By contrast, the latter aspired to the 'conquest of labour', insisting that Jewish enterprises employ Jews and exclude Arabs. In due course, the eviction of Palestinian *fellahin* (labourers) following Zionist land purchases prompted attacks on Jewish settlements of all kinds.

In this context the 'Arab Jews' came under stress. Sephardi Jews sought to distance themselves from Zionist activity. In the early years of the twentieth century, non-Zionist Jewish and Arab leaders sought, on the basis of existing good neighbourliness, to find a shared, peaceful *modus vivendi* for the future of their communities, even a common front against the Ottoman Turks; it is a sad irony on a historic scale that it was the growing influence of Zionists that prevented it. Political Zionism rendered Arab-Jewish *rapprochement* in Palestine impossible. Later, Arabs in revolt against Britain's 'facilitation' of Zionism in Palestine did not discriminate between one group of Jews and another. Most Jews thus found themselves, if only for reasons of self-defence, identifying more closely with the Zionist cause.

We may conclude that Zionism was a marginal, unrepresentative form of late-nineteenth-century Judaism. Insofar as it was known at all, to many contemporary Jews it was not merely eccentric but fantastic, divisive, even dangerous. It is worth stressing that, in these first decades, Zionism's critics were Jews, not gentiles. There could have been no clearer distinction between anti-Zionism and anti-Semitism.

Emigration, settlement, regeneration

The Zionist colonial project was part ideology, part movement. In its first three decades or so, the actual Zionist colonisation of Palestine was slight: the mass migration of Jews out of Europe went elsewhere. Nonetheless, by 1914 it was unwelcome enough for the resident Arab population – largely Muslim, but also Christian – to resist it and to inspire an incipient Palestinian national consciousness.

The early 1880s had seen the first wave of Jewish emigrants. For the most part they were escaping from the upsurge of violent anti-Semitism in Russia. This first *aliyah* comprised around 25,000, most of whom settled in the towns, though a few established agricultural settlements.

Among them were ideologues such as Ze'ev Dubnow, who led a group of emigrants from Odessa. He wrote: 'The ultimate aim is to build up this land of Israel and restore to the Jews the political independence that has been taken from them... The Jews, with weapons in their hands if necessary, will announce with a loud voice that they are masters of their ancient homeland.'[39]

There is no mention here of indigenous inhabitants, Arab or otherwise; but there is no mistaking the colonial aspiration of conquest, by force if needed. Dubnow's dramatic prophecy dates from 1882. However, only after Herzl founded the Zionist Organisation in 1897 did the prospect of a Jewish majority, through mass immigration, begin to be seriously envisaged. But not easily accomplished. Between 1882 and 1914 around 100,000 Jews emigrated to Palestine (where 20–30,000 Jews already dwelt). Over half of these, however, did not actually settle but left again.[40] Jewish immigrants of the first and second *aliyahs* struggled, dependent on financial support from abroad. Meanwhile, most of the former, mainly Sephardi, Jewish community – still a majority of all the Jews in Palestine – lived in Jerusalem, indifferent towards Zionism.

We may compare Palestine with other destinations for the great, turn-of-century Jewish emigration. The Statue of Liberty was inaugurated in New York harbour in 1886, welcoming the desperate of Europe: 'Give me your tired, your poor, your huddled masses yearning to breathe free.' And huge numbers of East European Jews offered themselves. By 1914, around two and a half million went to America; tens of thousands went to South America and the British overseas dominions; hundreds of thousands more settled in the cities and towns of Central and Western Europe.[41] Only a tiny minority of Eastern Europe's Jews turned to Zionism. For the great majority of those who left their homes in Central and Eastern Europe, the Promised Land was – as long as it remained welcoming – America, not Palestine.

◆

Even so, emigration to Palestine was taking place long before the First World War. Jewish settlers, at the very heart of the Zionist project, began to change the facts on the ground. As the twenty-two-year-old David Ben-Gurion, himself among Jews recently arrived in Palestine, wrote to his father in 1909: 'Settling the land – that is the only real Zionism. The rest is just self-delusion, idle chatter, and time-wasting.'[42]

The Zionist goal was indeed to acquire land for settlement. Transfers of land required, of course, owners able and willing to sell, as well as Jews willing and able to buy. The existence of the former arose from Ottoman reforms in mid-century, especially the Land Code of 1858. This new law had unintended consequences of great significance in the history of Zionism. The reform allowed individuals in Palestine to register the lands they cultivated and so claim them as their own; this enabled them to buy and sell (and to assume the tax burden associated with that ownership, which was the point of the reform). In practice, heads of villages and also Bedouin chiefs undertook the registration, while urban notables of prominent Arab families used their local influence to gain access to land. Substantial areas thus often ended up in the hands of absentee landlords. They acquired the properties as investment and had little attachment either to the land or to the people who lived and worked on it. When the opportunity came, many did not hesitate to sell.

A Jewish National Fund (JNF) was established in 1901, under the control of the World Zionist Organisation. It began to buy up tracts of land in the coastal plains and valleys of Palestine 'for the eternal possession of the Jewish people'. In funding the JNF, Jews in the diaspora were following the precedent of Baron Edmond de Rothschild. In 1882, he had subsidised the first community of Zionist immigrants. Only a very small proportion of Palestinian land was alienated at this time, but by 1914 it was already clear that Zionism was advancing by land purchase. Absentee landlords, mainly prominent Arab families, were happy to sell, mainly because Zionist demand was pushing up prices. Meanwhile, neither sellers nor buyers were greatly concerned about the fate of tenant farmers. Nor were they inhibited by the prohibitions of the Ottomans. As one commentator puts it, 'By means of bribery and other forms of persuasion, the energetic heads of the embryonic Zionist movement succeeded in circumventing the categorical opposition of the Ottoman government to the settlement of Jews in Palestine.'[43]

Arthur Ruppin was head of the Palestine Office established in Jaffa in 1908. He bought land all over the country for exclusive Jewish use, fully aware of the significance of his work. 'Land,' he wrote, 'is the most necessary thing for establishing roots in Palestine... Since there are hardly any more arable unsettled lands, we are bound in each case to remove peasants who cultivated the land.'[44] As Kenneth Stein (a long-established scholar of Arab-Israeli tensions) sardonically observes, the Jewish purchaser was generally interested in having his newly acquired land delivered 'free of tenant encumbrances'.[45] In 1907, Weizmann underlined the Zionists' need so to sever the Arabs from their land, in words of threatening condescension. 'The Arab retains his primitive attachment to the land, the soil instinct is strong in him, and by being continuously employed on it there is a danger that he might feel indispensable to it with a moral right to it.'[46]

Not all Zionists agreed. Epstein, as we have seen, was advocating something quite different. Buy uncultivated land first, he proposed. As for cultivated, 'this will be acquired not to expel the tenants but on condition of having them remain on the land, and improving their lot by introducing good agricultural methods... We shall benefit the residents, not furtively with bribes or gold in order to rid ourselves of them, but in true material and spiritual ways.'[47] When, in the early days, Jewish settlers allowed Palestinian tenant farmers to remain on the land and continue working it, the latter acquiesced in arrangements that entailed little more than transfer of ownership.

The second *aliyah* trampled on Epstein's sentiments. It also overrode another variant of Zionism embodied in Poale Zion (Workers of Zion), a socialist political party with origins in Russia. Looking for a synthesis of Zionism with Marxism, one of its Russian founders, Ber Borochov, looked to a time when middle-class Jews would emigrate to Palestine in sufficient numbers to build up the means of production there and so attract working-class Jews. In turn, these would come to be the vanguard of a revolutionary movement.[48] At a Poale Zion conference in Jaffa in 1906, Marxists advocated support for Arab workers, as brothers in struggle.

But the synthesis foundered. Recognising the historical force of *nationalist* as well as *class* struggles did not remove the contradiction. And the pursuit of political independence for Jews in Palestine was not compatible with the principles of inclusive socialism. Realising that orthodox Marxist concepts developed in Russia did not apply to Palestine, Poale Zion members in Palestine broke from their Russian roots. They accepted cooperation between bourgeoisie and proletarians in place of class struggle; and their adoption of Hebrew further illustrated a decisive shift towards Zionism and away from Marxism. So, too, did their need to defend themselves against Arab opposition. As Borochov put it himself, 'Emigration alone does not solve the Jewish problem. It leaves the Jew helpless in a strange country.'[49] In a context of light or non-existent Ottoman policing, settlers began to form guards to protect their properties. Thus, to quote the Israeli historian Benny Morris, 'armed might was now backing up purchase and cultivation; settler was becoming soldier.'[50]

In short, the social, economic and cultural conditions for an inclusive working class based on common interests did not exist in Palestine. Marxist Zionism yielded to its own internal contradictions, Arab opposition to the Zionist project, and vigorous opposition from Ben-Gurion within the Zionist movement. The exclusion of Arabs from Jewish unions, as from the land, continued. The second *aliyah* insisted on the 'conquest of labour': Jewish settlements and businesses in Palestine were not to employ Arabs if there were Jews seeking the same jobs. Thus Marxist ideas from Russia came up against the reality of experience in Palestine. By 1914, Poale Zion had merged with its erstwhile rival, the Hapoel Hatzair (Young Worker) party, which was less ideological, more pragmatic, not seeking class conflict but stressing the exclusion of non-

Jewish labour from the Zionist economy and the regenerative role for Jews of manual labour.

◆

Regeneration was a far more ambitious commitment than emigration and settlement, but it characterised this pre-war period. In the words of Shimon Peres, 'to counter anti-Semitism, Zionism posited, the Jews have to change themselves and, hence, how the world sees them'.[51] The young Ben-Gurion wrote: '*Eretz Yisrael* is not just a geographical concept... *Eretz Yisrael* must be a process of repairing and purifying our lives.'[52] There was a conviction that Jews were a community in urgent need of change. In the homeland, there would be a regenerated people who would not only fulfil the historic role of Judaism but also present to the world a redefinition of what it was to be Jewish.

Max Nordau, who was Herzl's right-hand man and the organiser of the early Zionist congresses, emphasised the need for physical change. The Jews had become weak and degenerate. Zionism would improve the race through agricultural labour, accompanied by gymnastics and body-building in the open air of the ancestral homeland. In Nordau's own words, 'in no other race or people can gymnastics fulfil such an important educational function, as it must do among us Jews. It is needed to straighten our backs, in body and character alike.'[53] This view was consistent with a broader contemporary preoccupation with race. And the notion that Jews shared a distinct homogeneous biological origin, and had a distinct racial potential, was popular in all currents of the Zionist movement. The Jewish pioneer was to be nurtured as a new man: liberated, Hebrew-speaking, strong, and fearless in battle. Weizmann dreamed that 'Palestine and the building up of a Jewish nation from within, with its own forces and its own traditions, would establish the status of Jews, would create a type of 100 per cent Jew.'[54]

Zionists of this period sought to transform the diaspora middleman, trader, intellectual, into a man of the earth. Jews had to work their own lands (or hire other Jews to work them). Farming – energetic, self-reliant – was the key. However, by no means all Jewish settlers of the second *aliyah* were committed to farming: of the 35–40,000 pre-war immigrants, only about a third took to the land.[55] Nonetheless, it was in this pre-1914 period that the *kibbutz* movement was conceived and prototypes were founded – Jewish settlements of equals, voluntarily joining together to redeem the land. And to defend it.

Leo Pinsker had urged Jews to seek security and salvation through 'auto-emancipation'. The pioneers of the second *aliyah* went further, ideologically committed to a brand of (exclusive) socialism as their means of fully liberating themselves. They were specifically committed too – as Pinsker had not been – to Palestine. Here was their own soil, the only proper place for national or racial regeneration. Conquest of land, conquest of labour: these were the means by which a new class, or race, of working Jews would be produced. Both socialist and non-socialist Zionists idealised rural society and the life of the working farmer. For the Marxist Zionist Borochov, the ambition did not stop at this point, for there would eventually be an extraordinary social change: 'It is the Jewish immigrants who will undertake the forces of production of *Eretz Yisrael*, and the local population will assimilate economically and culturally to the Jews.'[56] This vision of reverse assimilation was fantastical; but it captures something of the aspiration of first-generation Zionists.

Resistance and Palestinian nationalism
While there was some accommodation on the part of native Palestinians, these early years before the First World War were marked more by resistance, and the birth of a Palestinian national consciousness.

From the early days of Jewish immigration there were clashes, often bloody, between the new settlers and their Arab neighbours. A Jewish visitor to Palestine reported in 1898 on 'countless fights between Jews and Arabs'.[57] From the first *aliyah,* there were disputes between immigrant Jews and Palestinian residents. In 1882, when a Jewish guard accidentally shot dead an Arab worker, some 200 Arabs descended on the Jewish settlement, throwing stones and vandalising property. At Petah Tikva, in 1886, Arab villagers reacted against the loss of land they considered theirs (sold to Jews by Jaffa money-lenders to whom they had become indebted) by attacking this, Palestine's oldest Jewish settlement. Ottoman troops had to intervene.

Jewish settlement, in line with the Basel Programme which post-dated its early days, was embryonic colonisation. Arabs objected to Jewish immigrants, many of whom made little secret of wanting to found a Jewish state in the heart of the Arab world. The clash of cultures, already noted, provided further grounds for concern. Most settlers knew nothing of the Arabic language. They dressed differently, worshipped (if at all) differently, and generally behaved differently. Yet the major cause of tension and violence throughout the period 1882 to 1914 was conflicting interest. In this context, relations between the two communities soured. What rankled above all was that 'though still a small minority, the settlers quickly began to behave like lords and masters'.[58]

Zionists were not taken by surprise. As we have seen, forecasts of conflict had been made by some of its leading figures. Ahad Ha'am had been among the first to foresee that the Jews could never succeed in building some tranquil Jewish Switzerland, in the centre of the Arab Middle East. Herzl had himself written a warning against piecemeal immigration. In *The Jewish State* he argued that the future lay with the wholesale grant, by one or more of the Great Powers, of Jewish sovereignty over 'a portion of the globe', because '*an infiltration is bound to end badly*'. Infiltration, he explained, continues 'till the inevitable moment the native population feels itself threatened'.[59] This was not so much prophecy as a description of what was already happening in Palestine, even before his seminal pamphlet and the inaugural Zionist Congress.

Before the start of the First World War, Weizmann was warning of the dangers of a renascent Arab nationalism. He wrote in 1913: 'The Arabs are beginning to organise... They consider Palestine their own...

We shall soon face a serious enemy.'[60] In sorrow and in anger, educated Arabs articulated the complaints of their fellow Palestinians. In 1899, Herzl received a letter from Yusuf Diya al-Khalidi, representative for Jerusalem in the Ottoman parliament established in 1876. Its subject was Palestine. He asked Herzl: 'By what right do the Jews demand it for themselves?' He concluded with an appeal to the Zionist leader: 'For the sake of God, leave Palestine in peace.'[61] Earlier still, a group of Arab notables from Jerusalem had petitioned the Sultan, complaining that the Jews were depriving the Arabs of all lands, were taking over their trade and were bringing arms into the country.[62]

July 1908 brought a major event in the internal political history of the Ottoman Empire: the overthrow of the Sultan in the revolution of the Young Turks. The loosening of autocracy ignited nationalism throughout the Empire. In Palestine it led to a considerable increase in Arab attacks on Jewish settlements. In one such incident, the young Ben-Gurion was involved, armed with a pistol. In the twenty-seven years preceding 1908, thirteen Jews were killed by Arabs, though only four in what might be described as 'nationalist circumstances'; 1909 saw the first organised effort by Jewish settlers to arm themselves; in just five years thereafter, however, a dozen Jewish settlement guards were killed by Arabs. Local, specific, incidents were developing into something like nationalist resistance.[63]

After 1908, Arab newspapers began to voice radical demands. The struggle against Zionism became a central issue for Palestinians. Khalil al-Sakakini was a Christian Arab intellectual, born in Jerusalem in 1878, and a perceptive observer of the first decades of Zionism in action. He was not anti-Semitic. He respected what the Jews did as a people; he focused his criticism on Zionism. He wrote in 1914: 'If I hate the Zionist movement, it is only because it is attempting to found its existence and independence on the destruction of others.'[64] Zionism was trying to destroy Arab unity, he argued. Zionists 'want to break the chain and divide the Arab nation into two sections to prevent its unification and solidarity.'[65]

Another Arab spokesman was Najib Nassar. A Christian Arab, Nassar was an advocate of Palestinian resistance to Zionism, before the First World War and after. His Lebanese family moved to Palestine at the end of the nineteenth century. He graduated (in pharmacy) from the American University in Beirut. It is an irony that Nassar's anti-Zionist campaign came in response to the purchase of land around Tiberias, at the turn of the century, by a socialist Jewish immigrant, Haim Kalvarisky, who was convinced that Zionism would succeed only if there was agreement between Jews and Arabs. Nassar's incipient campaign was carried first by newspapers in Beirut and Cairo, before he responded to the abolition of censorship in the Ottoman Empire in 1908 by opening his own twice-weekly newspaper, *Al-Karmil*, in Haifa. Later, in 1911, he published *Zionism: Its History, Aims and Significance*, the first book in Arabic to expose the threat posed by Zionist colonisation, which he presented as a quasi-military movement. In these pre-war years of popular discontent and the crystallisation of a nationalist, anti-Zionist political consciousness, he called on Arab youth to dissuade Arab absentee landowners from allowing land to be transferred to Jewish ownership. He expressed his goal, in 1913, as 'preserving the country for its people'.[66]

We should note the wider context. Arab nationalism was directed against the Turks, not only against the Zionists. As early as 1905 Najib Azouri, a Maronite Christian who had been assistant governor of Jerusalem, wrote: 'The Arabs, whom the Turks tyrannised, have become conscious of their national, historical and racial homogeneity, and wish to detach themselves from the worm-eaten Ottoman trunk.'[67] But there was no mistaking the incipient core conflict in Palestine. Azouri saw what was coming, even before the Young Turks' revolution, and with no anticipation of world wars and the explosion of international interest in the region. 'Two important phenomena ... are emerging at this moment in Asiatic Turkey,' he wrote. 'They are the awakening of the Arab nation and the latent effort of the Jews to reconstitute on a very large scale the ancient kingdom of Israel. These movements are destined to fight each other continually until one of them wins.'[68]

'Palestine' under the Ottomans did not exist as a separate, distinct, administrative district. Yet, in the decade before the First World War, the term came into common usage among educated Arabs, as is emphasised by the founding by Christian Arabs in 1911 of a daily newspaper, *Filastin*, in Jaffa. *Filastin*'s editor, Isa al-'Isa, another Christian graduate of the American University in Beirut, expressed 'concern, bordering on an obsession' with Zionism, so his paper gave much more attention to Zionism than to any other matter.[69] A letter published in *Filastin* in 1911 was already prophetically describing Zionism as 'an omen of our future exile from our homeland'.[70] *Filastin* was repeatedly shut down by the Ottoman government; but it would re-emerge during the subsequent British period when it became the most influential Arabic publication in the territory. With the First World War about to break, the concept of Palestine was winning recognition among its inhabitants. One popular candidate declared, on the eve of elections to the Ottoman Parliament in 1914: 'If I am elected as a representative, I shall devote all my strength, day and night, to doing away with the damage and the threat of Zionists and Zionism.'[71] Indeed, in those elections, 'almost all candidates ... made resistance to Zionism the central theme of their campaigns'.[72]

Claims to national identity have always been contested. For their part, Zionists were most reluctant to acknowledge Palestinian nationhood. To be sure, Palestinian national consciousness lagged behind the Zionists' own conviction that the Jews represented an emergent nation – primarily because it grew in reaction to unwelcome Zionist immigration and settlement. But more importantly, as Israeli historian (and Oxford professor) Avi Shlaim has stressed, the non-recognition of a Palestinian national entity was a feature, in the Zionist movement, of 'fundamental and enduring importance in its subsequent history'.[73] The Zionists' demand for self-determination rested on their claim that the Jews were a nation; their argument for a homeland or state in Palestine could not afford to encompass recognition of a rival nation, with a competing claim to that land.

In 1912 Amin al-Husayni, later to emerge as the foremost Palestinian nationalist leader of the inter-war-years-period, was a teenager studying in Cairo. Years earlier his father, Tahir, Mufti of Jerusalem, had complained to the Ottoman authorities about Jewish immigration into Palestine; in response, in 1897 they had set up a commission under Tahir to monitor land sales to Jews. Now Amin, himself a devout Muslim, worked in Cairo with a Christian Palestinian to form a society to oppose Zionism. This society was small, and short-lived, but it offers an instance of embryonic Palestinian nationalism unfettered by the divisions of religious denomination.

By 1914 opposition to Zionism, from Muslim and Christian Arabs and at a number of levels of Palestinian society, was no secret. The fundamental, if as yet small-scale, collision in Palestine was between the coloniser and the colonised. This low-level colonialism was nurturing a conflict which would later tend to be perceived as that of two competing nationalisms. Though relatively few of the pre-war Jewish immigrants were themselves Zionists, shared experience would in time promote an enhanced sense of shared identity among Jews in Palestine. Meanwhile, political – increasingly national – consciousness for Arab Palestinians grew as a direct response to what they experienced.

Zionism and diplomacy for Palestine

What might diplomacy achieve? Might a Great Power – either unaware of, or dismissive of, Palestinian opinion – before long give open support for Zionism, authorise the Jewish national home, and expose Palestine to the unrestricted settler colonialism advocated in the Basel Programme? For the two decades preceding the outbreak of the First World War, Zionism was a cause with two faces. We have dwelt so far on practical Zionism, Zionism on the ground. This called for migration, land acquisition and settlement. We turn now to the Zionism of high politics. Rather than *ad hoc* colonisation, this entailed diplomatic relations with, and sought support from, the Great Powers as the key to reaching the same goal.

We thus concentrate on the last years of Theodor Herzl, before his death in 1904. This political emphasis on establishing close links with representatives of the Great Powers was grounded in Herzl's personal conviction, noted above, that what he called the 'infiltration' alternative was both inadequate and counter-productive. He insisted that the Zionist project could not succeed without international recognition. He thus set out to gain approval and endorsement for Zionism, in the form of a charter, from one or more of the European powers of his day. A charter would recognise Jewish sovereignty over the designated territory and set in motion a centrally funded, irreversible, internationally sanctioned, mass migration.[74]

Herzl has been described as a man who combined 'wild fantasies with an uncanny flair for practical action'.[75] He was endowed with exceptional organisational talents. He had convened the First Zionist Congress in Basel. This in turn founded the World Zionist Organisation as a permanent institution that could speak for the movement. As Michael J. Cohen puts it in his 1987 book *The Origins and Evolution of the Arab-Zionist Conflict*, Herzl had 'the audacity to practice diplomacy in the name of a people as yet without its own country'.[76] And it was, in the event, Herzl's own voice that came to speak for Zionism. He set out – literally, travelling in person – to try to persuade one Great Power after another to grant the sovereignty he craved, and so give the Jewish homeland project the support it needed to have from the gentile world.

Since Palestine formed part of the Ottoman Empire, Herzl hoped to persuade the Sultan to part with that, specific, 'portion of the globe'. He first visited Constantinople in 1896 but succeeded neither in meeting the Sultan nor in persuading his advisors of the merits of the Zionist cause. This was only to be expected. After the first, 1882, arrival of Russian Jews, Constantinople issued numerous prohibitions: against Jewish tourism, settlement, land purchases and construction in Palestine. Later, however, Herzl did meet the Sultan, on three occasions in 1901 and 1902. His pitch for a deal remained what it had been on his first visit: he would arrange for world Jewry to amass sufficient funds to pay off Turkey's national debt, in return for approval of a designated Jewish homeland in Palestine.

But these face-to-face meetings, too, came to nothing. For one thing, Herzl had not won a great response from wealthy diaspora Jews and thus did not have the funds to furnish his proposed deal. In England, for example, the prosperous Anglo-Jewish establishment was unwilling to embrace Zionism. Sultan Abdul Hamid II was impressed by his Jewish visitor, commenting that 'Herzl looks like a prophet, like a leader of his people.'[77] But he was not prepared to accommodate a Jewish homeland. Small, scattered communities of Jewish migrants would be free to settle where they liked ... *except* in Palestine (an exception which was to be ignored by landowners bent on benefiting from the high prices offered by Zionist buyers). In 1902, a charter on such restricted lines was on offer. Herzl, however, would not accept anything short of unlimited immigration, with Palestine as the immigrants' destination, and so nothing came of it.

Undaunted, Herzl continued to seek audiences with crowned heads of Europe. He had already met the German Emperor, in Jerusalem in 1898, hoping to persuade him to apply pressure on the Sultan. But Wilhelm II was so vague that Herzl abandoned hope of any substantial contribution from that quarter. A more controversial diplomatic initiative was his visit in August 1903 to St Petersburg, capital of the state regarded by Zionists as the driving force of anti-Semitic persecution. Herzl hoped in this instance that Russia would put pressure on the Sultan. Denied an audience with the Tsar, he tried to persuade Nicholas II's two key ministers, Witte and von Plehve, to make it easier for great numbers of Jews to leave the country. Yet again nothing was achieved. Von Plehve, Minister of the Interior, was founder of the notorious anti-Semitic Black Hundred gangs and a major organiser of pogroms. We may infer that he preferred having the Jews remain, as diversionary targets for right-wing extremism, to having them leave. Nor subsequently was anything gained by Herzl from a journey to Italy, where he met both King Victor Emmanuel II and the Pope.

Herzl's emphasis tended to isolate him in the movement. Ahad Ha'am was dismissive, insisting that 'the salvation of Israel will come through prophets, not diplomats'.[78] Weizmann, too, who at this time prioritised emigration and settlement, was a vocal critic of Herzl, seeing his grand political pragmatism as misguided and lacking the zeal of the Zionist pioneer. The overall fruitlessness of Herzl's efforts was therefore to be welcomed. For Weizmann, Zionism was not a political mechanism but a life-giving force. The correct means for achieving a Jewish homeland in Palestine was not the opening of doors through diplomatic initiative but, rather, settlement on the ground by a people with national and moral purpose. As he said in 1907, 'do not reduce politics to a mere approach to governments and to asking their opinion about Zionism'.[79]

But in the end Herzl was right. It may appear somewhat ironic that it was Weizmann, so long a critic of his predecessor's strategic priorities, who would effectively capitalise on Herzl's most significant diplomatic breakthrough when he, acting very much as Herzl had done, just ten years later persuaded the British government to issue the Balfour Declaration. Indeed, Herzl had achieved success by the time of his death in 1904. He had brought Zionism to the attention of European governments. Although, as we have seen, the British offer in 1903 of a haven in East Africa for desperate Jewish refugees was eventually rejected, Weizmann himself was generously to acknowledge that Herzl had accomplished something remarkable: 'This was the first time in the exilic history of Jewry that a great government had officially negotiated with the elected representatives of the Jewish people. The identity, the legal personality of the Jewish people had been re-established.'[80]

Herzl's leadership of the Zionist movement was brief, yet of considerable significance. As a man of action, he bulldozed his way through the intellectual debate of his contemporaries. And there would be more to Herzl's influence than public activity. An 1895 diary entry reveals a darker side regarding the existing inhabitants of Palestine: 'We shall have to spirit the penniless population across the border by procuring employment for it in the transit countries, while denying it any employment in our own country. Both the process of expropriation and the removal of the poor must be carried out discreetly and circumspectly.'[81] The concept of 'transfer' in Zionism has a long history.

Nonetheless, though he had crystallised a new, Zionist, ideology, Herzl had not, for the most part, convinced contemporary Jewry. Far from it. And though he doggedly put its case to European governments, by the time of his death (and, still, ten years later in 1914) there was no substantial prospect of a Jewish homeland in Palestine. Perhaps his critics were right, and Herzl's strategy of peripatetic diplomacy was doomed. Ben-Gurion lamented, in 1908, 'we Jews don't have a foreign government to come to our aid'.[82] Before the First World War, no Great Power stepped forward as sponsor, or looked likely to. After Herzl's death, it seemed that the Zionist movement had entered a period of stasis.

2

ZIONISM IN 1914

'A maverick in the history of modern nationalism.' Arthur Hertzberg[1]

Across late-nineteenth-century Europe and into the twentieth century, the Jewish Question was serious and urgent. Accomplished men of intelligence and action such as Theodor Herzl and Chaim Weizmann were passionately seeking solutions, which they honestly believed were offered by political Zionism. But by 1914 Zionism had convinced very few Jews that it had found the answer. Jewry as a whole had not turned to Zionism. It remained an eccentric, marginal – and to many Jews, spurious – ideology. It was hard for Zionists themselves to believe it had a sustainable future.

What follows is an evaluation of what was still, twenty years after the Basel Programme was formulated, a largely powerless phenomenon. It focuses on aspects which were open to criticism (and were criticised, especially by Jews). But as we shall see shortly, more damning and significant criticism is to be levelled at the government of one of Europe's Great Powers, the British Empire, for adopting it in 1917 without due care and attention.

The movement
Emigrant European Jews were not for the most part powered by Zionist zeal; they wanted only to escape persecution and pogrom, and to find a refuge and a better life. In this light, Palestine was not very attractive.

Many immigrants of the first two *aliyahs* left Palestine after only a brief stay. The explanation for this was, in part, very simple. In Palestine conditions were harsh. Western Europe and America offered relative comfort. 'Instead of assured individual emancipation in the West,' writes Michael Cohen, 'Zionism offered only the ill-defined prospect of collective, national transformation in the future.' He concludes, 'the appeal of Zionism to the Jewish masses was very limited'.[2]

Nonetheless, on the ground there was progress. Jewish immigration into Palestine was still a trickle rather than a flood but, according to Chaim Weizmann's biographer, 'the pioneers of the second *aliyah* were creating a new kind of reality' inspired by their socialist-Zionist faith.

Again, there is no certainty as to numbers. The first census in Palestine was conducted by the British in 1922, but there is broad acceptance that the total population of Palestine by 1914 was at least 700,000. Of these, around 85,000 were Jews, though Gudrun Krämer (a German scholar specialising in Islamic history) questions this figure – 'often cited in Western accounts' – and implies that Jewish numbers were at least matched by the 81,000 Christians in Palestine at this time.[3] Of those 85,000 Jews a majority (about 50,000) were of the old *yishuv*, largely Orthodox, devoted to religious pursuits, and unlikely to be Zionists.[4]

But Zionist ideas were finding practical expression, tempered by Palestinian realities. And there is no doubting the impact on Palestine's indigenous inhabitants of the already-accomplished Jewish immigration, land acquisition and settlement. A Palestinian commentator predicted in 1911 that 'if the government does not set a limit to this torrential stream, no time will pass before you see that Palestine has become a property of the Zionist Organisation and its associates'.[5] It was a further two decades before Jewish immigration actually began to resemble a 'torrential stream', but there is here a fearful perception of what might come about.

These were political fears aroused by a professedly secular political movement. It is hard to detect anti-Semitism in the concerns being raised by members of Palestine's majority Arab population. Muslim and Christian, they opposed not Jews but Zionism.[6]

Meanwhile, diplomacy had achieved very little. Though by this time few regarded the Turks as a significant force, Ottoman Imperial rule continued into 1914, with Britain still seemingly intent on propping it up, as had been the practice for many decades. Neither the Sultan nor the Young Turks had shown interest in abandoning 'a portion' of this part of the globe to unrestricted Jewish immigration and autonomy; and no Great Power was putting pressure on them them to do so.

The ideology

It is worth pointing out that serious study of the content of Zionism was not a task that British decision-makers were about to embark on before committing themselves to it. Nonetheless, we pause here to consider three core assertions within Zionist ideology: that the Jews were a nation; that their history entitled them to return to Palestine; and that theirs was a secular – political, not religious – project.

First, were the Jews a nation? There were no doubts in Weizmann's mind. In 1917 he declared: 'It is strictly a question of fact that the Jews are a nationality.'[7] But in that same year the British Liberal politician (and himself a Jew) Edwin Montagu could write, just weeks before the issue of the Balfour Declaration: 'I assert that there is not a Jewish nation.'[8] Who was right?

There is a problem here, in that there is no hard definition of 'nation'. Nationhood (unlike statehood) is a largely subjective matter. A nation is, at heart, a group of people who feel that they are one. Such feeling may arise from shared experience, language, or ethnicity: religion too, as in the Roman Catholicism of the Poles for example, though a common faith is neither necessary nor sufficient. Weizmann said of the Jews that 'an overwhelming majority of them has always had the conviction that they were a nationality'.[9] But the evidence, such as it is, seems to point the other way. For example, innumerable individual Jews opted in the nineteenth century for intermarriage and/or conversion.

Over the centuries there was a widely shared, though not constant, experience of discrimination, if not persecution; however, the breadth of the diaspora meant there was no single shared history but multiple and diverse histories, occurring over many centuries. Distances between communities were hard to bridge, and differences were thus more likely to develop. In the late nineteenth century, considerable distance separated sporadic barbarities in the east of Europe from the comparative calm of the centre and west. We have noted the divisions between Sephardic and Ashkenazi Jews in Palestine, and tensions between immigrant Jews and already-established Jewish communities. In Western Europe, there were further divisions based, in one form or another, on class. Accomplished, assimilated and established Jews in Britain, for example, had no strong sympathetic sense of common nationhood with either Jewish revolutionaries in Russia or with the mass of Jews seeking to enter Britain, which Balfour's 1905 Aliens Act was designed to keep out.

Moreover, Jews had no single language. Yiddish emerged and thrived in the East, but assimilated Jews in Central and Western Europe were at home with the vernacular languages of their respective nation states. For this reason, Weizmann laid particular emphasis on the cultivation of Hebrew as a binding national language. In inter-war Palestine, language would be used to create a degree of nationhood previously lacking. Not without difficulty, however. As a child in the 1940s, Amos Oz did not much care for Hebrew – 'not a natural enough language' – and writes that his parents spoke Russian or Polish to each other in his presence 'and presumably dreamed in Yiddish'.[10]

Some early Zionists adopted contemporary race theories. For Nathan Birnbaum, an early Zionist intellectual, the Jewish nation was an ethnic entity. But the reality was that the Jewish people had grown in number in earlier centuries partly through proselytising and conversion. Thus was added another element of diversity to those arising from the facts of the diaspora and the cultural/linguistic variations associated with them. Edwin Montagu was to object to the proposed formation of a Jewish Legion, to fight as a distinct unit with Allied forces during the First World War, on the grounds that 'a Jewish Legion makes the position of Jews in other regiments more difficult, and *forces a nationality upon people who have nothing in common*'.[11]

Other Zionists of Herzl's day were aware that many among their fellow Jews would have to be *persuaded* that there was a Jewish nation of which they were a part. So, for example, Leo Pinsker, president of the Hovevei Zion groups, wrote in 1882: 'We must prove that the misfortunes of the Jews are due, above all, to their lack of desire for national independence; and that this desire must be aroused and maintained in them if they do not wish to exist for ever in a disgraceful state – in a word, we must prove that *they must become a nation*'.[12] Weizmann recognised in 1918 that the Jews lacked 'that national unity which is expressed and secured by possession of a homeland, a common language, and common institutions'.[13]

It is impossible to say with any precision what proportion of the world's Jews regarded themselves as a nation in, say, 1914. But attempts have been made to estimate support for Zionism among Jews at that time. An estimate of a low single figure percentage does not seem unreasonable, given the relevant factors: the high degree of assimilation in Central and Western Europe and in the USA; the degree of inertia – or preference for revolutionary politics – of Jews in Russia; and the relatively small number of Jews emigrating to Palestine (and even fewer remaining there) since the first *aliyah*. Shlomo Sand, Professor Emeritus of History at Tel Aviv University, observes that in Germany in 1914 Zionists accounted for less than 2 per cent of 'Germans of Jewish origin', and in France less than that.[14] By this time, it appears, only a tiny minority of Jews adopted the Zionist call to nationhood and homeland.

And it would seem that, throughout our period, Zionism remained the cause of only a minority within world Jewry. One indication of the level of support for this singular ideological offshoot of Judaism was the proportion of Jews worldwide who paid to register as members of Zionist organisations. Registering entailed 'buying a shekel': that is, paying the membership fee. This nomenclature had been chosen at the First Congress in Basel in 1897. It was inspired by God's instruction to

Moses in Exodus 30: 11–16.[15] The notional exchange rate for a shekel was, for example, 1 franc, 1 mark, 1 shilling, 25 cents, 50 kopeks. As late as 1935, the proportion 'buying' was no more than a third in Palestine itself; in Poland, the largest Jewish community in Europe, one in ten; in the USA, the largest in the world, a mere one in thirty.[16] Of course, many other Jews will have sympathised, but even after Hitler's rise to power in Germany, Zionism was – by this measure – actively supported as the answer to the Jewish Question by only a small minority of the nation whose cause it claimed to embody.

We should be clear as to how far the question of *self*-identifying nationhood mattered. In one serious respect, it mattered not at all. Easily located and identified by *others* as different if not alien, Jews were being singled out for discrimination and subjected on occasion to violent persecution, long before the 1930s. In other respects, however, it did matter. If there was no Jewish nation, the whole Zionist project was jeopardised. There could be no appeal, in 1917, say, for privileged treatment in a post-war world of 'national self-determination'. There was no need for a national home for a nation that did not exist.

For the most part, the Jews of early-twentieth-century Europe did not act as if they believed that they formed a separate nation. Those who regarded themselves as Jewish Britons and Jewish Germans, for example, as distinct from British Jews and German Jews, had adopted the nationality of their home state. By the time Weizmann was writing his *What is Zionism?* pamphlet in 1918, the 'nationalisation' of the Jews – that is, the adoption by Jews of loyalty to their adopted nation – had advanced so far that, as Weizmann himself lamented, 'Jews have just shed their blood for every belligerent country'.[17] Emancipation and secularisation had opened up unprecedented opportunities for assimilation which countless Jews took – just when political Zionism was insisting that they were, and should remain, a people apart.

•

Second, how did Zionism portray the history of the Jews?

Every tribe, people and nation writes its own history. Zionists had a particular need to demonstrate Jewish nationhood and to use history to justify that nation's aspirations. Shlomo Sand writes that 'national mythology determined that the Jews – banished, deported or fugitive emigrants – were driven into a long and dolorous exile [from Palestine, by the Romans] causing them to wander over lands and seas to the far corners of the earth until the advent of Zionism prompted them to turn around and return *en masse* to their orphaned homeland'. He maintains that 'only this myth' would provide moral legitimacy to the settlement of the 'exiled nation' in a land inhabited by others.[18]

The issue of the 'exile' is particularly important, because 'return' depended on it: no exile, no return.

Not surprisingly, this version of Jewish history was written into the Declaration of the Establishment of the State of Israel, in May 1948. Here we read that 'Palestine was the birthplace of the Jewish people', that 'here they first attained to statehood' and 'after being forcibly exiled from their land, the people kept faith with it throughout their dispersion and never ceased to pray and hope for their return to it'. In this light, it was 'by virtue of our natural and historic right' that the Jews declared the establishment of the state of Israel.[19]

Like much effective propaganda, the Zionist version of Jewish history contains recognisable, persuasive truths – along with omission, exaggeration and distortion.

Zionist history does not emphasise the inconvenient fact that the Jews were themselves colonisers of an already inhabited land. During the second millennium BC, Palestine was inhabited by a number of pagan tribes, among them the Canaanites. It was toward the end of this period that the Jews invaded, and settled.

Far from Palestine, a Jewish community existed in Babylonia continuously from the sixth century BC. When Cyrus freed the Jews from their captivity in 539 BC, many stayed and never sought to 'return' to Zion. Long before 70 AD there were other large Jewish communities outside Judea. Egypt provides examples, particularly Alexandria and Cairo. Scattered Jewish communities were connected by Eastern Mediterranean trading networks. Olive oil from Galilee was exported in large quantities to Jews in the diaspora regions of Syria, Babylonia, Egypt, Anatolia and elsewhere. Sand concludes that both 'before and after the fall of the Second Temple, there were Jewish believers all over the Roman Empire, as well as in the Parthian territory in the east, in numbers vastly exceeding those of the inhabitants of Judea. From North Africa to Armenia, from Persia to Rome, there were thriving Jewish communities'.[20]

In this light, two shibboleths of the Zionists are challenged: the diaspora did not simply result from 'exile'; nor was there a single Jewish 'homeland'.

The fact of the exile itself has been keenly contested by Jewish writers.[21] At the very least, 'exile' appears to have been simplified and exaggerated by those sympathetic to Zionism. The Romans never deported entire peoples. It did not make sense to uproot cultivators and taxpayers, nor were the means available for such operations. Nowhere in the abundant Roman documentation is there any mention of a deportation from Judea after the revolt of 66–70 AD. There is even less information on the aftermath of a second Jewish rising, the Bar Kokhba revolt of 132 AD (nor is there a Zionist explanation as to how a people who had been exiled in the previous century could revolt again). Cassius Dio, a Roman statesman and historian born twenty years afterwards, wrote an account of the latter revolt, but he mentioned no deportations. There were temporary restrictions on the local populace and a temporary exclusion of circumcised men from Jerusalem, but the Judean masses were not exiled in either 70 AD or 135 AD.

Two thousand years ago the area of modern Palestine comprised three geographical and political components: from north to south, Galilee (including Nazareth), Samaria, and Judea (including Jerusalem and Bethlehem). There is no evidence that either Galilee or Samaria joined the revolt against the Romans. While 'exile' from Judea took the form, for some, of migration (following revolt) into the wider existing Jewish diaspora, for many others it entailed migration northwards into Galilee. Here, from this time, two Jewish communities co-existed: the former inhabitants, and migrants from Judea who included some influential rabbis. Continuing to reside in this northern region of Roman-occupied 'Palestine', Jews were taxed, but otherwise largely ignored by the authorities.

Misrepresentation of exile from Palestine arose fairly late, argues Sand, 'and was due mainly to the rise of Christian mythology about the Jews being exiled in punishment for their rejection and crucifixion of Jesus'. Thereafter, 'the myth of exile began to be slowly appropriated and integrated into Jewish tradition'. There was no constant yearning for a physical 'return' of 'exiles' to Judah. Individuals might choose to travel to Jerusalem, but the few who proposed a collective migration for the purpose of living a full Jewish life there 'were exceptional or eccentric'.[22] Jewish deportees from Spain in the late Middle Ages migrated to cities all around the Mediterranean, but only a few chose to go to Zion. As noted above, even in the early twentieth century Israel Zangwill's Jewish Territorial Organisation saw no necessary link between the search for a homeland and Palestine: 'we do not attach any real value to our supposed "historical rights" to that country'.[23]

Jewish experience in the post-70-AD diaspora has been distorted by generalisation. The Zionist version of history presents these Jewish communities, over many centuries, as uniformly powerless and constantly subjected to persecution. There were, of course, some solid grounds for this view. Ghettoisation is a historical fact, as are innumerable episodes of persecution (and apprehension of persecution, even in its absence). The pogroms in Russia, where so many Jews were living, were an accompaniment of modern political Zionism and, up to a point, explain it. This much is certainly not myth. Nonetheless, Zionist history was knowingly misleading. In many different communities, in many countries over many centuries, there was much diversity of experience.

There were sustained periods, in some regions, when Jewish communities thrived. For several centuries in the Islamic High Middle Ages, c. 850–1250 AD, Judaism and Jews flourished in a number of Islamic states. There were 2,500 Jews living in twelfth-century Constantinople, for example: craftsmen and merchants for the most part but also lawyers who served independent Jewish courts. Synagogues were legally protected; anti-Semitic acts were forbidden. Another case relates to a more surprising location, perhaps. Describing Eastern Europe in the nineteenth century, Chaim Weizmann's biographer Norman Rose acknowledges that, 'in a very real sense', the Pale could be experienced as 'a sort of Jewish National Home'. Jews in this region were bound together by the common language, Yiddish, as well as by an ancient heritage. Furthermore, Zionist history de-selected the plentiful evidence that Muslim and Jew, Arab and Jew, could co-exist, if not in perfect harmony then for long periods of mutual acceptance within, for example, the Ottoman Empire.

Zionists feared for the Jews. Herzl asserted that Jewish lives were everywhere becoming 'daily more intolerable', and that persecution 'is the case in every country and will remain so'.[24] But he exaggerated. It was anti-Semitism at varying levels that would persist, alongside other racial prejudices, not universal persecution. The pogroms in Russia were dreadful. But the unforeseeable awfulness of what happened, decades later, to Jews on a European mainland under Nazi rule should not be the prism though which we view earlier times or other countries. Recalling his great-grandfather's journey in the steamship *Oxus* to Palestine in 1897, Ari Shavit writes: 'The worst catastrophe in the history of the Jewish people is about to occur... So, as the *Oxus* approaches the shores of the Holy Land, the need to give Palestine to the Jews feels almost palpable.' Shavit continues: 'The Zionism that emerges in 1897 is a stroke of genius... The Herzl Zionists see what is coming... In their own way they act in the 1890s in order to pre-empt the 1940s'.[25] But this is self-serving anachronism; myth, not history.

A glance at the life and thought of Albert Einstein is instructive here. He was born in Germany in 1879. Before the First World War, his experience of discrimination was limited. He rejected German citizenship not because of Germany's anti-Semitism but because of his contempt for its authoritarianism and militarism. Though he was disturbed by rising anti-Semitism in the 1920s, his support of Zionism was limited and conditional. He despised all narrow nationalisms, including Jewish. In the event, he was delighted to accept refuge in the USA in 1933.

The Dreyfus Affair in 1890s France shocked Herzl and many others. But after years of scarcely bearable injustice and suffering, Dreyfus was eventually cleared, reinstated and promoted. Though his own assimilation had been so problematical, he nonetheless had contempt for Zionism. He dismissed it as an 'anachronism'.[26] By the time of Dreyfus's death, another Jewish Frenchman had come to prominence in a rather different way. Leon Blum took office in 1936 as Prime Minister.

The Jewish population in England was untypical: it was small and urban. But here, by the early nineteenth century, many Jews were mixing with others socially, and succeeding not only in business but in the academic world. A century later, the prominent historian Eric Hobsbawm, whose eminence and assimilation led to his being made a Companion of Honour, delighted in his Englishness and, though Jewish, never had time for Zionism. 'It was not such a good idea,' he wrote dismissively; and Theodor Herzl 'would have done better to stay with the *Neue Freie Presse* as its star columnist.'[27] To be sure, in the 1930s Oswald Mosley's British Union of Fascists adopted Nazi-style anti-Semitism. But they were thwarted by indifference, opposition and proscription. The English variety of fascism was violent and nasty, but never the outdoor pursuit of more than a few thousand members.

The prime location for Jewish assimilation – at every extent from 'mutual acceptance' to 'melting-pot' – was the USA. As the German Jewish socialist Judah Levin wrote: 'The eloquence of the Bible [and] the emotion aroused by our ancient memories ... speak for the Land of Israel'; but 'the good life recommends America'.[28] In America, along with the promise of material well-being, were the most favourable conditions for that assimilation of Jews which Zionists railed against.

From the late nineteenth century, most Jews did not act on any longing to 'return' to Palestine, after 1,800 years of 'exile' from their homeland. Even in the later 1940s, by no means all survivors of the genocide saw Palestine as their preferred refuge. Primo Levi, for example, regarded Italy as his one true home, returning there to devote his life as a writer to exposing the horror he had witnessed in Auschwitz. Before that period, in the earlier twentieth century, Zionists were for the most part not being listened to, or not being heard. (The two most articulate and influential of them, Herzl and Weizmann, were ironically among the most assimilated Jews of their generation.)

In the aftermath of the First World War, the Jewish national mythology was not taken seriously in Palestine itself by gentile contemporaries less wedded than the British government to Zionism. Zionist claims that the Jews had a right to Palestine were summarily dismissed. For example, General Congreve, who commanded British forces in Egypt and Palestine, wrote contemptuously that 'we might as well declare that England belongs to Italy because it was once occupied by Romans'.[29] In the judicious report produced by the King-Crane Commission in 1919, we find the following comment, devastating through understatement, on Zionism's version of Jewish history. 'The initial claim, often submitted by Zionist representatives, that they have a "right" to Palestine, based on an occupation of 2,000 years ago, can hardly be seriously considered.'

The Arab view was wearily summarised in their response to the 1922 British White Paper. 'We have shown over and over again that the supposedly historic connection of the Jews with Palestine rests upon very slender historical data. The historic rights of the Arabs are far stronger than those of the Jews. Palestine had a native population before the Jews even went there, and this population has persisted all down the ages and never assimilated with the Jewish tribes, who were always a people to themselves. The Arabs ... have been settled on the land for more than 1,500 years.'[30]

For some, the deepest flaw in the Zionist version of Jewish history was its dependence on the Bible (rather than, say, archaeology) for evidence. As Sand puts it, the *holy* books became a *national* text, 'the birth certificate attesting to the common origin of the "people"'.[31] Rejecting sceptical claims that it is a multi-layered literary construct, Zionism presented the Bible not as a theological treasure but as a reliable historical record.

◆

The status of the Bible lies at the heart of our third question: was Zionism secular?

Herzl acknowledged that, 'we feel our historic affinity only through the faith of our fathers'.[32] Yet he insisted that Zionism was a political, nationalist and *secular* movement. To this assertion, the counter by conservative American rabbi Arthur Hertzberg is powerful. 'Even at its most hard-headedly secular, the Zionist movement ... is unimaginable without its profound mystique about Zion – and these emotions derive not from any modernist philosophy but from the Bible.'[33]

Moreover, the ambitions of the first Zionists were not expressed in secular terms. Ze'ev Dubnow, the early settler, looked ahead thus: 'Then will the glorious day come, as prophesied by Isaiah in his promise of the restoration of Israel.'[34] And the Polish rabbi and sponsor of colonisation Zvi Kalischer insisted: 'Our duty is to labour not only for the glory of our ancestors but for the glory of God who chose Zion.'[35]

The Bible stands at the heart of this issue. There is no doubting its significance for Zionism. Shimon Peres wrote of Ben-Gurion: 'His point of departure was the Bible.'[36] It was the original language of the Bible, Hebrew, which the Zionists would adopt as the lingua franca to bind polyglot Jewish communities in mandated Palestine. Ben-Gurion's proposed boundaries for 'our country', Palestine, arose from biblical references. He did not disguise the implications. 'If I was an Arab leader,' he said in 1956, 'I would never make terms with Israel. That is natural:

we have taken their country. *Sure, God promised it to us*, but what does that matter to them?'[37]

For nineteenth-century Jews, as for their predecessors, the Hebrew Bible had a unique authority. It presented a narrative of their relationship – at times, conversation – with God. What contemporary Christians, including Zionists, term the Old Testament contains, for example, the following verses:

Genesis 17: 8
'And I will give unto thee and to thy seed after thee, the land wherein thou art a stranger, all the land of Canaan, for an everlasting possession.'

Numbers 33: 50–53
'And the Lord spake unto Moses ... Speak unto the children of Israel, and say unto them, When ye are passed over Jordan into the land of Canaan, then ye shall drive out all the inhabitants of the land from before you ... And ye shall dispossess the inhabitants of the land and dwell therein: for I have given you the land to possess it.'

There follows an awful, divine, warning in verse 55:

But if ye will not drive out the inhabitants of the land from before you, then it shall come to pass that those which ye let remain of them shall be pricks in your eyes, and thorns in your sides, and shall vex you in the land wherein ye dwell.[38]

Deuteronomy 1: 6–8
'Behold I have set the land before you: go in and possess the land which the Lord sware unto your fathers, Abraham, Isaac, and Jacob, to give unto them and to their seed after them.'

Grounded in numerous biblical texts, a driving force of Zionism was belief that the Jews were God's Chosen People and that Palestine was not merely a former home but a Promised Land. In 1904, Weizmann himself acknowledged that the Jews' credentials were in a key sense unique: 'We are Jews, our destiny is different from that of any other people, we are a chosen nation.'[39] Ben-Gurion saw Judaism as a faith rather than as a religion (citing his rejection of the rabbinate, the clerical establishment and the hierarchical church). Yet as Shimon Peres puts it, his Judaism 'comprised the Promised Land, the Hebrew language, the vision of the biblical prophets [and] the belief in one God'.[40] Religious observance may largely have been swept away; but what remained was not purely secular. In the age of nationalism, historic claims to territory took on a new guise, but their religious dimension did not disappear.

In the event, Zionism emerged as a hybrid. Arising from the need to protect victims of persecution, it was primarily a colonial project for the acquisition of territory and statehood. A secular, political ideology provided Zionism with mainstream currency and legitimacy. By contrast, an ideology infused with religious messianism would have been idiosyncratic in an increasingly secular age and aroused less sympathy outside Jewry. Yet Zionism sought to meet the aspirations and interests of Jewish communities defined for centuries, by reference to their Bible, as religious, God-fearing and unique: a Chosen People for whom there was a Promised Land.[41]

This composite character was to serve Zionism well. When global circumstances changed, decision-makers in Britain were to be attracted both by the secular dimension – comfortably advocating 'national self-determination' for the Jews after the First World War – and by the notion of an abused religious community fulfilling its destiny by returning to the land which the Old Testament God had granted them.

◆

We may conclude that, though sincerely promoted, each of these three propositions was to an extent a contentious fabrication. What mattered of course was not so much whether propositions were 'true' as the extent to which they were adopted. And by whom. It was to be of historic significance that British imperial decision-makers, with their huge potential at the time of the First World War for transforming the fortunes of peoples, came to accept – uncritically – three core Zionist assertions: that the Jews were a nation which had been exiled from their country by the Romans; had suffered for 1,800 years in the diaspora; and now had the need and the right to 'return' to Palestine as their national homeland.[42]

It is not hard to imagine an alternative future in which, beyond 1914, Zionism remained marginal or faded into obscurity. But circumstances changed, new possibilities opened up, and in 1917 it was endorsed by the British government. And an explanation of that endorsement lies, in part, in the prevalence of another form of Zionism among the decision-makers of that later day.

Christian Zionism

'Then the Lord thy God will turn thy captivity, and have compassion upon thee, and will return and gather thee from all the nations... And the Lord thy God will bring thee into the land which thy fathers possessed, and thou shalt possess it.' Deuteronomy 33: 3, 5

As now, Christians and Jews not only shared belief in one God, they shared a religious text. And familiar passages from their Old Testament, such as this one, led a number of influential Christians in Britain in the nineteenth century to advocate a return of the Jews to Palestine. Christian Zionism produced as many strands as the Jewish Zionism with which Herzl's name would later be associated. At its core though was an apparently philo-Semitic theology based, primarily, on God's unconditional, eternal, promise to Abraham of the whole land of Canaan and, more generally, on a vision of the future extrapolated from Old Testament prophecy.

In broad terms, such Christians held that their God had a continuing relationship with, and purpose for, the Jews. In particular, the Jewish people had a divine right to possess the land of Canaan/Palestine. Christian Zionists believed, and prayed, that at some point in this process of repossession the Jews would be brought to faith in Jesus Christ and so become part of the Church. A London Society for Promoting Christianity Amongst the Jews had been founded in 1809. 'Restoration' and 'conversion' of the Jews lay at the heart of Christian Zionism, the glorious outcome of which would be the Second Coming of Jesus Christ, heralding the fulfilment of God's purpose and the end of time.

During the Victorian era, this new current developed in English Protestant and literary circles. By the middle of the century, hundreds of Anglican clergy in England were Christian Zionists, advocating not only evangelism but also humanitarian work among the needy Jews of Europe. But it was among the laity that the major Christian Zionists emerged; and none was more influential than Lord Shaftesbury. Better known as a politician for his philanthropic initiatives in Parliament, Shaftesbury was also for more than thirty years president of the British and Foreign Bible Society, and the founding president of the Palestine Exploration Fund (PEF). This brought together a number of distinguished British academics and clergy (including the Dean of Westminster Abbey) and for many its purpose was, as Shaftesbury put it in his inaugural address, to prepare Palestine 'for the return of its ancient possessors'.[43]

It was Shaftesbury too who adopted the description, later exploited by Zionists, of Palestine as 'a country without a nation, for a nation without a country'. This was a period of general rising interest in Palestine. George Eliot's last completed novel, *Daniel Deronda*, 1876, is a proto-Zionist work: the eponymous hero discovers his Jewishness in adulthood and is inspired to seek a new life in Palestine.[44] And by this time there were new means available for travelling there. Just four years after the founding of the PEF, Thomas Cook took his first group to Jerusalem; within thirty years, his company had arranged for 12,000 tourists, among them Christian evangelicals, to visit the Holy Land.

As we shall see later, Christian Zionism not only survived into the twentieth century but appears to have been a strong influence on several decision-makers in the British government towards the end of the First World War. Christian Zionism and Jewish Zionism overlapped not so much theologically as instrumentally: that is, regarding the Jews' longing for Palestine. There is more than one irony in this relationship. Christian Zionism was an essentially religious commitment among Christians, whereas Herzl's Zionism was a professedly secular ideology and movement among Jews. More remarkable is the fact that Zionism was supported and encouraged by Christians long before it gained widespread acceptance within Jewish communities. This second irony was to be of huge political significance: it may be argued that the 1917 Balfour Declaration owed more to Christian Zionists than to any weight of worldwide Jewish support for a national home in Palestine (the Zionist goal of Herzl and Weizmann).

One further irony emerged, during and after the First World War. With English Christian opinion tending to be strongly pro-Zionist, some British officials in Palestine regarded Arab Christians – perhaps 10 per cent of all Palestinian Arabs, and among the most prominent and articulate – not as co-religionists and potential allies, but as a dangerous obstacle. Consequently, Arab Christian opposition to the Balfour Declaration, and that community's nationalist appeals to the British government, would be fruitless.

David Lloyd George (1863–1945)
British Prime Minister, 1916–1922

THE BRITISH ADOPTION
OF ZIONISM, 1914–1917

'The policy of His Majesty's Government is anti-Semitic, and in result will prove a rallying ground for anti-Semites in every country of the world.' Edwin Montagu[1]

Overview

After August 1914, in the new context of a world in turmoil, Zionism's fortunes and prospects were unexpectedly and improbably transformed. Though not immediately, the First World War changed everything. In an age of empire, this was at heart a war between empires. At its end, the victorious empires shared out the territories of those they had defeated. In particular, the British formally acquired Palestine from the Ottoman Turks. By that time, in the Balfour Declaration of November 1917, they had declared their support for Zionism.

This represented an astonishing, unanticipated, turn in British policy, brought about by the war. In December 1916, political crisis in Britain brought to power David Lloyd George, already drawn to Zionism. At just this time, Palestine – to which he was emotionally attached – looked as though it could be prised from the Turks. Given the worrying wartime context elsewhere, of stalemate on land and crisis at sea, it now appeared to make sense to issue an appeal for help to 'world Jewry'. Lloyd George and many of those around him believed that Jews in America and in Russia, especially, were highly influential and that they would support the Zionist plan for a Jewish national home. They would welcome

Balfour's promise that the British would 'facilitate' this project; they would do everything possible to keep America and Russia committed to the war on Britain's side; and they would thus enable Britain both to secure victory and to support Zionism in Palestine.

In the event, as a wartime *cri de coeur*, the Declaration failed. Based on fantasy, it proved fruitless. Its issue did not change the course of the war. However, Lloyd George remained committed to it; and its retention, afterwards, would change the course of Jewish and Middle Eastern history.

BRITAIN AND PALESTINE

It is of more than passing interest that, during the premiership of Herbert Henry Asquith, the British did not seek to acquire Palestine. It was certainly not the government's priority. Palestine was a land of relative insignificance that could be dealt with once the war was over. If we review four relevant documents of this period, 1914–16, we see that, under Asquith, the prevalent official British view was that Palestine was a region of limited strategic value; and that, assuming the war was won, the British and French could then conclude acceptable arrangements for this and all the lands of the Ottoman Empire.

First, a caution. We must beware hindsight and too narrow a focus. Before and during the First World War, Palestine was not the defined, separate entity that appeared on the post-war map and foreshadowed the state of Israel. For the Ottomans, it was a remote region of limited importance. For Zionists, this was a once Promised Land from which the Jews had been exiled. But for the Arabs it was a part of Greater Syria and an integral part of the extensive Arab world which Europeans termed the Middle or Near East. Far from being a distinct territory, Palestine had long been, in the laconic words of a reflective British Arabist in 1946, 'a somewhat arid prolongation of Syria'.[2] When, in 1920, the Arabs declared their leader, Faisal, King of Syria, there was a general Arab assumption that this territory included Palestine. It was only months later, when the French deposed Faisal to take control of Syria, that Arab nationalists from the south focused their attention on (the now British) Palestine.

In other words, it was to be a fateful post-war decision, and a break with continuity, for the British and the French not to cultivate a *united* Arab world but instead to *divide* that world and seize the pieces they each wanted. There was much bitterness among Palestinian Arabs when they found themselves, for the first time, a distinct political unit cut off from the rest of Syria.

But this lay in the future. During the war, and before Asquith's fall, there were indications that the British would be content, afterwards, with both Arab unity and a considerable degree of Arab independence.

The Future of Palestine, January 1915

Early evidence of British strategic thinking and war aims came in January 1915, shortly after the Ottoman Empire entered the war. The British Cabinet considered a memorandum titled 'The Future of Palestine' put forward by one of their number, Herbert Samuel.[3] Samuel was the only Jewish member of this Cabinet: indeed, he was the first Jew to serve at this highest level of British government. He was also a Zionist, and his paper was a heartfelt appeal to his colleagues for Britain to acquire Palestine as a homeland for the Jews.

Samuel was nothing if not direct. 'A feeling is spreading,' he insisted, 'that now, at last, some advance may be made towards the restoration of the Jews to the land to which they are attached by ties almost as ancient as history itself.' This required 'the annexation of the country to the British Empire'. Then 'in course of time, the Jewish people, grown into a majority and settled in the land, may be conceded such degree of self-government as the conditions of that day may justify.'

Samuel appreciated that he had to convince his colleagues that such a vision was in line with, and would further, British interests. He struggled, however. His five 'arguments' contained more hopefulness

Sir Herbert Samuel (1870–1963)
British Cabinet Minister, 1909–1916; High Commissioner
of Palestine, 1920–1925.

than sound strategic calculation. For example, he blithely maintained,
in wishful thinking to which many of his colleagues in London would
fall prey, that British administration would bring so many benefits that
the present Arab inhabitants of Palestine would 'not merely acquiesce,
but rejoice, in the change'. In addition, according to Samuel, possession
of Palestine would raise Britain's prestige – 'would add lustre even to the
British crown' – and win for England 'the lasting gratitude of the Jews
throughout the world'.

More prosaically Samuel argued that, in a post-war settlement, it
would be wiser for Britain to seek 'compensations' in the Ottoman lands
of Mesopotamia and Palestine than in Germany's African possessions,
for fear of arousing 'intense bitterness among the German people'. We

may note the implication that bitterness among Arabs would be of no comparable concern. As for imperial strategy, Samuel had just one argument: that his proposal would help to secure the Suez Canal (though he somewhat undermined his case by acknowledging that 'Palestine in British hands' would thereby itself be open to attack).

Samuel ended as he had begun, with a fervent appeal to support 'the Jewish race'. Palestine might be able to 'hold' in time up to 4 million of the world's 12 million Jews and 'the character of the individual Jew, wherever he might be, would be ennobled'. 'The Jewish brain,' he concluded, with a flush of racial pride, 'is a physiological product not to be despised.'

Unfortunately for Samuel and his cause, the Prime Minister was not interested. Asquith did not support Zionist ambitions. He dismissed his ministerial colleague's advocacy as a frenzied ('dithyrambic') outburst; and 'despatched Samuel's memorandum to the wastepaper basket'.[4]

Zionism would have to wait. It was significant that there was at least one zealous Zionist at the heart of public affairs, and a triumph of sorts that Zionist goals were being discussed in Cabinet and were thereby reaching a wider circle of British decision-makers. But Asquith's government saw no strategic value in Palestine – so, no gain from its acquisition – and was unmoved by Zionism.

This episode illustrated that something important would have to change, in the course of the war and/or the course of British politics, for Zionism to receive in London the endorsement it needed.

Report of the de Bunsen Committee of Imperial Defence: Asiatic Turkey, June 1915

The indication, in the story of Samuel's paper, that 'Palestine in British hands' had no priority in the strategic thinking of this imperial power, was emphatically confirmed a few months later. On 8 April 1915, Asquith asked an interdepartmental committee to determine what British policy should be towards the Ottoman Empire. In particular, what should be British strategic priorities in the aftermath of war (and victory)? Chaired by Sir Maurice de Bunsen, the committee published its report less than three months later. It is full of interest, but one assessment above all catches the eye. In a concluding paragraph it says: 'Still less do the Committee desire to offer suggestions about the future destiny of Palestine.'[5]

The committee's analysis was to have considerable influence on subsequent British policy-making, albeit in matters *other* than the future of Palestine. With the security of and access to India always at the back of their minds, the committee was in no doubt that Mesopotamia was the major British concern regarding the territories of the Ottoman Empire. Moreover, 'mankind as a whole' would benefit from Britain's development of Mesopotamia (Iraq), in which the British would bring back into cultivation 12 million acres of fertile soil; meanwhile, 'we could develop oil fields'. The acquisition of Baghdad would 'guard the chain of oil-wells along the Turco-Persian frontier'. Relating to this, 'one of the cardinal principles of British policy in the Middle East' is 'our special and supreme position in the Persian Gulf'. No mention of Palestine here.

Nonetheless, more was probably required to keep British interests safe: a 'back door into Mesopotamia from the Eastern Mediterranean'. Conceding that the French had a lasting interest in the best port of that coast, Alexandretta, they recommended as second-best Haifa, which was 'capable of development into a sufficiently good port, and of connection by railway with Mesopotamia'. So, the committee imagined securing for Britain the lands contained in a cartographical triangle 'whose base is from Aqaba to the Persian Gulf, and whose sides run from Acre on the west, and Basra on the east, to Mosul at the apex'. This was the marginal importance of (one part of) Palestine: that one of its harbours should be developed, so as to provide secondary support for British interests elsewhere, in Mesopotamia.

Early in the report, the British Empire's nine strategic 'desiderata' are enumerated. Number One is 'final recognition and consolidation of our position in the Persian Gulf'. The ninth and last is 'a settlement of the question of Palestine and the Holy Places of Christendom'. To underline Palestine's minor significance, this item is one of three 'which may, for the moment, be set aside', to be dealt with later 'in concert with other Powers'. We notice that insofar as there was British interest in Palestine, it was religious and also historic. This history was not only ancient but also recent. With disputes over the Holy Places, especially Jerusalem, among the causes of the Crimean War, these sites again needed international deliberation. However, the committee concluded that 'His Majesty's Government should be prepared to *make no claim themselves* to the possession of the Holy Places, and to leave their future to be decided as a separate question, in discussion with those who stand for the national and religious interests involved.'[6]

The report is revealing about Britain's attitude to France, the most important 'other Power' referred to here. When it was written, in the middle of 1915, Britain and France were allies, committed to standing side by side against Germany in a conflict for which neither end nor outcome was in sight. There is little apprehension that France, with whom the *entente cordiale* was quite recent, might (again) become a threatening imperial rival. The committee ruled out a successful bid by France for sole control of the Holy Places, since 'the world-wide interests affected by the destiny of the Holy Land will not allow this'. Britain acknowledged that France would claim a 'liberally defined Syria', but there was no reason to fear serious French ambition in Palestine. Nor was there any anticipated threat from Russia (to Palestine, as distinct from Mesopotamia).

Reading this report, we seek in vain any endorsement of Herbert Samuel's argument, above, that Palestine was needed for the protection of the Suez Canal. Rather, we may infer that there was such confidence in British Egypt's capacity to provide all the security the canal needed, as there had been for thirty years, that there was no need to waste words on the issue. In 'The Future of Palestine', Samuel did not specify a threat to Britain's strategic position, but we may assume that he had France uppermost in mind. But the Committee of Imperial Defence had few such concerns. It was bound to speculate about a future war in the area against France (and Russia). But to imagine was not to anticipate. Rather, the assumption was that European countries would recognise each other's imperial spheres of interest in the region and agree compromises. In particular, it was asserted in this report that any difficulty in securing a deal with France 'should not prove insuperable'. The Sykes-Picot Agreement was negotiated just a year later.

In short, in 1915 the Committee for Imperial Defence did not see 'Palestine' as a priority. Haifa would be an asset; the Holy Places would need attention. But the acquisition of the whole territory was not regarded as being in Britain's strategic interest.

There is more to this report than is generally acknowledged. Writers on the period tend not to go far beyond quoting from the solitary, late, paragraph devoted to Palestine: 'It will be idle for HMG to claim the retention of Palestine in their sphere.' However, we need to acknowledge also the thinking and the calculations behind this conclusion. A product of its age, the report was certainly cynical. The casual discussion of 'partition' and 'annexation' is striking. But its authors were thorough, and they looked carefully at the long-term implications of each of the strategic options they considered.

The Balfour Declaration, issued two years later, was by contrast romantic in its vision and naïve in its neglect of consequences.

The McMahon letter, 24 October 1915

'Oceans of ink' have been spilled on the subject of another British documentary relic of 1915, the first full year of the First World War.[7] The letter in dispute was part of a lengthy correspondence between Sir Henry McMahon, British High Commissioner in Egypt, and Hussein bin Ali, Sharif of Mecca, whose Hashemite clan claimed descent from the Prophet Muhammad.[8] It would prove to be the first of three separate agreements that the British concluded for the post-war partition of Ottoman Arab lands, between 1915 and 1917. 'One of the challenges of British post-war diplomacy', comments historian Eugene Rogan with a degree of understatement, 'was to find a way to square what were, in many ways, contradictory promises.'[9]

Different parties have, unsurprisingly, accorded the McMahon letter different levels of significance. This controversy will continue. We consider it here for the light it sheds on, first, Britain's relationship with the Arabs at this stage of the war; second, the status of Palestine at this time; and, third, on Arab rejection of the Balfour Declaration which was to follow two years later.

McMahon wrote: 'I am empowered in the name of the Government of Great Britain to give the following assurances... Great Britain is prepared to recognise and support the independence of the Arabs within the territories included in the limits and boundaries proposed by the Sharif of Mecca... I am convinced that this declaration will assure you beyond all possible doubt of the sympathy of Great Britain towards the aspirations of her traditional friends, the Arabs, and will result in a firm and lasting alliance, the immediate result of which will be the expulsion of the Turks from Arab countries and the freeing of the Arab peoples from the Turkish yoke.' There was a political deal here. Recognition of an independent Arab Kingdom, under Hussein, would be in return for the Hashemites leading an Arab revolt, with British support, against Ottoman rule.

How extensive would this kingdom be? Hussein had earlier asked for all of Greater Syria as well as Mesopotamia and the Arabian Peninsula. In reply, the exceptions that McMahon stipulated, elsewhere in the same letter, did *not* include Palestine. They were: Cilicia (the southern coast of Turkish Asia Minor); the area of Syria west of the towns of Damascus, Homs, Hama and Aleppo (sought by the French); and Baghdad and Basra (which the British wanted for themselves). Britain would substantially recognise Arab independence across a region defined by Sharif Hussein. Palestine was not mentioned at all; it fell within Hussein's boundaries.[10]

It is worth emphasising that, according to this British pronouncement of late 1915, Palestine was not to be detached from Syria. It lay south of the specified Syrian towns, not west. As Joseph Jeffries, political correspondent for the *Daily Mail*, was to observe in 1939: 'There was no mention of its exclusion. We gave our word that on its soil the Arabs should be free of all foreign control save such as they chose of their own free will.' He added: 'For this reason, today, more than twenty years after this Anglo-Arab treaty was concluded, the treaty remains of momentous importance to Palestine.'[11] Jeffries exaggerated: this was not, strictly, an Anglo-Arab treaty. But it was an official, written, wartime pledge. It preceded the Balfour Declaration by two years. Later, after the Arab Revolt against the Ottomans and the Ottoman defeat, Arabs expected it to be honoured. In the end, the question whether or not Palestine was, or was to be, included is academic: the British reneged on the whole promise.

The Sykes-Picot Agreement, May 1916

The Sykes-Picot Agreement, the following year, retains a reputation for secret, imperialist double-dealing and cynical manipulation of subject peoples and their resources – a reputation that may exceed what it deserves.[12] Our special interest lies in what it says, or does not say, about (British) imperial interest in Palestine at that time, two years into the war.

The agreement was to share out the Ottoman territories, apart from a Turkish Turkey (Anatolia) and an Arab Arabia (to include Mecca and Medina). The negotiators Sir Mark Sykes and François Georges-Picot drew 'a line in the sand' from the coast of the eastern Mediterranean to the north-western frontier of Persia (Iran). In place of Ottoman rule, there would be 'protected' Arab states, both north and south of the line. These would be subject to, respectively, French and British influence (financial, economic, political). Moreover, as illustrated on an accompanying coloured map of the region, within each sphere there were to be special zones, for 'direct administration or control': a blue zone in the north (including Alexandretta, the north-east Mediterranean port, and Damascus) for France; and a red zone in the south (the north-western shores of the Persian Gulf and extending north through Basra to Baghdad) for Britain. The signatories agreed that no changes in these arrangements should be made by one party without the prior consent of the other.

That was the partition plan. In the light of the de Bunsen committee's findings, which in general it closely resembles, one detail catches the eye: the allocation of Mosul to the northern, French, sphere. This probably reflected a classic British imperial priority: to avoid sharing an Asian frontier with Russia. In fact, Mosul itself had not been mentioned by name in de Bunsen's list of nine priorities. It was regarded in that report as of secondary importance, the army valuing its 'good hill stations for white troops', while its native Kurds afforded 'excellent material for recruits'.

Palestine is not mentioned by name on the map. Rather (much of) what became the post-war mandated territory is shown, and referred to, as merely 'the brown area'.[13] This, it was agreed by Sykes and Picot, would come under 'international administration', the form of which would be decided later after consultation with Russia, other allies, and the Sharif of Mecca. This outcome may reflect an unwritten assumption: that what mattered in 'the brown area', which included Jerusalem, was authority relating to the Holy Places. However, there was one special case: it was agreed that 'Great Britain be accorded' Haifa, the sole location in Palestine that the de Bunsen committee had focused on. Haifa, along with neighbouring Acre, was to be an addition to the British red zone. This was part of a British enclave in the far north of the Palestine 'allied condominium', close to the southern border of the French zone. This was a nice case of inter-empire accommodation. Haifa, the agreement spelled out, would serve as the Mediterranean terminus for Britain's railway link eastwards to Baghdad in distant Mesopotamia.

In trying to assess the significance of the Sykes-Picot agreement, in view of Britain's policy towards Palestine just a year or so later, three aspects are of interest. First, there is confirmation that Palestine as a territory had, in general, a very low priority. In not taking this negotiating opportunity to push for its inclusion in the British sphere – let alone 'the red zone' – Sykes was expressing the consistent, considered, view of Asquith's government. Palestine was not a strategic priority for British imperial interests. Haifa was the exception, as 'the back door' to Britain's primary region of interest, Mesopotamia and the Persian Gulf.

Second, this agreement is merely one indication of the government's thinking, while war was raging (and would continue to rage for two more years). While profound imperial strategic interests were constant, the context remained in flux; similarly, international agreements such as this would, as the context changed and once victory was won, be subject to review and adaptation.

Third, here was evidence, in no way surprising, that the British and French governments could talk about the future of the Middle East in a business-like manner, recognising the interests of each other. There was nothing naïve about these dealings. As the de Bunsen report had put it the previous year: 'It is of course obvious that British desiderata in Asiatic Turkey are circumscribed by those of other Powers, and that any attempt to formulate them must as far as possible be made to fit in with the known or understood aspirations of *those who are our Allies today, but may be our competitors tomorrow*'.[14] There would be rivalry, certainly; but hard-nosed compromise would remain both desirable and achievable. There is no sense in 1915 or 1916 that the French might pose a threat to British interests, in the region generally or to Suez in particular, after the war. The Sykes-Picot arrangement over Palestine was a pragmatic arrangement: neither party fully obtained what it wanted, yet together they could find a compromise.

Lastly, we note insistence on the need for secrecy regarding these dealings with the French: in particular, the terms had to be kept from Arab leaders.

◆

The question remains: why Palestine? Or rather, why did British policy suddenly change from indifference towards Palestine to a determination to acquire it? Asquith's British imperial government repeatedly demonstrated that Palestine was not a strategic priority: in rejecting Herbert Samuel's paper; in accepting the recommendations of de Bunsen's committee on imperial defence; in accepting implicitly Palestine's allocation to a post-war Arab state, in the McMahon letter; and in negotiating the Sykes-Picot Agreement with France.

Yet the conventional view remains that the British felt an overriding strategic need for Palestine, relating to the defence of Suez and more. To be sure, Winston Churchill, guided by Zionism, had written in 1908 that 'a strong, free Jewish state astride the bridge between Europe and Africa, flanking the land roads to the East, would be ... an immense advantage to the British Empire'.[15] Zionism moreover would offer a convenient propaganda device by which the British could disguise a fundamentally imperialist purpose. This is the line of reasoning accepted by many historians. According to James Barr, a prolific historian of the Middle East, for instance, 'by publicly supporting Zionist aspirations to make Palestine a Jewish state, they could secure the exposed east flank of the Suez Canal while dodging accusations that they were land-grabbing'.[16] And Jonathan Schneer writes: 'Of course ... for imperial-economic-strategic reasons, Britain meant to keep the primary governing role in Palestine for herself'.[17]

Much of this is questionable: there are grounds for challenging the easy assumption that continues to be made. It is true that the British had taken control over Egypt in 1882 in order to safeguard the canal as a critical stretch of the sea route to India. As a consequence, they had fallen out with France. A period of vexatious colonial rivalry ensued, and in 1898 the two powers came close to open warfare over Fashoda, on the Upper Nile (Egypt's life-line). Egypt straddled the Suez Canal, but the canal's eastern bank was exposed: the Ottomans were not a threat, but the French, in pursuit of their own Greater Syria, might be.

However, a surer guide to Anglo-French relations during and after the First World War is the *entente cordiale* which in 1904 marked the resolution of outstanding imperial rivalries between the powers. This understanding expressed the shared view that on balance the British and the French had more to gain as allies than as foes, especially in view of the threat to each from Germany. Their fighting side by side against a common enemy from 1914 was therefore no abnormal, unexpected, alignment; it had been anticipated and prepared for (and was the restoration of a previous alliance against a common foe, Russia, in the Crimean War). In the event, French Prime Minister Georges Clemenceau's post-war fears of Germany did far more to bring the French and British together than Near-Eastern rivalry did to separate them.

Meanwhile, Asquith's government had no appetite for Palestine. And it accepted France as a power with whom it could do business: for the foreseeable future, in war and peace, in the Middle East and elsewhere. France was certainly not perceived as a danger serious enough to overcome Britain's reluctance to take on still more imperial responsibilities. In the sobering words of the de Bunsen Report, 'Our Empire is wide enough already, and our task is to consolidate the possessions we already have.' In this light, Palestine was not a strategic priority.

Not, that is, before the change of Prime Minister. In December 1916, a major domestic political crisis in Britain removed Herbert Asquith, Prime Minister at the outbreak of the war, and brought David Lloyd George to power as his successor. By late 1916, Asquith was coming under increasing pressure. In the last years of peace, he had achieved much – in social welfare, for example – but he was failing now as a war leader. He had survived the 'shell shortage' crisis, but he continued to lack vigour and enterprise in pursuit of victory. Towards the end of 1916, with the slaughter on the Somme fresh in everyone's mind, a cross-party triumvirate of leading politicians – Lloyd George, Asquith's Liberal War Minister; Edward Carson, leader of the Ulster Unionists; and Andrew Bonar Law, leader of the Conservatives – urged the irresolute Prime Minister to institute, beneath him, an elite War Cabinet, consisting of themselves. This pressure, along with considerable support in the press for a change of national leadership, induced Asquith to step aside. On 6 December 1916 he was replaced as Prime Minister by Lloyd George, by chance already an enthusiastic Zionist, though this had nothing at all to do with his rise to power.

Quite coincidentally, there was a tipping of the military balance in one, remote, theatre of war. By early 1917 there were no signs of the war's end. Where Britain and France faced Germany on the Western Front, there was stalemate. There were indications that the Germans would win the war at sea. But the Ottoman Turks had become vulnerable. In January 1915, an Ottoman army had invaded Sinai, though it was held before threatening Suez. For much of that year, the focus of the Middle Eastern Front turned to the Dardanelles and Gallipoli, where an ambitious strategic action by British and ANZAC forces ended in defeat and withdrawal. 'The Turk' was underestimated at this time, along with 'the African' and 'the Arab'. There followed in 1916 the surrender of British forces to the Ottomans in Kut, south of Baghdad; and a sustained contest for Sinai.

But then the military situation improved. A contributory factor was the Arab Revolt. In June 1916, encouraged by the British, the Arabs rose, under Faisal Hussein, against the Turks. This revolt, supported by T.E. Lawrence, added to pressure on the Ottomans and gave Britain the advantage. At the year's end, British and ANZAC forces at last had victories to report. In December 1916, the British secured El Arish. This was the one theatre of operations where British armies were actually advancing. In January 1917, they completed the recapture of Sinai. Palestine was opened up.

Lloyd George's coming to power at just this time was to have profound and long-term consequences for the Near East. In the middle of the war, the government of a Prime Minister indifferent to both Palestine and Zionism was replaced by another, committed to both. The coincidental reversal of British military fortunes was such that, within days of taking office, Lloyd George was able to give fresh impulse to plans for an advance from Egypt. Asked by his chief whip 'What about Palestine?' the Prime Minister replied, 'Oh! We must grab that.'[18] In June, Lloyd George told Allenby to take Jerusalem by Christmas. He did.

BRITAIN AND ZIONISM:
THE BALFOUR DECLARATION, 1917

The promise was conveyed in a letter – dated 2 November 1917 and signed by Arthur Balfour, the Foreign Secretary – to Lord Rothschild, prominent among British Jews and honorary president of the Zionist Federation of Great Britain and Ireland. A single sentence of sixty-seven words, it was published in *The Times* a week later, on 9 November:

His Majesty's Government view with favour the establishment in Palestine of a national home for the Jewish people, and will use their best endeavours to facilitate the achievement of this object, it being clearly understood that nothing shall be done which may prejudice the civil and religious rights of existing non-Jewish communities in Palestine, or the rights and political status enjoyed by Jews in any other country.[19]

In these words, the British gave an endorsement of the Zionist project for Palestine which would have been scarcely imaginable before the war or indeed in the earlier years of the war. It is to be explained by individual responses to changing circumstances. It is a tale not of inevitability or necessity but of coincidence and contingency.

To make sense of this extraordinary British policy initiative, we must try to uncover what Lloyd George, Balfour and other key decision-makers thought, wanted, or hoped. Impersonal forces shape history; so, too, in times of flux, do the private motives and public decisions of individuals.

In mid-1917 the general military situation remained bleak for Britain. Progress of any promise was exceptional in the Middle East. The Ottomans might appear vulnerable, but the Germans held firm in northern France on the Western Front and still had the advantage, potentially decisive, in the war at sea. The situation called for imaginative, if not desperate, measures. Lloyd George had to win the war. Chaim Weizmann persuaded the new Prime Minister that an appeal to the Jews of America and Russia, based on the offer of a homeland in Palestine, would help to achieve this primary goal. And so the Balfour Declaration was made.

The previous year, in March 1916, Foreign Secretary Lord Grey had believed that 'the Jewish forces in America, the East and elsewhere' were 'largely, if not preponderantly, hostile to us'.[20] In particular, it seemed that up to 3 million Jews in the USA had no wish to fight alongside anti-Semitic, Tsarist Russia. But in March 1917 the Tsar abdicated; and in April the USA declared war on Germany. Chaim Weizmann saw his opportunity. He advised the Allies to declare outright support for Zionism.

Weizmann persuaded the British that the Jews in both Russia and the USA were crucial to their respective countries remaining in the world war. According to him, in Russia, the Jews would put pressure on the Provisional Government to keep fighting Germany and prevent the Russian grain trade from being diverted to hungry Germans. In America, they would support President Wilson and vanquish the continuing opposition to full involvement in Europe's war.

Under considerable pressure to break the stalemate against Germany and to secure victory, British policy-makers were susceptible to Zionism. They surrendered to its blandishments and, however improbably, they offered Palestine as a homeland in the future, in return for present help. Only eighteen months after Grey's sombre assessment, Balfour, who succeeded him as Foreign Secretary, addressed the Cabinet meeting of 31 October 1917, at which the declaration was at last approved. He assured his ministerial colleagues that 'the vast majority of Jews in Russia and America, as indeed all over the world, now appear to be favourable to Zionism'.[21]

The reality was very different from the picture that Weizmann so skilfully painted. The power of 'international Jewry' was a fiction: consciously or not, an anti-Semitic delusion. For Michael Stanislawski, Professor of Jewish History at Columbia University, the Jews in the United States had 'virtually no political influence'; and in Russia 'absolutely no influence'.[22] The associated supposition was that this 'international Jewry' leaned towards Zionism. However, as noted earlier, by 1914, of around 3 million Jews in America, just 12,000 were enrolled as members of Zionist societies. More would have sympathised, especially perhaps when the United States entered the war in March 1917, but American Zionism could be regarded as 'little more than a sect'.[23] Yet it was on this basis that Britain decided to sponsor the Zionist cause.

The main point here, however, is not whether world Jewry could, or did, win the war for Britain (it could not, and did not). Rather it is that the Balfour Declaration was made, in a time of crisis, as a loosely worded, no-cost, short-term appeal for help. What lay behind its issue? We look now at the roles of the two key players, Lloyd George and Weizmann; at Balfour himself, and the role of anti-Semitic nimbyism; at the memorandum written by Cabinet member Edwin Montagu; at Christian Zionism and its influence on imperial strategy; and then more closely at the text itself.

◆

David Lloyd George

Lloyd George has been impishly described as 'a master of improvised speech and of improvised policies'.[24] It is, of course, always very difficult to know what people think, or thought; and it is notoriously difficult in the case of politicians, who do not always say or write what they believe to be true. But the effort should be made here. Lloyd George was not only the man who authorised the sending of Balfour's letter but also, and more importantly, the Prime Minister, *after* the war, who insisted that, rather than being shelved, the Declaration should be included in full in the terms of Britain's League of Nations mandate for Palestine. His leadership at this time shows how individuals in power can, if the conjunction of events allows, make decisions that change the course of history.

Among Lloyd George's primary interests at this time were Palestine, the Jews and Zionism. C.P. Scott, editor of *The Manchester Guardian,* wrote of Lloyd George in his diary: 'Palestine was to him the one really interesting part of the war.'[25] The contrast with Asquith could hardly have been greater. And the new Prime Minister had told Scott that Britain 'could take care of the Holy Places better than anyone else'.[26]

Realism and romanticism are inter-woven in Lloyd George's memoirs.[27] Palestine was cherished as 'a historic and a sacred land, throbbing from Dan to Beersheba with immortal traditions'. For him, Palestine was essentially Jerusalem and the Holy Places. When briefed at the post-war Paris Peace Conference on the contemporary geography of Palestine, Lloyd George 'could not move beyond the Christian Zionist worldview of his youth' and 'insisted on reciting, from his memory of childhood Sunday School lessons, the Biblical cities and lands of Bible times – some of which no longer existed'. He admitted that as a child he 'was taught far more about the history of the Jews than about the history of my own land'.[28] As for the Jews, 'this race of wanderers sought a national hearth and a refuge for the children of Israel' wrote Lloyd George, 'in the country which the splendour of their spiritual genius has made for ever glorious'.

Lloyd George first became aware of the Zionist movement during the time of the El Arish and British East Africa offers. Years later, after the Ottomans declared war, he told his colleague Herbert Samuel that he was keen to see a Jewish state established in Palestine. He met Weizmann for the first time over a working breakfast with Samuel in January 1915. Weizmann 'appealed to my deep reverence for the great men of his race who were the authors of the sublime literature upon which I was brought up'. Lloyd George was Samuel's sole supporter in the Cabinet when it considered Samuel's paper at that time. In March 1917, Weizmann met Lloyd George (by now Prime Minister) again, along with Balfour; and Weizmann 'gained the impression that the statesmen who really mattered were unshaken in their support for a British protectorate over Palestine'.[29]

His impression was sound. As Lloyd George put it, later: 'during the summer of 1917, with my zealous assent as Prime Minister, Mr Balfour entered into negotiations with Lord Rothschild on the subject of the Zionist aims'.[30] Florid and overblown as some of Lloyd George's sentiments strike us, we may infer a strong emotional commitment, since childhood, to biblical Palestine and a genuine fascination with the Jews, their spokesman, their history and their prospects. He appears to have relished lending support to a deserving, oppressed, people (albeit somehow considered, simultaneously and incongruously, a people of intangible global agency).

Evidence of Lloyd George's enduring support for Zionism comes from the House of Commons in 1930 – many years after he lost office – in the wake of severe disturbances in Palestine the previous year. The Passfield White Paper of 1930 drew attention not only to general Arab concerns about levels of *authorised* Jewish immigration into Palestine, but also to their specific concern that *illegal* immigration was continuing, unchecked. Lloyd George scoffed. 'This White Paper is a one-sided document. It is biased. Its whole drift is hostile to the mandate. It breathes distrust and even antagonism of the Jewish activities... You have only got to look at one or two things with which they are dealing. Take immigration. There is criticism of the Jews because some of them went there temporarily and remained, attracted by the country.'[31]

There were the immediate practical concerns, too: the exigencies of war, and the need for help, in 1917. In his memoirs, Lloyd George urges his readers to remember that 'the issue of the war was still very much in doubt'. The Allies had two strategic goals in 1917: to enforce the blockade of the Central Powers, and to speed up the war preparations of the USA. In this context, of the need to sway world opinion, an appeal to the Jews seemed reasonable, and worth trying. Lloyd George thus writes of 'the decision to come to terms with Jewry'. The timing of the declaration 'was determined by considerations of war policy... It was part of our propagandist strategy for mobilising every opinion and force throughout the world which would weaken the enemy and improve the Allied chances.'

Lloyd George also had security concerns, especially regarding his wartime allies the French. He was among those who believed that a Zionist Palestine would help to secure the Suez Canal's eastern approaches (a belief not widely shared in the military, as we shall see). We may note that there are hints, too, of a somewhat different calculation. The Cabinet Secretary Maurice Hankey was to write that 'the new Prime Minister wanted assets to bargain with, against those of the enemy'. Among these 'obtainables' – including German East Africa, for example – was Palestine. Seeking such 'assets' justified, for Lloyd George, 'the side-shows' of the war.[32] In this testimony, Palestine might serve only as a post-war bargaining chip. But other indications of Lloyd George's motivations tend to rule out this type of reckoning, the more so because after the war Britain would be competing with France.

Drawn to the romance of Zionism, Lloyd George was happy also to exploit it. It offered an agency and a cloak. When Lloyd George decided to launch the invasion of Palestine 'he was well aware that such a move would certainly spark accusations of imperialism'. So 'he decided that support for the stateless Zionists' aspirations was a good way to thwart French ambitions in the Middle East and silence [President Woodrow] Wilson simultaneously'.[33] It is likely that two strategic calculations lay behind Lloyd George's adoption of (and post-war commitment to) Jewish 'national self-determination': it would disguise his passion for Palestine and, in his hands, Britain's on-going commitment to colonisation east of Suez; and it would help to cover the costs.

Lloyd George was fiercely anti-French. He confided to C.P. Scott that a French Palestine was out of the question and that he was altogether opposed to a condominium. His antipathy to France appears to have been irrational, and not based on reasoned strategic calculation at all. His erstwhile colleague, Asquith, offered his own explanation, writing that 'Lloyd George thinks it would be an outrage to let the Christian Holy Places ... pass into the hands of agnostic, atheist France.'[34] We might add that the Welsh non-Conformist's suspicion of the Roman Catholic Church – arguably accounting for his lack of sympathy with

Irish nationalism – would have led Lloyd George in a similar direction. Perhaps religious prejudice mattered at least as much as political calculation.

The French, moreover, had declared their own interest in Zionism. On 4 June 1917, Jules Cambon of the French Foreign Ministry wrote to the Zionist activist Nahum Sokolow. From a British perspective, the letter grew in menace as it proceeded. 'It would be a deed of justice and of reparation,' wrote Cambon, 'to assist, by the protection of the Allied powers, in the renaissance of the Jewish nationality in that land from which the people of Israel were exiled so many centuries ago.' He continued, 'The French Government ... cannot but feel sympathy for your cause.'[35] Not only the French: there was a belief in London that, by September 1917, 'the German government were making very serious efforts to capture the Zionist movement', according to Lloyd George. It was 'considerations' such as these which 'impelled the British Government towards making a contract with Jewry'.[36]

A contemporary Greek tragedy throws further light on Lloyd George's *modus operandi*. In early 1919, Britain's victorious Prime Minister attended the Peace Conference at Versailles. Once again, he was to be moved by prejudice and by the charisma of a great advocate. On this occasion, it was the 'energetic, persuasive, indefatigable' Greek Prime Minister, Eleutherios Venizelos. His Greek cause was, in a number of respects, comparable to that of Chaim Weizmann's Zionism. He too sought – in the name of history, civilisation and justice – to serve his people by re-creating something of the glory of the ancient world. Venizelos insisted on a Greater Greece, in the wake of the collapse of the Ottoman Empire and at the expense of the Turks. The country which he proposed would incorporate Thrace (between the Aegean and Black Seas) and a huge piece of Asia Minor including Izmir. The Canadian historian (and great-granddaughter of Lloyd George) Margaret MacMillan notes regarding Venizelos that, as with Weizmann, 'only a few wondered whether his influence over the peacemakers was a good thing'.[37]

Lloyd George was not one of the few. Capable, it has been said, of 'massive misjudgements of people', he sprang to the side of Venizelos.[38] For him, too, the Greeks were a nation of the modern, western, world; they would civilise the backward Turks; Greece had served British interests in the war; this was an issue of national self-determination; and Greece could be a partner, to keep the eastern Mediterranean safe in British interests. Like Weizmann, Venizelos knew how to compromise and seem reasonable, so he did not insist on Constantinople, or Cyprus. But these were details. 'Greece was golden; Turkey was shrouded in darker memories,' writes MacMillan.[39]

There is a further parallel with Zionism, regarding legacy. The Greek leader's performance was captivating – but it also endangered the Greeks and threatened peace in the Middle East. Venizelos lit a fuse that caused not only the immediate Greco-Turkish War of 1919–22 but also enduring hostility between Greeks and Turks. No more than in Palestine did Lloyd George foresee such conflict and disorder.

Lloyd George's personal commitment to Zionism in Palestine was a necessary condition for the Balfour Declaration. He was a mercurial, impulsive, intuitive leader: passionate, articulate and persuasive. He did not act in 1917 out of studious analysis of British interests and post-war imperial strategy – nor, indeed, of Zionist ideology. Nor did he act (as Joseph Chamberlain may have done in 1903) out of sympathy on hearing of persecuted Jews in Central and Eastern Europe. Rather, devoted to an imagined Palestine and a notion of resurrecting something of a splendid past, Lloyd George fell easily under the spell of Weizmann and succumbed to the Zionist dream.

We may infer that, broadly, his heart and his head moved him in a single direction. Lloyd George wanted Palestine, and he wanted a Jewish homeland there. Although it was a wartime improvisation, Balfour's Declaration was no passing whim. There were months of gestation before his pledge was formulated, approved and published. There was enough belief here to help account for Lloyd George's retention of the Declaration after the war. Nonetheless, his responses to both Weizmann and Venizelos – to the cause of the Jewish homeland, and to the cause of Greater Greece – look less like cool statesmanship than caprice. Improvising policy for an immediate goal, such as insisting on the use of convoys in 1917 to protect British shipping in the Atlantic, was one thing; and in this case it helped to win the war. Improvising policy for the long term, such as lending uncritical and open-ended support for Zionism, was another; it brought about, in his beloved Palestine, civil unrest, violent conflict, and the embarrassment of imperial failure.

Chaim Weizmann

Weizmann's greatest contribution to Zionism was his persuasiveness when dealing with the major players. Weizmann was the most influential Zionist spokesman after Theodor Herzl. David Ben-Gurion was later to write to him: 'I know you are the champion of the Jewish people, not because you have been elected ... but because you were born for it.'[40] According to Lloyd George, 'the fact that Britain at last opened her eyes to the opportunity afforded to the Allies to rally this powerful people to their side was attributable to the insistence, the assiduity and the fervour of one of the greatest Hebrews of all time, Dr Chaim Weizmann.'[41] Like his friend Ahad Ha'am, though unlike Herzl, Weizmann had believed that Zionism should focus not on diplomacy but on promoting popular Jewish migration and settlement. And yet it was he, more than any other Zionist leader, who won the Great Power endorsement Herzl had advocated but failed to win. So impressed was Lloyd George by Weizmann's personality that he prophesied to Herbert Samuel, 'When you and I are forgotten, this man will have a monument to him in Palestine.'[42]

In 1892, Weizmann had left Russia for Germany to study. He moved to England in 1904 and became a lecturer in chemistry at Manchester University (soon after which he had an encounter with Arthur Balfour, recounted below). He became a leader among British Zionists, visiting Palestine for the first time in 1907. He adopted British citizenship in 1910. At the outbreak of the war, the War Office invited British scientists to report all discoveries likely to be of military value. Weizmann's

Chaim Weizmann (1874–1952)
Zionist leader and first President of Israel, photographed in New York, 1921, with Albert Einstein and two fellow Zionists, Nehemia Mossessohn (far left) and Menachem Ussishkin (far right).

expertise lay in a fermentation process that could produce large quantities of acetone (essential in the manufacture of cordite, the propellant used by British forces). The Admiralty promoted its large-scale manufacture. Weizmann's process was a huge success; and Weizmann made the process available to the British for the duration of the war, without payment.[43]

To this extent, chance and circumstances brought Weizmann to London. There, partly through his contribution to the British war effort, he earned the confidence of British leaders. Weizmann took full advantage of his connections and engaged in more than two years of lobbying. He tirelessly confronted British Jewish opposition while at the same time courting the Cabinet, the Foreign Office and Lord Rothschild.

By the autumn of 1917, Weizmann had access to politicians, editors and civil servants across the capital. Professional expertise converged with political ambition and opportunism, just as the general political climate was turning in the Zionists' favour.

Weizmann had extraordinary charisma; he was able to persuade even the sceptic. A case from after the Second World War well illustrates this prodigious charm. Richard Crossman, then a newly elected Labour MP (subsequently a Cabinet minister), was asked to serve on a committee to investigate the situation in post-war Palestine. An assimilated Jew, he was initially sympathetic to the Arab cause. While serving in the British army, he had recently been among the first British officers to enter the former Dachau concentration camp in Bavaria. But it was an encounter with Weizmann that turned him to Zionism. Weizmann struck Crossman initially as a man 'of the fanaticism and power attributed to Lenin'. He made an immediate impression. Weizmann spoke, in Crossman's words, 'with a magnificent mixture of passion and scientific detachment'.[44] Like so many before him, Crossman was won over.

◆

Over several decades, Weizmann was a formidable and, it appears, irresistible advocate of Zionism. He was shrewd, too. Before and during the First World War, while happy to exploit the sympathetic Christian Zionist sensibilities of many men in British public life, he also adopted a view of British strategic interests that would enhance Zionism's appeal to them. Before the outbreak of war, in 1911 Weizmann not only played the strategic card but also presented the Jewish national home as a means of guaranteeing the future prosperity of the territory. 'Palestine is a natural continuation of Egypt, and the barrier separating the Suez Canal from Constantinople,' he wrote. And, he added, 'it will be the Asiatic Belgium, especially if it is developed by the Jews'.[45] In the succeeding years, key British policy-makers listened to Weizmann; and they liked what they heard.

At the start of the war, Britain appeared to Weizmann to be the only belligerent power in Europe that might one day be persuaded, if the circumstances were right, to adopt the Zionist cause. By now a British subject himself, Weizmann argued that the movement should hope for an Allied victory. After Turkey entered the war, he reprised his earlier argument. He told C.P. Scott (won over by him the previous year) that Jewish settlement in Palestine 'would develop the country, bring back civilisation to it, and form a very effective guard of the Suez Canal'.[46] This, as we know, fell on Asquith's deaf ears; but it would be different when Lloyd George replaced him.

How differently events might have unfolded if the Palestinians had possessed in London, during these critical years, an advocate for Arab nationalism who was as skilful and eloquent as Weizmann. Such an advocate would have struggled to overcome prevailing racial prejudice; the level of development, and role in history, of the 'Arab' could not stand alongside that of the 'Jew'. But the absence of any such figure was a considerable weakness from which the Arab Palestinian cause would suffer during the inter-war mandate years, too.

Arthur Balfour, anti-Semitism and nimbyism

Arthur Balfour once made a curious general comment on his decision-making. 'I can remember every argument, repeat all the pros and cons, and even make quite a good speech on the subject. But the conclusion, the decision, is a perfect blank in my mind.'[47] Balfour rarely seemed to take himself or anything else seriously. In this light, any attempt to identify his thinking and personal motivation has to be conjectural and inconclusive. But we may learn something valuable about the British elite's complex attitudes to Judaism and to Zionism.

Balfour was Foreign Secretary in 1917 and signatory to the historic letter to Lord Rothschild. Jonathan Schneer has written in depth on the Balfour Declaration; he writes persuasively that Weizmann's argument 'worked upon the minds of anti- and philo-Semites alike, among the British governing elite', desperate as they were for any advantage in the wartime struggle.[48] The case of Balfour indeed suggests that one individual could hold both positive and negative feelings toward the Jews. Brought up on the Old Testament, Balfour had long had a sympathetic interest in Jewish history. His niece wrote later: 'I remember in childhood imbibing from him the idea that Christian religion and civilisation owes to Judaism an immeasurable debt, shamefully ill repaid.'[49] He had been baffled by the Zionists' rejection of land for settlement in British East Africa.

Balfour met Weizmann almost a decade before Lloyd George did: an unexpected encounter, early in 1906. During the general election of January/February 1906, Balfour, then Prime Minister, fought to retain his northern seat, in Manchester. While he was campaigning, his agent (himself Jewish) suggested a meeting with the thirty-two-year-old Weizmann, who was then a lecturer in the chemistry department at Manchester University. Balfour asked to see him; and despite the demands of the election, an interview was set up. The result was an immediate rapport. Weizmann had a profound effect on Balfour. They became friends. It was, writes Margaret MacMillan, 'a strange friendship – the intense, committed Jew from the Pale, and the charming, worldly Englishman who had drifted through life with such ease – but for Weizmann and Zionism it was crucial'.[50]

Balfour's high regard for Zionism increased the more he learnt about it. Indeed, he later claimed to have personally adopted it. On leaving the USA in midsummer 1917 – having met the American Zionist leader Justice Louis Brandeis and been assured by him that 'there would be active sympathy there' for Zionism – he proclaimed, 'I am a Zionist.'[51]

And yet Balfour as Prime Minister had presided over the passage of the Aliens Act, in August 1905 (to come into effect on 1 January 1906). This followed the recent 'invasion' (Balfour's description) of Britain, especially the East End of London, by tens of thousands of East European Jews fleeing persecution in Eastern Europe. Public opinion and the press had demanded an end to the immigration. Balfour's legislation – though it referred to 'aliens' – targeted these Jews. The Act was condemned by

Arthur Balfour (1848–1930)
British Prime Minister, 1902–1905, and British Foreign
Secretary, 1916–1919.

Jewish critics in Britain as an act of anti-Semitism. It was clear that Jews
were no more welcome in Britain, where they sought refuge, than in the
Russia from which they fled. If the Aliens Act is not it itself evidence of
personal anti-Semitism, it remains the case that Jews were to be excluded
from the country that Balfour governed because of the prevalence of
anti-Semitism among his fellow countrymen.

The two initiatives of Balfour, in 1905 and 1917, while seemingly
contradictory, may have been complementary. There is no reason to
doubt his sympathetic awareness, since childhood, of the plight of
contemporary Jewry. But his overriding and consistent view (confirmed
in both acts) was that the Jews should not find a home *in England*. 'We

have a right,' he insisted, 'to keep out everybody who does not add to the strength of the community.' It would not have been advantageous to embrace 'an immense body of persons who, however patriotic, able and industrious ... remained a people apart'.[52] In 1906, the focus was negative, on not admitting Jews to Britain; in 1917 it was more positive, on admitting them to Palestine. Also 'positive' in this sense had been the offer, by Balfour's own government in 1903, of British East Africa, albeit another refuge far away from Britain's own shores. At the heart of Balfour's personal beliefs and public acts – as for so many policy-makers of his time and later – was nimbyism.

Justice Brandeis is a significant and comparable case. Born in Kentucky to Jewish immigrants from Bohemia in 1856, he was brought up in a secular home. His assimilation was such that after shining at Harvard, and a successful career as a lawyer, he was appointed the first Jewish member of the Supreme Court. In conversation with Balfour in 1919 he stressed that he came to Zionism 'wholly as an American', for his whole life 'had been free from Jewish contacts or traditions'. But he had become aware of 'the vast number of Jews, particularly Russian Jews, that were pouring into the United States year by year'. Then a Zionist pamphlet had by chance come his way: and this led him to 'the conviction that Zionism was the answer'.[53]

The record of this discussion continues: 'Mr Balfour interrupted to express his agreement, adding, "of course, these are the reasons that make you and me such ardent Zionists".' The Jews of Central and Eastern Europe had a problem, these two prominent men agreed; but the solution did not lie in their entry into the USA or Britain. For Balfour and perhaps Lloyd George and others, we may conclude that altruism and self-interest pointed in the same direction: Palestine. There, *Arab* nimbyism was not to be indulged. Arab objections would be overridden. Speaking in Paris in July 1919, Balfour reflected, with lordly cynicism, that the British 'had not been honest with either French or Arab, but it was now preferable to quarrel with the Arab rather than the French, if there was to be a quarrel at all'.[54]

That political, if not personal, nimbyism lay at the heart of the Balfour Declaration is further illustrated by Leo Amery, a secretary to the Imperial War Cabinet who was largely responsible for drafting the final British text. In a contemporary letter to Sir Edward Carson, he wrote that 'an anti-Semitism which is based partly on the fear of being swamped by hordes of undesirable aliens from Russia ... will be much diminished when the hordes in question have got another outlet'.[55]

Among others in Balfour's circle, the British negotiator of the Sykes-Picot agreement comes across as both anti-Semitic and pro-Zionist. Mark Sykes is described by his grandson as having had views on the Jews which were merely 'the anti-Semitic opinions of a man of his time and class'. Yet the young Mark's anti-Semitism could be quite venomous. When travelling by boat to the Boer War, he described the majority of passengers on board as 'Jews of the most repulsive type; in fact, it is for these beasts that we are fighting. They jabber about the mines all day long; I hope they will be made to pay. I would extort the last farthing from the most jingo loyal Jew in the British Empire before I'd fine a traitorous gentile.'[56]

However, the First World War was a different affair. Sykes talked to Herbert Samuel, who showed him his 1915 paper 'The Future of Palestine'. He was impressed. Now, we are told, Sykes 'realised that the Jews were dangerous only if they were alienated, in which scenario, because their power and influence were world-wide, they might do damage to the Allied cause'.[57] There were no indications here of sudden compassion for Jews having to flee persecution and pogroms in Eastern Europe. Sykes's support of Zionism seems to have owed nothing to sympathy, but everything to calculation founded on racialist generalisation.

A belief in the international omnipotence of Jews was prevalent in British government circles. Winston Churchill was another who held it. He wrote an article in February 1920 which began by asserting that a 'world-wide conspiracy' or 'sinister confederacy' of 'international Jews' was seeking to destroy European civilisation (though it ended with praise for Zionism as 'a new ideal' that was simple, true and attainable).[58] Such a powerful global community had to be appeased – so if it wanted a national homeland, Britain must offer one. This groundless assumption was itself an indication of anti-Semitism.[59] Yet it was one with which Weizmann, ever ready to exploit others' self-interest, was happy to confront Sykes, Lloyd George's government and later the powers assembled for the Paris Peace Conference.

A fusion of gentile interests had earlier been noted by Herzl. He had written in 1896 that 'the governments of all countries scourged by anti-Semitism will be keenly interested in assisting us to obtain the sovereignty we want... If we only begin to carry out the plans, anti-Semitism would stop at once and for ever.'[60] Such beliefs lay behind his dealings with the notoriously anti-Semitic Russian Minister of the Interior, von Plehve. And we can see it at work, too, in Balfour's cordial first meeting with Weizmann. Christian Zionism, for all its philo-Semitic dimensions, carried also an anti-Semitic prejudice. Lord Shaftesbury was committed, as we have seen, to supporting the return of Jews to Palestine; but this did not prevent him from describing the Jews as 'admittedly a stiff-necked, dark-hearted, people, and sunk in moral degradation, obduracy and ignorance of the gospel'.[61]

A plausible conclusion is that behind the Balfour Declaration, issued at a critical wartime moment in 1917, lay a congruence of Zionism with British, casually anti-Semitic, nimbyism.

The Montagu Memorandum, August 1917

Edwin Montagu declared, shortly before the issue of the Balfour Declaration, 'the policy of His Majesty's Government is anti-Semitic'.[62] He was reported to have been close to tears in the Cabinet. It is of singular significance that the most passionate opposition in the British government to the issue of Balfour's historic letter was that of its only Jewish member.

Montagu, Minster of Munitions in 1916, was from July 1917 Secretary of State for India. He believed wholeheartedly in assimilation. His own achievements and position strengthened the belief of innumerable Jews in Britain, and elsewhere, that assimilation into a gentile society was not only possible but taking place. A level of continuing anti-Semitic prejudice was to be expected – but staying where you were was far preferable to emigration to an undeveloped, notional Jewish homeland.

Anxiety looms at the start of the memorandum. British support for a Jewish national home in Palestine 'will prove a rallying ground for anti-Semites in every country of the world'. He marshals four arguments in support of this deep concern.

First, a designated Jewish homeland would confirm the gentile prejudice that all Jews were restless aliens. It would mean that Jews would be regarded as foreigners everywhere else. 'When the Jew has a national home,' he adds, 'surely it follows that the impetus to deprive us of our rights of British citizenship must be enormously increased.' Other countries would find an outlet for their anti-Semitism by seeking to export their own Jews. 'Palestine will become the world's ghetto.'

This apprehension is at the heart of Montagu's claim that the Balfour Declaration would be anti-Semitic. Whatever its *provenance* – the real or imagined motivations of its creators – it would have an anti-Semitic *effect*. Assimilation, achieved by Montagu and so many like him, would be undermined.

Second, 'I assert that there is no Jewish nation.' Moreover, Montagu argues that, through their service to the country, Jews in Britain have earned the right to be regarded not as British Jews but as Jewish Britons. Assimilation is working.

Third, in a Palestine dedicated to the so-called Jewish nation, Muslims and Christians – from now on regarded as foreigners in the land of their birth – would have to leave, in order to make way for innumerable Jewish immigrants (though 'there are three times as many Jews in the world as could possibly get into Palestine, if you drove out all the population that remains there now').

Fourth, Palestine is special not just for Jews but for Muslims and Christians. 'I deny that Palestine is today associated with the Jews or

Edwin Montagu (1879–1924)
British Secretary of State for India, 1917–1922.

properly to be regarded as a fit place for them to live in.'

Montagu's conclusion is forceful. Zionism 'has always seemed to me to be a mischievous political creed'; 'it seems to be inconceivable that Zionism should be officially recognised by the British Government'; 'I would be almost tempted to proscribe the Zionist organisation as illegal and against the national interest.'

Weizmann is not mentioned in the memorandum, but Montagu took the opportunity a little later to tell Lloyd George: 'You are being misled by a foreigner, a dreamer and an idealist who sweeps aside all practical difficulties.'[63] To no avail. His heartfelt (and prophetic) arguments were almost wholly ignored. And Weizmann was allowed to wait outside when the Cabinet held the meeting, on 31 October 1917, at which the decision to issue the declaration was made.

Lloyd George was later to refer somewhat patronisingly to Montagu's stinging memorandum and its author. 'There were one or two who were not so favourably inclined to the policy. One in particular doubted the wisdom from the Jewish point of view: that was Edwin Montagu.'[64] But where lay wisdom? A fascinating exchange with Balfour suggests that the Secretary of State for India was a shrewder judge of the import of the Declaration than its author, the Foreign Secretary. Montagu declared, 'Let us not for Heaven's sake tell the Muslim what he ought to think; let us recognise what they do think' – to which Balfour replied, 'I am quite unable to see why Heaven or any other Power should object to our telling the Muslim what he ought to think.'[65]

Montagu was *almost* wholly ignored. The Declaration's concluding (albeit unenforceable) provision for safeguarding 'the rights and political status enjoyed by Jews in any other country' appears to have been a concession to Montagu and other non-Zionist Jews in Britain. But for the most part, and in its essence, Montagu's last-minute appeal was side-lined. 'Poor Edwin Montagu!' comments Jonathan Schneer.[66] But this is unwarranted condescension. There was nothing pitiable about this prominent man and courageous advocate. He took the matter personally and felt that the Zionists were trying to push assimilated British Jews back inside the ghetto. Moreover, it seems in retrospect that in many respects he was right in what he wrote.

In the British government, Montagu was not quite a solitary critic of the Balfour Declaration. Lord Curzon, Leader of the House of Lords and former Viceroy of India, was also dismissive of the Zionist proposal and sympathetic towards the native Arabs. Curzon insisted at a Cabinet meeting in October 1917 that Zionism was no more than 'sentimental idealism'.[67] As for the Arabs, 'what is to become of the people of the country?' he asked. They 'and their forefathers have occupied the country for the best part of 1,500 years, and they own the soil'. He added, with foresight, 'they will not be content either to be expropriated for Jewish immigration or to act as hewers of wood and drawers of water for the latter'.[68] We may surmise that the insights of both Montagu and Curzon were shaped in part by their experience of India and its huge Muslim population.

More telling than Curzon's support was the anti-Zionist feeling among many British Jews – that is, Jewish Britons – other than Montagu. Thus, for example, two leaders of the Board of Deputies wrote a letter to *The Times* in May 1917 'reiterating their opposition to any theory of the Jews as a homeless nationality'. They warned against giving Jewish settlers in Palestine special rights and feared 'the most bitter of feuds with their Arab neighbours'.[69] In the light of this letter, Montagu's memorandum and the indifference shown towards Zionism at this time by the overwhelming majority of Jews globally, the fundamental claims of the Zionists – that the Jews were a nation and in need of a national homeland – looked fragile. But they were good enough for Balfour.

Christian Zionism and Imperial Strategy

Napoleon Bonaparte had sensed how valuable a friendly presence in Palestine could be for a European Power. During his Syrian campaign he became the first European political leader to propose a sovereign Jewish state in Palestine. France, he proclaimed in 1799, offered Jews 'Israel's patrimony' as 'rightful heirs'. This was, he told the Jews, the time to 'claim the restoration of your rights' and 'your political existence as a nation among the nations'.[70] Napoleon's Zionism was more calculated than Christian, but it made political sense. As in his post-Revolutionary Concordat with the Pope, Napoleon recognised the usefulness of other peoples' faiths.

By contrast, Lord Shaftesbury was later to see the restoration of the Jews to Palestine as serving both religious and strategic goals. A strategic conviction lay behind his Christian Zionist argument for a Jewish national homeland, with Jerusalem its capital (remaining under Ottoman rule, but with British protection). Such an arrangement would be agreeably cost-free, with the Jews peopling the land and the Ottomans continuing to administer it. But it would give Britain an imperial advantage over post-Napoleonic France for control and influence in the Middle East.

Years later, Lloyd George and Balfour were the two main individual decision-makers in 1917, and they both shared Shaftesbury's outlook. They operated in a cultural context. They both knew their Old Testaments. Lloyd George once told Weizmann that he 'knew the map of the Holy Land better than he did that of France'.[71] For Balfour, too, the Bible remained from childhood a living reality. Weizmann observed that 'the fact that England is a biblical nation accounts for the spiritual affinity between them and the Jews'.[72] Lloyd George had adopted Zionism and, when he replaced Asquith, he gathered round him men of a similar outlook: for example, Alfred Milner and Jan Smuts. The prejudices and inclinations of a number of key individuals – inside and outside the small War Cabinet, and in top administrative positions – coalesced, to have a profound influence on policy and events.

Smuts, like other Boers, had been brought up on the Old Testament and always believed that the Jews would return to their ancient land. He had led the Boers in their war against the British, when Milner had been Britain's High Commissioner in South Africa. A dozen years later, Zionism was something that the former foes could agree on. Powerful assistant secretaries in the War Cabinet – Mark Sykes, William Ormsby-Gore and Leo Amery – adopted Zionism. Meanwhile, in the Foreign Office, under Balfour, there was Lord Robert Cecil, another friend of Zionism.

In short, as Lloyd George put it in his memoirs, 'men like Mr Balfour, Lord Milner, Lord Robert Cecil and myself were in whole-hearted sympathy with the Zionist ideals'. Later critics of Zionism have highlighted the significance. So, for example, expatriate Israeli historian Ilan Pappé notes that 'for both Christians and Jews ... the colonisation of Palestine was an act of return and redemption', and argues that a Christian-Jewish alliance turned 'the anti-Semitic and millenarian idea of transferring the Jews from Europe to Palestine' into a project of settlement, at the expense of the native people of Palestine.[73]

The combination of Jewish and Christian impulses could serve British imperial interests. There would be a 'European' outpost in the Eastern Mediterranean, 'civilising' the indigenous Arabs. This would secure in the Near East not only a potential economic asset (if it attracted international Jewish capital) but also, some believed, an immediate strategic asset as Eastern protector of the Suez Canal.

In the event, Christian Zionism appears to have been a more powerful influence than strategic calculation. Weizmann acknowledged that he would not have succeeded had he based his arguments on British self-interest alone. And a comment made by Balfour himself, a decade later, is most telling. In a Cabinet meeting on 5 March 1928, he began by observing that Palestine 'lies at the very place where the Power responsible for the security of the Suez Canal would wish to place it', and that a mandated territory 'must add strength to the Empire'. Nevertheless, he went on, 'this was not a consideration which influenced most British Zionists in 1917. It certainly did not influence me.'[74] Balanced and considered, this judgement by the author of the Declaration represents a convincing disavowal of the strategic argument as the prime motivation in Britain's claim to Palestine.

As one British official of the time put it, 'Palestine for most of us was an emotion rather than a reality.'[75] Balfour, Lloyd George and the other decision-makers were, for complex reasons, some of them ignoble, committed to Zionism. Its instrumental value as a cloak for the extension of the British Empire in a strategically sensitive region of the Middle East was recognised but, it seems, secondary. Philo-Semitism pointed the same way as anti-Semitism. 'The return' of an alien race to their ancient home would be in line with biblical prophecy and would also help to solve the Jewish Question by concentrating in one – distant – place all Jews who wanted or needed to emigrate from their adopted lands.

The Declaration: The Text

The Balfour Declaration has had such historic significance – albeit beyond the imaginations of its makers in November 1917 – that its text merits review and, first, restating.

> His Majesty's Government view with favour the establishment in Palestine of a national home for the Jewish people, and will use their best endeavours to facilitate the achievement of this object, it being clearly understood that nothing shall be done which may prejudice the civil and religious rights of existing non-Jewish communities in Palestine, or the rights and political status enjoyed by Jews in any other country.

Essentially, the Declaration envisaged an act of post-war colonialism in a territory which would, in place of one imperial master, acquire another ... which was committed to its settlement by a third party.

Though in a number of respects ambiguous, it was very carefully drafted. Labelled Balfour's, the Declaration was in fact a co-production, in provenance, and wording, of leading Zionists and moving forces in the British government. According to former *Daily Mail* journalist Joseph Jeffries, writing in the late 1930s, a Zionist programme had been produced as early as October 1916 as a basis for discussion with Whitehall. Following the entry of the USA into the war in April 1917, this seems to have strongly influenced a statement of war aims in the Middle East, issued 'under the auspices' of the British government and directed towards the Jews of America. The statement proposed the recognition of Palestine as the Jewish national home, into which there would be full and free rights of immigration for Jews of all countries.[76]

Meanwhile, a meeting had taken place in London in February 1917, attended by Sykes (by now Secretary to the War Cabinet) and Samuel, with other leading Zionists and Lord Rothschild. Then, in April 1917, Cecil (in charge at the Foreign Office in Balfour's temporary absence) advised Weizmann that 'it would strengthen the British position' if the

Zionists would ask for a British Palestine. The two already knew each other: after meeting Weizmann in 1915, Cecil had become, in his own words, 'a Zionist by passionate conviction'.[77]

There followed a remarkably frank speech by Weizmann, on 20 May, addressed to the English Zionist Federation. He said that 'while a Jewish Commonwealth in Palestine is our final ideal ... the way to achieve it lies through a series of intermediate stages'. Then, foreshadowing the Balfour Declaration by six months, he continued: 'I hope ... that the fair country of Palestine will be protected by such a mighty and just power as Great Britain... I am entitled to say that His Majesty's Government is ready to support our plans.'[78] Jeffries concludes that everything 'had been privately arranged' – already, in the middle of 1917.

In June and July, with Weizmann abroad, the text of a letter in support of Zionism, for the British government to issue, was carefully drafted by other leading Zionists. Prominent among them was the Polish writer and diplomat Nahum Sokolow, who shared leadership of the Zionist movement with Weizmann after 1917. Balfour's Declaration was issued only after much discussion and many drafts. Eventually, Rothschild submitted a final draft to the Cabinet in early August; after further tinkering, Balfour placed his notice in *The Times*.

In adapting the draft proffered by the Zionists in July, British officials softened the wording. First, recognising '*Palestine as the* national home *of* the Jewish people' became 'establishment *in Palestine* of *a* national home *for* the Jewish people'. Second, while the Zionist draft saw as essential 'the grant of internal autonomy to the Jewish nationality', the Declaration promised respect for 'the civil and religious rights of existing non-Jewish communities'.[79] No borders for this new Palestine were defined. The British did not explain 'views with favour' or specify what form 'their best endeavours' would take.

Margaret MacMillan relates that, at the 1919 Peace Conference in Versailles, 'from the start, Jews and non-Jews alike, politicians, diplomats and journalists, talked in terms of a Jewish state'.[80] This interpretation of the Balfour Declaration was confirmed by Zionists of the time.

Thus, when Ben-Gurion asked Weizmann, 'Why didn't you demand a Jewish state in Palestine?' Weizmann replied: 'We didn't demand one because they wouldn't have given us one. We asked only for conditions which would allow us to build a Jewish state in the future. It is simply a matter of tactics.'[81] More remarkable is evidence confirming that this was indeed what the British envisaged. So, for example, Balfour told a Jewish audience, three months later, 'my personal hope is that the Jews will make good in Palestine and eventually found a Jewish state. It is up to them now.'[82] Similarly, in July 1921, at a meeting in Balfour's home, he and Lloyd George told Weizmann that the Balfour Declaration 'had always meant the eventual creation of a Jewish state.'[83]

The Arab population was to have – keep – no equivalent homeland and was consigned to a secondary role. This is implicit in the very concession to the Zionists of a homeland/state in Palestine; and it can be inferred from the omission of *political* rights where the guarantee of 'civil' and 'religious' rights is made. Over and above this, the Declaration makes no mention of the Arabs by name. Though a great majority of the residents of the territory, they were merely subsumed in the expression 'non-Jewish communities'. The naming of Jews alone, and reference to others only in subsidiary relation to them, was confirmation of prevailing notions of the racial and social hierarchy. 'The Arab' might be 'noble', for a few such as Kitchener. But Balfour himself articulated the far more widespread and disparaging British (and Zionist) view when, in 1919, he declared: 'Zionism ... is rooted in age-old traditions, in present needs, in future hopes, of far profounder import than the desires and prejudices of the 700,000 Arabs who now inhabit that ancient land.'[84] And yet Balfour could then, without shame, assure the House of Lords in 1922 that 'I cannot imagine any political interests exercised under greater safeguards than the political interests of the Arab population of Palestine.'[85]

We may speculate as to why the British, having laboured so long over it, issued a text that was in some respects so opaque. It seems likely that, first, the wording had to be (just) enough to win over the world's Jews, without unduly alarming other Powers or indeed, at that time, the Arabs of the region to whom other promises had been made. Second, with the war not yet won – the Declaration began, after all, as an instrument for winning it – the British may have wanted to keep their options open. Being as loosely worded as it was, it could do little harm. It could be revisited, if or when the war was won.

◆

What are we to conclude? Weizmann saw the Balfour Declaration as 'the Magna Carta of Jewish liberties'.[86] Zionists were delighted – even if it was, in November 1917, only the end of the beginning. Ten years later Weizmann was still expressing his surprise at the turn of events. Talking in Czernowitz (Chernivtsi) in the Western Ukraine in December 1927 he said with genuine emotion – if nonchalance, regarding the facts – 'We Jews got the Balfour Declaration quite unexpectedly; or, in other words, we are the greatest war profiteers. We never dreamt of the Balfour Declaration; to be quite frank, it came to us overnight.' He went on to say something more remarkable in revealing the pressure he had felt, during the intervening years, to bring the Jewish national home into existence – at a time when world Jewry was largely either indifferent or hostile to the project. 'I trembled lest the British Government would call me to ask, "Tell us, what is this Zionist Organisation? Where are they, your Zionists?". For these people think in terms different from ours. The Jews, they knew, were against us.'[87]

Zionists' surprise and delight (albeit qualified by the burdens of responsibility and isolation) were matched by Arabs' shock and dismay. The verdict of Edward Said, a pioneer of postcolonial study, is restrained but bitter. 'The declaration was made (a) by a European power, (b) about a non-European territory, (c) in flat disregard of both the presence and wishes of the native majority resident in that territory, and (d) it took the form of a promise about this same territory to another foreign group, so that this foreign group might, quite literally, *make* this territory a national home for the Jewish people.'[88]

Sympathetic to the Arabs through close reporting of events at the time, Joseph Jeffries published his own assessment of the Balfour Declaration and its effects in late 1938.

1. Its publication broke our pledged word to the Arab race.
2. Its object was to establish the Jews in a privileged position in Palestine without the assent of the population, as a prelude to the absorption of the latter, under plea of their cooperation, in a future Jewish state.
3. It was written in great part by those who were supposed only to have received it, and was deliberately worded so that the truth might be hidden by it, its guarantees to the Arabs be useless and its promises intangible.
4. It was ostensibly a recognition of Zionist aspirations to return to Palestine under the sanction of historic rights, but in reality it was the published clause of a private bargain by which war spoils were to be given in payment for war-help.

Jeffries's analysis, though partisan, is in most respects substantially unexceptionable. In his final overall verdict, he did not hold back. 'The Balfour Declaration,' he wrote (shortly before the Munich Agreement), 'is the most discreditable document to which a British Government has set its hand within memory.'[89]

There are grounds for concluding, as many have, that the Declaration was neither legal nor just. But Balfour's fateful letter is open to other charges: it embodied an irresolvable contradiction; it brought no advantage at the time; and it was linked to flawed assumptions about British imperial needs in the future.

First, the contradiction. Lord Grey had been Asquith's Liberal Foreign Secretary (that is, the Conservative Balfour's predecessor). His comments are all the more withering for being couched in understatement. On 27 March 1923, he said: 'I think we are placed in considerable difficulty by the Balfour Declaration... It promised a Zionist home without prejudice to the civil and religious rights of the population of Palestine. A Zionist home, my Lords, undoubtedly means or implies a Zionist Government ... and as 93 per cent of the population are Arabs, I do not see how you can establish other than an Arab Government without prejudice to their civil rights.'

Grey went on to ask the government to publish and review all 'engagements relating to the matter which we entered into during the War'. Having been in post at the time of the McMahon correspondence with Sharif Hussein, he argued that 'from the point of view of honour' it should look fairly at each pledge 'and the date at which it was given.'[90]

Second, the lack of advantage. As a wartime diplomatic ploy, the Declaration failed. There was no gain in Russia which, from November 1917, was led by Bolsheviks committed to making a separate peace with Germany. In America, Jews were deeply divided over Zionism; and in any case President Wilson preferred planning for world peace, founded on general principles and a League of Nations, to making any public singular commitment to the Zionist cause. In short, the Balfour Declaration was issued in vain. Neither Russian nor American Jewry changed the course of the war. It was won by Britain and her Allies by other means.

Third, imperial security. The British did not need Palestine. The meticulous assessment of Palestine's potential, under Asquith, proved sound. Palestine was to become a liability. The previous, relatively sanguine, official assessment regarding any post-war French challenge was justified at the war's end. France had no capacity to compete with British interests in far-off Egypt or Palestine. Exhausted by the conflict on the Western Front, France looked to Britain for post-war support in minimising the local threat from a resurgent Germany.

All the hard-nosed calculation of the committee of Imperial Defence – and the realistic calculations of Sykes and Picot – made the Balfour Declaration appear an extraordinary piece of whim and wishful thinking. Yet it was this document that Lloyd George advocated (and his coterie approved) within a year of his taking office. Neither the acquisition of Palestine nor the endorsement of a Jewish national home there served the British Empire. The verdict of Elizabeth Monroe, Head of the British government's Middle East Information Division during the Second World War and later Middle East correspondent for *The Economist*, was that, 'measured by British interests alone, it was one of the greatest mistakes in our imperial history'.[91]

What Balfour and Lloyd George approved in November 1917 would have been out of the question had their respective predecessors, Grey and Asquith, still been in power. In the extraordinary context of mid-1917, Lloyd George and others made their decisions. The Prime Minister appeared to hold no doubts. But he was a master of casuistry – as two extracts from his memoirs testify. First, 'the democratic powers of Europe and America have always advocated emancipation of the subject races held down by the great empires'; second, 'no race has done better out of the fidelity with which the Allies redeemed their promises to the oppressed races than the Arabs'. The prejudice and wishful thinking of Lloyd George, and of others involved too, appear to have been the product largely of ignorance (of Palestine, and of the Palestinian Arabs) and susceptibility (towards Weizmann).

As for the Arabs who would bear the consequences, officially they were not even told. It thus appears that the only people who remained ignorant of the Declaration were the existing inhabitants of Palestine 'who probably had not ten wireless-sets between them, nor any access to the newspapers' wrote Jeffries.[92] He concluded that General Allenby suppressed news of it: partly because an occupying army could not, legally, introduce a new political regime; and partly because the British government, knowing that the Declaration was a betrayal of the Arabs, preferred to conceal it from them until their newly conquered territory was fully under British control.

The Balfour Declaration was just one British ploy among many for winning the war (and possibly shaping the peace). It was an event that at the time created little public interest. Its failure as a diplomatic gesture to 'world Jewry' did no immediate harm. It might have been of only transient significance, as other wartime promises proved: it, too, could have been shed. But it was not. The lasting harm to British interests – including Britain's reputation first among Arabs and later, ironically, among Jews too – arose after the First World War, through its retention.

4

THE BRITISH COMMITMENT
TO ZIONISM IN PALESTINE,
1918–1922

'There exists an entire people who have held it for centuries and to whom it would never occur to leave.' Yitzhak Epstein[1]

Overview

Britain's post-war acquisition of Palestine came about in stages. In relation to international authority, the victorious powers discussed the partition of the Ottoman Empire first in Paris and then at the London Conference of February 1920. Meeting again at San Remo, in April that year, they formally, if provisionally, allocated mandates. Palestine was awarded to Britain, for example, and Syria to France. However, the mandated territories as yet had no agreed boundaries, and they had no settled form of words. The League of Nations Council finally approved the terms of the British Mandate on 24 July 1922. However, regarding the exercise of local power, there was no related turning point in Palestine itself. The British had conquered the territory and occupied it. The only change of significance was their replacing military with civilian rule in July 1920. Thus, we may focus on developments on the ground in Palestine, which had their own momentum from 1918, largely without reference to faraway decision-making.

Once the war was over, and won, wartime pledges could be shed. Others were.[2] But the Balfour Declaration, far from being dropped,

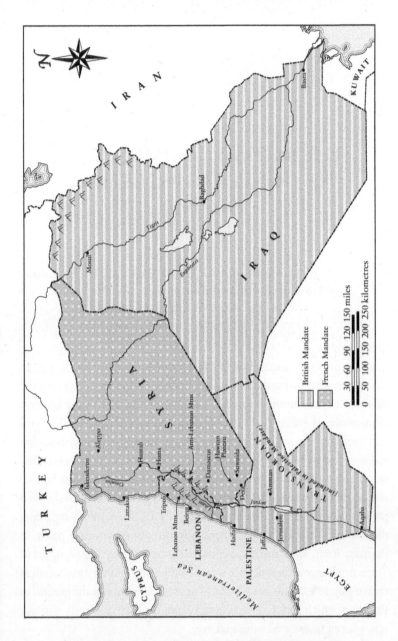

THE LEAGUE OF NATIONS MANDATES FOR THE
ARABIC-SPEAKING OTTOMAN PROVINCES

became embedded – even augmented – in British policy to Palestine. This continuing British commitment was made in the face of all-but overwhelming evidence and argument that a British-backed Zionist project for a Jewish national home would lead to inter-communal antagonism and, in time, a territory that would be ungovernable. Arab opposition was rekindled after the war and, as Jewish immigration resumed, soon manifested itself in demonstrations, petitions and outbreaks of violence. Disturbances in Palestine coincided with disturbances (of a comparable provenance) much nearer home, in Ireland. Warnings of 'another Ireland' were ignored, along with the findings of a succession of commissions of enquiry into unrest in Palestine.

The British government in London refused to hear what its men on the spot in Palestine were saying. Lloyd George, still in power, was wedded to the Balfour Declaration – even though the contradictions it embodied rendered its twin promises undeliverable. For him and those around him, everything pointed to retention: Palestine was both a glorious gain and a strategic asset; and 'national self-determination' for the Jews would provide a cover for imperialism, favour an oppressed people (who would help develop and pay for the territory), and help to solve the Jewish Question in a land far from Britain's own shores. Seemingly in denial about the level of uncompromising present and predictable future Arab opposition – and wishfully thinking that in due course the Arabs would welcome benefits which Jewish investment would bring – the British took none of the opportunities that arose to review and revise the Declaration. Instead, they ensured that it was written into the mandate awarded to them in 1922 by the newly formed League of Nations.

The issuing of the Balfour Declaration is understandable. The British were waging total war with as yet no certainty as to its outcome; any measure could be taken, straw clutched, in hope of increasing the chances of success. What is harder to understand is why, after the war, the British retained the Declaration, as issued, when reason pointed to at least revision and circumscription. It had done nothing to bring about success; it was crippled by contradiction; and, as events already strongly suggested, it would bring to Palestine conflict and costly disorder.

The context: Woodrow Wilson's Fourteen Points, and the origins of the mandate

The British ended the First World War on the winning side. But by now imperialism itself was under attack. Competing empires were deemed to have caused the war and the unprecedented slaughter. This critique was implicitly adopted by President Woodrow Wilson in the Fourteen Points that he published in January 1918. These were issued as a set of legitimate war aims, not only for the USA but for all belligerents. The Points were to prove very influential while Wilson was involved in the post-war peace negotiations and decision-making. Three are of special relevance to this study.

V. A free, open-minded, and absolutely impartial adjustment of all colonial claims, based upon a strict observance of the principle that in determining all such questions of sovereignty the interests of the populations concerned must have equal weight with the equitable claims of the government whose title is to be determined.

XII. The Turkish portion of the present Ottoman Empire should be assured a secure sovereignty, but the other nationalities which are now under Turkish rule should be assured an undoubted security of life and an absolutely unmolested opportunity of autonomous development.

XIV. A general association of nations must be formed under specific covenants for the purpose of affording mutual guarantees of political independence and territorial integrity to great and small states alike.

Much of Wilson's thinking was crystallised in the concept of 'national self-determination'. At first sight, this spelled the *end* of empire, since empire could be defined as 'rule by one nation over other nations'. In the event, it spelled a *re-packaging*. The British and the French were spared the task of dismantling their empires, mainly because they were, alongside the USA, the victors in the conflict and thus in a position to shape the aftermath. They benefited too from the prevailing notion that some peoples were more equal than others. Some nations were deemed to be advanced: more deserving and more capable of self-rule. Others were not (yet). The concept was thus applied, albeit imperfectly, in Europe, where the 'nations' of the former Austro-Hungarian Empire achieved 'self-determination' in, for example, Czechoslovakia and Yugoslavia. The Poles, too, were to enjoy independence again, in redefined Poland.

Conveniently for the victorious imperial powers, however, subjects of the Ottoman Empire and of the German Empire in Africa were not considered ready for self-government. This qualified negation of their political rights opened the way for Britain and France to move beyond Sykes-Picot and actually reap the rewards of victory. But there were conditions, formally, at least. Under a graded system of mandates, they were authorised by the League of Nations to administer their newly acquired territories – such as formerly Ottoman Syria, for France; German East Africa, for Britain – on condition that they did so in the interest of their inhabitants.

We shall see shortly how the League of Nations Covenant spelled out this condition; and how the terms of Britain's own mandate for Palestine ignored it.

THE CASE AGAINST COMMITMENT

The chronological perspective is important here. In this post-war period to 1922 there was no wave of anti-Semitism to compare with, say, the pogroms in Russia around the turn of the century. In Germany, Hitler was an obscure figure who had not yet launched in Munich his unsuccessful *putsch*. The USA remained open to Europe's Jews who, like the millions who had already done so, chose to migrate there. In these respects, a case for Zionism based *at this time* on persecution and an urgent need for a refuge was far from overwhelming.

We will take three perspectives: from Palestine, Ireland and London.

Palestine

There was no honeymoon period for the British in Palestine. After all, opposition to Jewish settlement predated the outbreak of the First World War. The British now had to contain fresh outbreaks of Arab anti-Zionist hostility. There were early signs that they had casually acquired a political problem that had no solution.

The British head of the Arab Bureau in Cairo informed London, as early as February 1918, that it was not just Arab 'notables' who objected. In Palestine, 'fear and dislike of Zionism has become general throughout all classes'.[3] When the Zionist Commission organised a grand procession in Jerusalem to mark the first anniversary of the Balfour Declaration, on 2 November 1918, a hundred or so Arab dignitaries, Muslim and Christian, handed a written protest to the British Governor of Jerusalem. It was measured and reasonable, even empathetic. 'Jews ... pretend with open voice that Palestine, which is the Holy Land of our fathers and the graveyard of our ancestors ... is now a national home for them... We Arabs, Muslim and Christian, have always sympathised profoundly with the persecuted Jews in their misfortunes in other countries... But there is a wide difference between this sympathy and the acceptance of such a nation in our country, to be made by them a national home, ruling over us and disposing of our affairs.'[4] Oppressed Jews continued to be welcome; Zionism was not.

Gertrude Bell, archaeologist, linguist, Arabist, author and poet wrote: 'Mr Balfour's Zionist pronouncement I regard with the deepest mistrust. If only people at home would not make pronouncements, how much easier it would be for those on the spot.'[5] Recorded views of British officials and army officers 'on the spot' in Palestine are close to unanimity. Just three weeks after the publication of the Balfour

Declaration, General Clayton, Chief Political Officer of OETA (Occupied Enemy Territory Administration), told the Foreign Office of the 'dismay' among Arabs who heard the news. And he expressed his fears in a private letter to Sir Mark Sykes in December. 'We are risking the possibility of Arab unity becoming something like an established fact and being ranged against us... Out and out support of Zionism,' he continued, would 'risk alienating the Arabs at a crucial time.'[6] It has been observed by one Palestinian historian of this period that Clayton, 'an intimate observer of the Arab East ... was more often than not right'.[7] By January 1918, even Sykes was acknowledging that 'a whole crop of weeds' was growing up.[8]

In April 1919, Chief Administrator of Palestine Major-General Money wrote to Lord Curzon: 'The Palestinians in fact desire Palestine for themselves, and have no intention of allowing their country to be thrown open to hordes of Jews from Eastern and Central Europe.' To implement the Balfour Declaration would require the British to use force 'in opposition to the will of the majority of the population'.[9]

We should recall the significance of Christian Arab sentiment. Muslim-Christian societies were an embodiment of resistance to the official British preference for having Palestinian society divided on religious lines. A memorandum sent by a newly formed Muslim-Christian Association from Jaffa in the autumn of 1918 reflected the prevalent mood. 'Palestine is Arab, its language is Arabic; we want to see this formally recognised. It was Great Britain that rescued us from Turkish tyranny and we do not believe that it will deliver us into the claws of the Jews. We ask for fairness and justice. We ask that it protect our rights and not decide the future of Palestine without asking our opinion.'[10]

Other sources, perhaps more surprisingly, sang a comparable tune. Zionists themselves could be completely open about what they wanted, and what it would cost. In June 1919, David Ben-Gurion was acknowledging that 'there is no solution to this question... We as a nation want this country to be ours; the Arabs as a nation, want this country to be theirs.'[11] Remarkably, even Arthur Balfour had recognised, in February 1919, that 'the weak point of our position is that in the case of Palestine we deliberately and rightly decline to accept the principle of self-determination. If the present inhabitants were consulted,' he continued, 'they would unquestionably give an anti-Jewish verdict.'[12]

Such a consultation exercise was about to take place.

The King-Crane Commission Report, August 1919

Expressions of critical concern by local inhabitants and by knowledgeable men on the spot were one thing. The findings of an independent, impartial, commission of enquiry were another. The Report of the King-Crane Commission of mid-1919 gave the British both the arguments and the opportunity to step back from its casual, context-driven, wartime commitment to the Zionists.[13] This remarkably thorough, wide-ranging and impartial assessment deserves to be looked at in some detail.

Henry King and Charles Crane, two Americans, landed in Palestine in June 1919 on a mission. They were required by the Peace Conference in Paris to find out how best to divide Ottoman territories and allocate mandates. They were charged with discovering 'the conditions, the relations and the desires of all the peoples and classes concerned'. The 'desires' of the Arab majority were of special significance. They remain of special interest, recorded less than a year after the end of the war, and before any formal and final decision was made regarding Palestine's future. In the event, the two Americans concluded that the people of the region wanted neither Britain nor France but the United States as overarching mandatory authority, for a *united* Syria and Palestine; and they wanted Emir Faisal – son of Sharif Hussein, leader of the Arab Revolt against the Turks, and liberator of Damascus – to be its head of state as constitutional monarch.

Two characteristics of this report make it persuasive. First, it is credible as evidence of the prevailing situation. It was thorough and balanced, written by two impartial outsiders, accomplished respectively in the fields of education and business, after conscientious investigation

Faisal Hussein (1885–1933)
Leader of the Arab Revolt against the Ottoman Empire,
1916–1918; King of Syria 1920; King of Iraq 1921–1933.

over several weeks. Second, the findings and conclusions of the report were clear, unambiguous and prophetic. 'The Muslim and Christian population was practically unanimous against Zionism, usually expressing themselves with great emphasis.'

The following is extracted from the two pages of the Report headed 'Zionism':

> The Commissioners began their study of Zionism with minds predisposed in its favour... They found much to approve in the aspirations and plans of the Zionists... If, however, the strict terms of the Balfour Statement are adhered to ... the extreme Zionist Program must be greatly modified... The fact came out ... that the Zionists looked forward to a practically complete dispossession of the present non-Jewish inhabitants of Palestine.

The non-Jewish population of Palestine – nearly nine tenths of the whole – are emphatically against the entire Zionist program... There was no one thing upon which the population of Palestine was more agreed upon than this. To subject a people so minded to unlimited Jewish immigration, and to steady financial and social pressure to surrender the land, would be a gross violation of ... the people's rights.

The Peace Conference should not shut its eyes to the fact that the anti-Zionist feeling in Palestine and Syria is intense and not lightly to be flouted. No British officer, consulted by the Commissioners, believed that the Zionist program could be carried out except by force of arms... Decisions, requiring armies to carry out, are sometimes necessary; but they are surely not gratuitously to be taken in the interests of a serious injustice.

Jewish immigration should be definitely limited and ... the project for making Palestine distinctly a Jewish commonwealth should be given up.

The complete Jewish occupation of Palestine ... would intensify, with a certainty like fate, the anti-Jewish feeling both in Palestine and in all other portions of the world which look to Palestine as the Holy Land.

In a confidential appendix 'for use of Americans only', the commissioners wrote: 'The Arabs are friendly toward the Jews long resident in the land who use the Arabic language; they will resist to the uttermost the immigration of foreign Jews and the establishment of a Jewish government.'[14]

'A serious injustice.' 'Will resist to the uttermost.' 'With a certainty like fate.' King and Crane found that there was overwhelming opposition from the 'non-Jewish population' of Palestine; that a Jewish State would increase anti-Semitism both in Palestine and elsewhere; that Zionism had to be restricted; and that in consequence the British should revisit the Balfour Declaration.

But the British Imperial Government did 'shut its eyes'. The case for a policy review was ignored, and an opportunity to improve Britain's standing among the majority of the population was missed. The British persisted with a policy condemned by King and Crane as both unjust and unworkable. The US government did not make the report public. When it was received by the Peace Conference in August 1919 it was shelved. But no one could shelve the reality in Palestine.

Joseph Jeffries, writing before the Second World War, is typically eloquent in his assessment.

> The American report was withheld, and once more the prestige of the West ... suffered in the Near East a shocking decline. The Commission had come to Syria acting with authority and vested in credentials. Everywhere the people had thronged to lay their case before the long-anticipated tribunal, and everywhere the commissioners had made meticulous enquiry. Honest dealing, the Arabs thought, was to be their portion now. They were being treated as intelligent persons, as men competent to discuss their own future, and no longer as dead stones which were to be built into the constructions the Allies meant to raise upon their soil. The Commission departed and the Arabs waited, at first with confident impatience and then with increasing disquiet. They waited and waited, but nothing was said, nothing done. By degrees the old silence and boycott closed round them again, worse this time because of their spent hopes.[15]

Violent resistance followed.

The disturbances of Nabi Musa, Jerusalem, 1920

There were clear indications that the 'facilitation' of Zionism would provoke conflict. At the end of February 1920, the head of OETA stated in an interview in an Arabic-language newspaper that Britain intended to implement the Balfour Declaration. This announcement (of a fact previously not widely known) led immediately to waves of demonstrations, shop closures and petitions, in Jerusalem and elsewhere. In Damascus, where the Second Syrian Arab Congress was meeting, it caused Palestinian delegates to call for a renewal of the struggle against Jewish immigration. And it is likely to have prepared the ground for the Nabi Musa disturbances in Jerusalem in April. These dramatically confirmed the hostility of Palestinian Arabs towards Jewish settlement and Zionist ambition, to which the King-Crane Report of the previous year had so deliberately drawn attention.

The holy city of Jerusalem had already seen a considerable worsening of Arab-Jewish relations in the previous year, and tensions remained high. Now, on 4 April, a crowd of perhaps 70,000 Muslims gathered for the annual festival of Nabi Musa, which coincided with the Jewish festival of Passover. In the Ottoman period, the festival had no political dimension. This time, however, a number of Muslim dignitaries called for resistance to the Balfour Declaration and denounced Zionism. Many pilgrims entered the Jewish Quarter in Jerusalem, whose inhabitants for the most part had no sympathy with Zionism. Predictably – though the local British authorities were to be criticised for not having taken precautions – three days of rioting and violent inter-communal confrontation followed. The clashes left dead and wounded on both sides. Arab assailants made no distinction between Jews and Zionists: members of the old community of Jews found themselves victimised by the (to them) unwelcome arrival of Zionism in their city.

Subsequently, a four-man British Court of Inquiry, under General Palin, produced a report full of foreboding.[16]

It is impossible to exaggerate the gravity of the position erected in Palestine... On the one hand we are faced with a native population thoroughly exasperated by a sense of injustice and disappointed hopes, panic stricken as to their future and ... in consequence bitterly hostile to the British Administration. They are supported and played upon by every element in the Near East of an anti-British character.

On the other hand, we have the Zionists, whose impatience to achieve their ultimate goal and indiscretion are largely responsible for this unhappy state of feeling, now bitterly hostile to the British Administration... They are ready to use their powerful foreign and home influence to force the hand of this or any future Administration. If not carefully checked they may easily precipitate a catastrophe, the end of which it is difficult to forecast.

At the heart of the problem was the Arabs' 'inability to reconcile the Allies' declared policy of self-determination with the Balfour Declaration, giving rise to a sense of betrayal and intense anxiety for their future'. Accompanying this was 'fear of Jewish competition and domination, justified by experience and the apparent control exercised by the Zionists over the Administration'.

The situation at present obtaining in Palestine is exceedingly dangerous and demands firm and patient handling if a serious catastrophe is to be avoided.

'It is impossible to exaggerate' ... or were these findings exaggerated? If we distinguish between tone and content, there are two grounds for concluding that they were not. First, similar findings are to be found in comparable contemporary reports, notably that of King and Crane. Second, with the advantage of hindsight, we can see central ingredients identified here which, though relatively dormant during the 1920s, later did much to shape the future of the mandated territory. These are: Arab disillusionment with the British (and wider Arab distrust of Britain in the region); Zionist provocation, and Zionist access to British decision-making; at the core, a British commitment to the Balfour Declaration which contained pledges which were contradictory and could not be reconciled; and apprehension of future 'catastrophe'. All this in 1920.

Like the findings of King and Crane, the Palin Report was not published. Herbert Samuel recommended that it should not be, though the decision was taken in London. The subsequent comment of Jeffries was wry and unflattering: 'To suppress the Palin Report, yet to continue with the policy which was responsible for the subject-matter of the Report, was not a piece of remarkably clear thinking.'[17] The situation was summed up, with remarkable frankness, by Theodor Herzl's former antagonist, Ahad Ha'am. As we have seen, he had placed the spiritual mission of Zionism before the political. He now wrote, in 1920, 'from the very beginning we have always ignored the Arab people'.[18]

◆

Notwithstanding Nabi Musa, two weeks later Britain and the other victorious powers met for the last time, at San Remo, and shared out the spoils of war. They allocated Palestine to Britain and recognised that the Balfour Declaration would guide British policy. However, their findings remained provisional until such time as mandates were drawn up and the League of Nations formally endorsed them. That was not to happen for another two years. In this intervening phase, from April 1920 to July 1922, few local observers could have been in any doubt as to what lay ahead if the British continued on their chosen course.

◆

A peace treaty with Turkey had not yet been signed. However, in the aftermath of Nabi Musa, the British chose in July 1920 to terminate not the Balfour Declaration but their military administration, OETA, which had been so critical of its impact on Palestine.

It is likely that Chaim Weizmann had some influence over the timing of this decision. Shortly before the San Remo conference he sent an indignant telegram to David Lloyd George, complaining that 'the overwhelming majority of British officials ... considered the Balfour Declaration a catastrophic policy mistake and were doing their utmost to undermine it'.[19] OETA had certainly been provocative. When in

March 1920 the Syrian General Congress proclaimed Faisal as King of Syria (including Palestine and Lebanon), OETA responded by recommending to London that Faisal be accepted as ruler of Palestine – 'and that the Balfour pledge be rescinded'.[20]

Weizmann was right about where local British sympathies lay. Following the 1920 disturbances, General Bols, Chief Administrator of Palestine, wrote to military HQ in Cairo. It was not the Arabs who were to blame for the troubles in Palestine, he argued with force, but the Zionist Commission. This, he wrote, had 'from the commencement adopted a hostile, critical and abusive attitude' to the British authorities. It sought, he went on, 'not justice from the military occupant but, in every question in which a Jew is interested, discrimination in his favour... My own authority and that of every department of my administration is claimed or impinged upon by the Zionist Commission... The situation is intolerable.' The Zionists, Bols continued, 'appear bent on committing the temporary military administration to a partialist policy before the issue of the mandate'. Bols called for the abolition of the Zionist Commission.[21]

The views of some OETA officers may have arisen in part from a pre-existing anti-Semitism; but they are likely to have been crystallised by what they saw and heard while on service in Palestine. Captain James Pollock provides another example. A Christian and a student of Arabic, he served in Palestine for most of the mandate years. In January 1919, in a letter home to his family, he had described British policies in Palestine as 'absolutely incomprehensible'.[22] On hearing of the appointment of Herbert Samuel as first British High Commissioner (before the League had actually approved the mandate), he wrote: 'Britain may be about to commit the greatest injustice that has ever been done by any nation in modern times.'[23] But Samuel's arrival appeased Zionists. Whether he succeeded in implementing the Balfour Declaration or not, he could not be accused of being anti-Semitic.

Disturbances in Jaffa, 1921, and the Haycraft Report

The clashes of May 1921 were on a larger scale. This time, Jerusalem remained calm. Jaffa was the main focus. Jaffa was significant as the seaport, forty miles from Jerusalem, where most Jewish immigrants into Palestine disembarked.

Arabs clashed with Jewish marchers in a May Day parade and went on to attack Jewish stores. In an especially gruesome episode, a mob attacked a hostel housing about 100 Jewish immigrants, killing thirteen and wounding twenty-six. Violence spread into the surrounding countryside. Arabs attacked Jewish settlements. One of these was Petah Tikvah, a flourishing Jewish colony of over 6,000 acres, funded by Baron de Rothschild. The attackers here were met with armed resistance, leaving twenty-eight Arabs dead. In all, there was a week of violence: in the end, forty-seven Jews and forty-eight Arabs were killed.

A commission of inquiry led by Sir Thomas Haycraft reported in the autumn. It worked its way painstakingly through the detail of the events. Its conclusions as to the cause of the troubles were unambiguous.[24] Early in the report, Haycraft stresses as the main factor 'Arab discontent with Zionist manifestations, and resentment against the new immigrants'. These new arrivals were regarded by Arabs not as people returning to their ancient homeland but as 'Russians and Poles'. He notes that Jewish witnesses chose to deny that Zionism was the issue, claiming instead that 'the Arabs are only anti-Zionist or anti-Jewish because they are primarily anti-British and they are merely making use of the anti-Zionist cry in order to wreck the British mandate'. But these witnesses did not impress Haycraft. 'We are satisfied that this is not the case,' he writes dismissively. 'The feeling against the Jews was too genuine, too widespread and too intense' to be accounted for in such a way.

The Report continues: 'There is a suspicion that the Government is under Zionist influence and is therefore led to favour a minority, to the prejudice of the vast majority of the population.' Indeed, 'any anti-British feeling on the part of the Arabs ... originates in their association of the government with the furtherance of the policy of Zionism'. The Report is consistent in theme. Rebutting Zionist claims that ordinary Arabs were actually content, and only stirred into mob violence by political agitators, it states that 'the general belief that the aims of the Zionists and Jewish immigration are a danger to the national and material interests of Arabs in Palestine is well-nigh universal amongst the Arabs, and is not confined to any particular class'. The primary Arab grievance was that the British administration was not acting fairly; that Britain 'was led by the Zionists to adopt a policy mainly directed towards the establishment of a National Home for the Jews, and not to the equal benefit of all Palestinians'.

Haycraft also issues a warning. 'This was no ordinary riot.' The civil administration had 'broken down under the pressure of popular violence'. And, Haycraft concludes, 'so long as the popular feeling described above continues, it will not be possible to maintain law and justice effectively'.

The Report stresses, more than once, that the disturbances were anti-Zionist, not anti-Semitic. 'There is no inherent anti-Semitism in the country.' Regrettably, the Zionist Commission had done nothing to reassure the Arabs regarding the Balfour Declaration. Instead it represented an *imperium in imperio* – a state within a state. In the past, inter-communal relations had been quite different. 'So long as the Jews remained an unobtrusive minority, as they did under the Ottoman Government, they were not molested or disliked.' The change came when it came to be believed, after the First World War, that the Jews were directing British government policy. The inhabitants of Palestine had been alienated. 'It has been impossible to avoid the conclusion that practically the whole of the non-Jewish population is united in hostility to the Jews.' Arab activists did not discriminate between Jews of the old and new *yishuv* (settlement). The former thus found themselves identifying ever more closely with the latter, in self-defence.

Though Haycraft states that 'it is not within our province to discuss Zionism', he strongly implies that Arab fears of Zionist ambition were well founded. He quotes Dr David Eder, Chairman of the Zionist Commission, describing him as 'perfectly frank in expressing his view of

Zionism'. In Eder's opinion, Haycraft continues, 'there can only be one National Home in Palestine, and that a Jewish one, and no equality in the partnership between Jews and Arabs'.

◆

In an afterword, Herbert Samuel, by this time High Commissioner, described this report as 'a very thorough and impartial review' of the 'unfortunate events' it described. Haycraft was, after all, the Chief Justice of Palestine. Its message to the British government in London could not have been clearer. Commitment to the Balfour Declaration, British endorsement of Zionism, and the writing into the mandate of the pledge to secure a national home for the Jews, brought deep unease to the Arab majority and the inevitability of communal conflict to Palestine.

The May Day riots in Jaffa shocked Samuel, representing as they did a major setback to British government. The first responsibility of any colonial authority was to maintain order, and to anticipate disorder. Samuel was weakened by the riots and their aftermath. His reaction was temporarily to suspend Jewish immigration, turning away boatloads of prospective settlers, thereby implicitly accepting the Arab analysis of inter-communal unease. This did not spare him criticism from Lloyd George and the British press.

Since the Jewish national home depended on immigration, the Zionists were extremely critical of its suspension. They went on to express 'utter outrage' when Samuel chose in a speech at Government House on 3 June to offer his own cautious interpretation of the Balfour Declaration. The pledge had meant, he said:

... that the Jews, a people who are scattered throughout the world ... would be able to found here their home; and that some among them, within the limits that are fixed by the numbers and interests of the present population, should come to Palestine ... to develop the country, to the advantage of all its inhabitants... The British

Government, the trustee under the mandate for the happiness of the people of Palestine, would never impose upon them a policy which the people had reason to think was contrary to their religious, their political, and their economic interests.[25]

From a chastened Samuel this was, at last and in the light of experience, a *defining* of the Balfour Declaration. For Weizmann, however, it was a *rejection* of it, since it precluded an eventual Jewish majority in Palestine. Samuel's speech appeared to leave the Arab majority to determine what was and was not acceptable regarding the Jewish homeland. It was notable, too, for referring to the Arab and Christian populations by name – as the Balfour Declaration deliberately had not – and for including among their rights the political and economic, as well as religious. Yet Samuel's balanced commentary changed nothing.

By this time, it was not just Weizmann who was uneasy. The May violence showed Zionists in general that their position in Palestine was still precarious. Their militia, the Haganah, began organising secret imports of arms. But redoubled Zionist determination to succeed in their project only widened the division between Palestine's two main communities. In May 1921 a Zionist official acknowledged that, 'We ourselves – our own movement – are speeding the development of the Arab national movement.'[26] The May riots had more than illustrated the problem; they had aggravated it.

The Deedes Letter, November 1921
It was increasingly clear to all the 'men on the spot' that Arab Palestinians would not accept the special status accorded to the Jews by a British administration wedded to the Balfour Declaration. In this light, we revisit an extraordinary exchange between two top British officials at this crucial time. It could have led to Articles 4 and 6 (recognition of the Jewish Agency; and its role in facilitating Jewish immigration) being taken out of the terms of the draft mandate.

Such an excision was advocated, astonishingly, by Sir Wyndham

Deedes, Civil Secretary in Palestine under Herbert Samuel. But he was overruled. Another opportunity to scale down the British commitment, and perhaps mitigate Arab opposition, was missed. Committed on paper, and potentially dependent in practice, the British in London baulked at confronting Zionism.

This is how it happened. First, after the riots of May 1921, Herbert Samuel recommended that draft Article 4 of the mandate should (in the words of the Colonial Office) be 'watered down' or 'sterilised', by recognition of a comparable non-Zionist, Arab, agency. Further riots marking the fourth anniversary of the Balfour Declaration, on 2 November 1921, confirmed him in this view.

Subsequently, Deedes wrote an extraordinary secret letter from Palestine to Sir John Shuckburgh at the Colonial Office. Deedes, it should be emphasised, was both a fervent Christian Zionist and a friend of Weizmann. By late 1921, however, he and Samuel were both exasperated by excessive demands made by the Zionist Commission (that is, the Jewish Agency). For a senior British colonial official, professional responsibility for public order overrode personal predilections, however strongly held.

On 21 November 1921, Deedes wrote that the Arabs could draw only one conclusion from the unfolding political situation: 'that HMG [His Majesty's Government] was bound hand and foot to the Zionists ... and that all legislation here was, and would continue to be, inspired by Zionist interest'. He continued: 'Something striking and emphatic requires to be done. The *anomalous position* assigned to the Zionist Organisation in the mandate *should be abolished*, and the administration should be left to govern this country with the help of a body in which *all* sections of the community would be adequately represented.'[27] Samuel's later proposal for a legislative council – a standard colonial mechanism for bringing leaders of major subject communities into the corridors of power – was intended to create such a body as Deedes advocated; but, as we shall see, Samuel proposed it in vain.

When Weizmann heard of this 'private and secret' letter, he

responded to Deedes. He conceded that 'Zionist ideals may have upset some Arabs and some British anti-Semites' (casually conflating as he did so anti-Zionism and anti-Semitism, a shameless rhetorical tactic that was to take root). But there must be no watering down, he insisted. 'I cannot ask the Zionist Organisation to commit suicide.'[28]

On the basis of previous comparable (missed) opportunities to adjust the British commitment, the outcome was entirely predictable and again very revealing. First, strong Zionist pressure was put on the Colonial Office. Weizmann had a two-hour meeting with Shuckburgh, after which Shuckburgh said of him, 'I have never known him before in so disturbed a frame of mind.'[29] Second, the British government cravenly ignored the pleadings of their highest-placed officials in Palestine – though both were ardent Zionists – and succumbed. Churchill informed Deedes that Article 4 of the mandate would stay as drafted, explaining that 'Zionists here would never accept such a proposal' as his.[30]

The incorporation in the mandate of a Jewish Agency, but not of an Arab equivalent, reinforced the impression and the reality that the British were not, and could never be, even-handed in their dealings with the two major communities in Palestine. Justice Haycraft's warnings had been grounded, clear and repeated. But there was to be no change in the direction of British policy in Palestine.

Ireland
The disturbances in distant Palestine occurred at a time of upheaval much nearer home.

'Trouble' in Ireland was shifting from wartime containment to open conflict. The onset of the First World War had served to contain tensions in the island, the whole of which had for long been under British rule; but its ending released them. Irish, largely Catholic, nationalists took their opposition to British rule to new heights. Protestant unionists, concentrated in the north, armed themselves to defend the *status quo*. If the pre-war plan for home rule for all Ireland went ahead, they would not succumb to a Catholic Irish majority. Elections in December

1918 saw victory for the Irish nationalists of Sinn Fein. Their elected representatives, assembled in Dublin, formed a breakaway government and declared their independence from Britain as the Irish Republic, claiming sovereignty over the whole island.

In the ensuing Irish War of Independence, 1919 to 1921, the Irish Republican Army fought British forces sent to restore imperial order. In the first seven months of 1921, around 1,000 were killed, and over 4,000 republicans interned. Eventually – in the same month as the Jaffa disturbances in Palestine, May 1921 – 'Northern Ireland' was officially conceived. The British imperial government formally acknowledged defeat when, in the Anglo-Irish Treaty of December 1921, it approved the creation of the Irish Free State.

Ireland demonstrated the depth and longevity of inter-communal rivalry based on competing claims to land and reinforced by religion. Here too the English had sponsored third-party colonialism: a large proportion of unionists traced descent from Protestant Scottish settlers in the seventeenth century. In Ireland, settler-colonialism had bred competing nationalisms. And here, now, just a quarter of a century before the creation of Israel, partition – a 'two-state solution' – was the only practicable response to irreconcilable conflict.

'The Irish Problem' had preoccupied governments in London for many years before the First World War. It erupted dramatically in the 1916 Easter Rising in Dublin. It clearly had to be confronted once again as soon as that war ended.[31] There was no lack of awareness among British policy-makers as to what was going on in the island.

Lloyd George knew Ireland from first-hand experience. Margaret MacMillan paints a typically vivid picture of him at the Paris Peace Conference. 'While he was in Paris, Lloyd George had to take time out for labour unrest, parliamentary revolts and the festering sore of Ireland. Yet he entered into the negotiations in Paris as though he had little else on his mind.'[32] MacMillan praises the Prime Minister's 'powers of concentration and recuperation'. One might, alternatively, lament the absence of any lateral thinking or, despite his own Welsh origins, sympathetic imagination for another subject people (whether Irish or Arab). Arthur Balfour knew Ireland, too, but failed to regard it as a warning. He had been Chief Secretary of Ireland in the late 1880s. He regarded Home Rule as a wicked proposal. No more than Lloyd George did he perceive an Irish nation or recognise Irish nationalist claims.

Senior military figures saw things differently. Field Marshal Sir Henry Wilson, himself a Protestant from the north of Ireland, commanded British operations there between 1919 and 1921 before becoming the highest-ranking British soldier in the Middle East. He declared in 1921 that the British had no business being in Palestine – he thought it had no strategic value – and that Britain would be well advised not to inherit or intensify its inter-communal strife. This was Ireland all over again, he observed: 'two peoples living in a small country hating each other like hell for the love of God'.[33] This soldier's analysis was straightforward, unsentimental and pragmatic. The Arabs required what the Irish had required: 'overriding authority so strong that it can enforce its will'. But, he concluded, the British were not in a position to exercise such authority and should thus withdraw.

The perspective of the British military in Palestine was partly determined by the diminishing prospect of their being able to maintain order. After the demise of OETA, officers continued, under the civilian administration, to criticise imperial policy, and to draw comparisons with Ireland. The head of the British army in Egypt and Palestine, General Congreve, advocated a major policy rethink in London. He was not anti-Semitic, he was even sympathetic towards a Jewish national home, but he deplored British concessions to Zionist impatience. He argued in a letter to Churchill, just after the May 1921 riots, 'if all the methods heretofore adopted to give effect to the Balfour Declaration' were persisted in, 'sooner or later the whole country will be in a state of insurrection', beyond the capacity of his forces to suppress.

For Congreve this was an issue not merely of physical capability but also of morality. The following month he wrote that the (Arab) majority 'means to fight, and to continue to fight, and has right on its side'. He, too, made a direct comparison with Ireland. 'Whilst the army officially is supposed to have no politics, it is recognised that there are certain problems such as those of Ireland and Palestine in which the sympathies of the army are on one side or the other. In the case of Palestine these sympathies are rather obviously with the Arabs ... the victims of the unjust policy forced upon them by the British Government'.[34]

But it was not only the military who thought, and feared, like this. After the riots of May 1921, Herbert Samuel himself, though committed to Zionism, confided to an official of the Zionist Commission that 'coercion could not be applied to this country, otherwise we should have a second Ireland'.[35]

It seems extraordinary, looking back, that lessons from Britain's own 'back yard' were not learnt and applied. The British persisted in acquiring Palestine and backing the Zionist project. In 1936, the Arabs rioted on a scale comparable to the Irish uprising. And the British authorities in Palestine – many of whom had served in civil or military posts in Ireland – adopted 'security tactics' previously adopted against the Irish: for example, police units operating in the frontline, and the use of special units that were given a free hand in a conflict in which the normal rules of war were disregarded. The British had acquired from Ireland not the political lesson that such situations were better avoided, only the military reaction that when nationalist revolt broke out it had to be put down.

There was something deliberate in Joseph Jeffries's choosing to recall Ireland in the very first paragraph of his vast study of Palestine between the wars. In 1938 he was writing while the Arab revolt was still being brutally suppressed, by forces resembling the Black and Tans whom Churchill and Lloyd George had inflicted on the Irish in 1920. This is how he began:

All the mistakes and misdeeds which fed eternal discontent in Ireland, and culminated in so much vain bloodshed and destruction there, have been reproduced in Palestine. It is almost as though the

Irish precedent, far from being kept in mind as a warning, had been remembered as a valuable example of success, and was being copied sedulously in every detail.[36]

London

The British government in London continued on its perilous course. The first chapter of Britain's administration of Palestine formally closed in the summer of 1922. In June the government updated its policy for Palestine in a White Paper. In July the League of Nations, meeting in London, finally awarded Britain the mandate to govern Palestine.

The Balfour Declaration loomed large in both these historic documents. The White Paper stated that it was 'not susceptible of change'. The preamble to the articles of the mandate went further: it endorsed Britain's commitment to the Declaration and incorporated it *verbatim*. The Declaration, far from being reversed – as circumstances and experience, reason, and contemporary informed opinion on every side seemed to dictate – was consolidated.

The 1922 White Paper

At first glance the 1922 White Paper comes across as it was intended to: as balanced and reassuring to all communities.[37] Closer reading uncovers the on-going partiality of its framers, Herbert Samuel, Sir John Shuckburgh of the Colonial Office, and the Colonial Secretary himself, Winston Churchill. It began by acknowledging 'uncertainty and unrest' and 'tension', in implicit reference to the May riots of 1921. Thereafter, however, it offered more to the Jews than to the Arabs.

It reaffirmed the Balfour Declaration, and the Jewish national home. Zionists could also welcome a substantial paragraph that congratulated them on what they had so far achieved. The White Paper assured the Jews that they were in Palestine 'by right'; and urged that the goal of a Jewish national home should be 'formally recognised to rest upon ancient historic connection'.

For their part, the Arabs were told that they had been worrying unnecessarily. Their interpretations of the Balfour Declaration were 'exaggerated'. After all, it was only 'a' home 'in' Palestine that was envisaged for the Jews. To be sure, Zionists were expected to assist in the *development* of the country; but they were to have no share in its *administration*. Arabs would not be subordinated to the Zionist project. In one specific respect, however, the British appeared to have responded to Arab fears. The White Paper stated that Jewish immigration 'cannot be so great in volume as to exceed whatever may be the economic capacity of the country at the time'. For the Arab population, the observance of the principle of 'the economic absorptive capacity' was to be treasured as a safeguard; but it would prove a feeble one.

Waving aside years of Arab protest and opposition, the British argued that Zionism, far from representing a threat, would have a benign impact on the whole of Palestine, and all its peoples. Somewhat disingenuously, the White Paper quoted, in support of this assertion, a statement from the Twelfth Zionist Congress (the first since 1917), which had met at Carlsbad in September 1921. This proclaimed 'the determination of the Jewish people to live with the Arab people on terms of unity and mutual respect, and together with them to make the common home into a flourishing community, the upbuilding of which may assure to each of its peoples an undisturbed national development'. Some Zionists may have believed this pious claim; for others, it was not convincing.

The White Paper contained one political initiative. 'It is the intention of His Majesty's Government to foster the establishment of a full measure of self-government in Palestine.' In line with this objective, an elected, representative Legislative Council would come into being.

At heart, the White Paper repeated the Balfour Declaration, including its bias and its contradictions. Notwithstanding its overall tenor, it was criticised by Zionists in three respects. First, the regulation of Jewish immigration according to the criterion of 'economic absorptive capacity'. In the event, however, there was little to be concerned about here. At one level this policy simply made sense. More importantly, no figures were cited; the economy was expected to grow; and there was to be no restriction on land purchases. 'Absorptive capacity' proved impossible to calculate; the policy proved unenforceable; and illegal immigration accompanied legal, largely unimpeded.

Second, the Legislative Council. Zionists well knew that Arabs would outnumber Jews if elected proportionally. This was not the time or place for democracy. 'The Jewish population was fearful of representative institutions.'[38] But they had nothing in fact to fear: this proposal was doomed, anyway, because the Arabs were determined to boycott any institution that implied their acceptance of the Balfour Declaration (and the mandate terms).

Third, the exclusion from 'Palestine' of territory to the east of the river Jordan. This provoked some rhetorical outrage, but there were few grounds for authentic grievance. In the early 1920s the Zionists were struggling to fund immigration and land purchase in the *de facto* Palestine of 1922 (from the Jordan's west bank to the Mediterranean). That was enough.

Overall, the 1922 White Paper was unquestionably sympathetic to the Jewish community and did nothing of substance to check the Zionist project.

The Arab reply was eloquent and, in the circumstances, remarkably restrained:

The fact is that His Majesty's Government has placed itself in the position of a partisan in Palestine of a certain policy which the Arabs cannot accept because it means his extinction sooner or later... We wish to point out that the Jewish population of Palestine who lived there before the war never had any trouble with their Arab neighbours... We see division and tension between Arabs and Zionists increasing day by day... Nature does not allow the creation of a spirit of cooperation between two peoples so different, and it is not to be expected that the Arabs would bow to such a great injustice. The Arabs should be confirmed in their national home as against all intruders.

However, the course of British policy hardly deviated. It is difficult not to see the 1922 White Paper as an opportunity lost. An opportunity, that is, to learn from what was taking place and to formulate a policy that circumscribed the Jewish national home to the extent that it could, possibly, be made tolerable for the Arab majority. The Balfour Declaration contained a promise so vague that a shrewd, pragmatic post-war 'clarification' could have been made – with prestige intact – by a government prepared to withstand Zionist complaints; in other words, by a government prepared to lead rather than be led. Zionism remained an ideology and movement to which a very small minority of Jews throughout the world were committed. The international Zionist organisation was not so powerful that it had to be appeased; it could not have withstood firm British resolve to delimit, while continuing to honour (and exploit), the commitment that Balfour had made.

But the framers of the White Paper did not deviate from Britain's open-ended commitment to Zionism. They substantially confirmed it. They knew well, by this time, that any document which stated that 'the Declaration ... is not susceptible to change' yet closed with the pious, if not risible, assertion that 'a policy on these lines ... cannot but commend itself to the various sections of the population', could not, in fact, 'commend itself' to the Arab majority.

The League of Nations Mandate, 1922

The League of Nations was not a truly representative world body – there was no USA, no USSR, for example – nor was it devolving authority to individual powers on terms of its collective deliberations. The League was dominated by Britain and France. The Council of the League was not permitted to draw up the terms of the mandates. The British mandate for Palestine was written by the British.[39]

First, however, came the Covenant, its 26 Articles the foundation document for the League: its constitution. It was drafted by a committee of men attending the Paris Peace Conference. This met several times in the early months of 1919. It was chaired by Woodrow Wilson, the

US President and the formulator, a year earlier, of the Fourteen Points which appeared to offer the world a new direction. The Covenant was adopted in April 1919 and came into force in January 1920.

It was mainly concerned with the principles and purposes of relations between member states, and with the League's mechanisms for preventing, in the wake of the First World War, future wars between states. In the case of mandates, great powers were mandated – entrusted – by the League to provide government in specified former possessions of the defeated powers. These subject peoples were regarded, in the words of Article 22, as 'not yet able to stand by themselves under the strenuous conditions of the modern world'.

We should contrast the Covenant on the one hand, and the terms of the British mandate on the other. The mandate diverged from the Covenant in important respects. Because it spelled out the terms of British rule in Palestine, it is central to our understanding of what followed. It was a focus for Palestinian opposition to Zionism from the outset and, increasingly over time, to the British administration itself. There was a unique question of legitimacy here, in the context of neighbouring mandated territories. Legitimacy conferred by the mandates system was in all cases questionable, but nowhere was it more so than in Palestine where the terms of the British Mandate appeared to defy the League's own founding principles.

Article 22 of the Covenant, patronising as it may appear to later generations, clearly delineated the responsibilities of the mandated powers. Peoples of the former Ottoman Empire were deemed to have 'reached a stage of development where their existence as independent nations can be provisionally recognised'; the 'well-being and development of such peoples form a sacred trust for civilisation'; they were to be administered only 'until such time as they are able to stand alone'; meanwhile, 'the interests of these communities must be a principal consideration'. In short, it was to be merely a matter of time (albeit unspecified), in the former lands of the Ottomans, before the new imperial regimes stood aside in favour of Arab national self-determination.

In passing, it is instructive to note the categorisation of peoples, which reflected the casual racial stereotypes of the age. Europeans were advanced enough for self-government, now; Arabs were less advanced, but far more advanced – and so worthy of Class A mandate status – than Africans, worthy of only Class B. Europeans in high office had little if any regard for the competence of Arabs (let alone Africans) and tended to treat them collectively with a degree of contempt.

Nonetheless, the Covenant expressed an unambiguous requirement to govern on behalf of these subject populations. By contrast, any doubts as to the enduring British priorities would have been dispelled by the terms (and emphasis) of their mandate for Palestine, endorsed by the League of Nations in July 1922. Though the preamble made initial mention of Article 22 of the Covenant, this was immediately followed – that is, effectively countered – by reference to Britain's pre-existing commitment to Zionism, made during the recent war. The document thus proudly proclaimed that 'the principal Allied Powers have agreed that the mandatory should be responsible for putting into effect the declaration originally made on 2 November 1917 by the government of His Britannic Majesty'.

A number of subsequent articles underlined this priority, as can be seen in these extracts.

2   'to secure the establishment of the Jewish national home ... and the development of self-governing institutions, and also for safeguarding the civil and religious rights of all the inhabitants of Palestine, irrespective of race and religion'

4   'an appropriate Jewish agency shall be recognised as a public body for the purpose of advising and cooperating with the administration of Palestine' and 'the Zionist organisation ... shall be recognised as such agency'

6   'shall facilitate Jewish immigration ... and encourage, in

cooperation with the Jewish agency referred to in Article 4, close settlement by Jews on the land'

11 'The administration may arrange with the Jewish agency to construct or operate ... any public works, services and utilities and to develop any of the natural resources of the country'

22 'English, Arabic and Hebrew shall be the official languages of Palestine'.

There was no mention of a comparable agenda for the Arabs, nor indeed mention of the Arabs by name at all, in spite of their being the overwhelming majority of the population living in Palestine. Instead, 'all the inhabitants', or the 'various people and communities' were to expect and experience an indefinite period of British rule which was hitched to the Jewish agency and to the cause of the Jewish national home.

In spite of everything that had been done and said and witnessed in Palestine between 1917 and 1922, and despite the vivid illustration in Ireland of the consequences of settler colonialism in any age, there was no watering down, here, of British support for Zionism. The British were not naïve newcomers to imperialism. They were experienced in empire and the defence of empire, unlikely to be moved by criticism based on either legality or morality. What is striking in this case is that the experience of rising Arab resistance and inter-communal disorder led neither to a review of self-interest nor to a pragmatic shift of policy in Palestine.

The Mandate Commission was supposed after 1922 to scrutinise the implementation of every mandate on a regular basis, on behalf of the League of Nations. But this was to prove a truly toothless tiger before the mid-1930s. So, for example, in 1930, following major disturbances in Palestine, the Commission accepted without demur what the British told it: that 'the obligations laid down by the mandate in regard to the two sections of the population are of equal weight; and that the two obligations imposed on the mandatory are in no sense irreconcilable'.[40] Yet the events of August the previous year had demonstrated that quite the opposite was the case.

◆

In its endorsement of Zionism, the mandate went further than both the Declaration and the 1922 White Paper. Palestine was to be the location of not 'a' but 'the' Jewish national home (Article 2). In other respects, too, the mandate took a step back from the White Paper to the Declaration. There was no reference here to 'political' (rather than 'civil' or 'religious') rights. The White Paper had appealed for Arab participation in the administration. Here, Article 2 again paid lip service to the development of self-governing institutions but only after restating, as Britain's primary purpose, securing the establishment of the Jewish national home. Nothing in the mandate recalled the statement in Article 22 of the Covenant that communities formally governed by the Ottomans had reached a stage of development 'where existence as independent nations can be provisionally recognised'.

The Zionists were handed what they had sought. The mandate's preamble included the following extraordinary passage: 'Whereas recognition has thereby been given to *the historical connection of the Jewish people with Palestine* and to the grounds for *reconstituting their national home* in that country.'[41] Seldom can such a contested history and questionable claim to nationhood have been authorised with such nonchalance at such a level. Chaim Weizmann had complained in the summer of 1921 that 'of the Balfour Declaration, nothing is left but mere lip service'.[42] But here was the Declaration, and much more, written into international law. In the event, Weizmann was not slow – or entirely fanciful – in taking the credit. 'The mandate,' he commented, 'was written for the greater part with my own blood.'[43]

Key sections of this founding document for Britain's undefined, immeasurable, future in Palestine consolidated a special, prioritised, relationship between this great power and a Zionist movement which could not have triumphed without it. This is why nationalist Arab Palestinians could not accept it. They had stated their opposition to Zionism, before and after the war. The mandate now confirmed their worst fears. They could take no political steps thereafter – such as participating in a legislative council – that would require or imply acceptance of it. Within ten years, a sympathetic British High Commissioner fully appreciated their position, and voiced it to his masters in London. But by then it was too late.

The entire period of British rule was haunted by the mandate. All parties were locked in by its terms. In retrospect, the British come across as having engaged in an act of self-defeating mischief. They ignored Point 12 of Woodrow Wilson; they contravened Article 22 of the Covenant from which their authority derived; and by incorporating the Balfour Declaration they persisted with a loosely worded commitment to the 'non-Jewish communities' which they could not meet. The mandates system was presented as self-terminating colonialism, to be practised according to the interests of the subject peoples. But in Palestine, which people?

THE CASE FOR COMMITMENT

How are we to account for the seemingly obtuse persistence of the British government at this time? Why did it adhere to an approach to Palestine which so many contemporary observers – including their own well-informed personnel – predicted would lead to an intensifying of inter-communal friction, further disturbance and a potentially fatal undermining of their own authority? By way of an answer, we look at two primary factors: first, there were no great changes of personnel (or of their thinking) in London; and second, it was thought that Jewish capital and enterprise, hitched to the Zionist goal, would serve an ambitious but indigent colonial power well.

The government in London

Lloyd George and many others of the 1917 government remained in power to October 1922. The Prime Minister's view of the world, and of what Britain wanted, did not change. In the aftermath of victory, he was not one to let facts stand in the way of prejudice and self-deception. He never visited Palestine except in his imagination; and he was not inclined to change his mind about acquiring it or supporting Zionism.

One of the other decision-makers, however, was not unconditionally committed to either Palestine or Zionism, and wavered before assenting to both objectives. Winston Churchill is an interesting case. His public pronouncements were consistent with his government's wartime and post-war position – favouring Palestine, favouring Zionism – but he clearly had doubts about both. In March 1921 he travelled to Palestine, one of the very few members of the Cabinet to do so. He was newly appointed Colonial Secretary, thus responsible for the soon-to-be mandated territory. He visited Jerusalem, and Zionist colonies where he saw Jewish pioneers in action. He was impressed. However, on entering Palestine he had been met in Gaza by Arab demonstrators denouncing Zionism; he later received an Arab memorandum asking the British to drop their pro-Zionist policy; and Musa Kazim al-Husayni, the former Mayor of Jerusalem, demanded that he revoke the Balfour Declaration and close the country to Jewish immigration.

In public, Churchill was unmoved. Responding to an Arab delegation, he said: 'It is manifestly right that the scattered Jews should have a national home ... and where else but in Palestine? ... We think it will be good for the world, good for the Jews, good for the British Empire.' He might have been reading from a Zionist script. He concluded unambiguously: 'You ask me to repudiate the Balfour Declaration and to stop immigration. This is not in my power, and it is not my wish.'[44]

But beneath it all the Colonial Secretary had his doubts. Churchill was not alone in the Cabinet in fearing a post-war Turkish revival: that Kemal Atatürk would sweep down on the Middle East and retake it by force. If that happened, he wrote to Lloyd George on 2 June 1921 (with the Palestine mandate yet to be ratified), the British would be unable 'to maintain our position either in Palestine or in Mesopotamia, and the only wise and safe course would be to take advantage of the postponement of the mandates and resign them both and quit the two countries at the earliest possible moment'.[45]

A few weeks later in the House of Commons, his colourful comparison of the Middle East with East Africa betrayed continuing apprehension: 'In the African colonies you have a docile, tractable population, who only require to be well and wisely treated to develop great economic capacity and utility; whereas the regions of the Middle East are unduly stocked with peppery, pugnacious and proud politicians and theologians, who happen to be at the same time extremely well-armed and extremely hard up.'[46] He was evidently aware that there was nothing 'docile' or 'tractable' about the peoples in Palestine, and that ruling them 'well and wisely' would not be easy.

Though a supporter of Zionism, Churchill harboured no illusions about it. He had observed in 1919 – in an early official recognition that population transfer was a central theme of more extreme Zionist policy – that 'the Jews, whom we are pledged to introduce into Palestine ... take it for granted that the local population will be cleared out to suit their convenience'.[47] Then, on 11 August 1921, Churchill made a remarkable address to the Cabinet. It was honest, well informed (by his visit earlier in the year) and sombre. He invited his fellow ministers to think again about the Balfour Declaration. 'The situation in Palestine causes me perplexity and anxiety. The Zionist policy is profoundly unpopular with all except the Zionists. Both Arabs and Jews are armed and arming, ready to spring at each other's throats... I have done and am doing my best to give effect to the pledge given to the Zionists by Mr Balfour... I am prepared to continue in this course if it is the settled resolve of the Cabinet.'[48] But no re-think ensued.

In the House of Commons a few years later in July 1926, Churchill famously defended his attitude towards the General Strike by declaring 'I decline utterly to be impartial between the fire brigade and the fire.'

It might have carried considerable weight if, on witnessing the state of affairs in Palestine in 1921, he – representing the fire brigade – had acted on the evidence of what had started the fire there.

◆

Britain's men on the spot were repeatedly overruled by London. They knew the reality of the deeply contentious unfolding situation in post-war Palestine, many months before the mandate was drawn up. They were not hindered by delusion. They reported what they found and what they saw and made their recommendations accordingly. Yet the men in Whitehall and Westminster chose to ignore unwelcome facts.

What divided them was the Balfour Declaration. As Gudrun Krämer puts it, British personnel in Palestine 'saw the Balfour Declaration as the main obstacle to establishing law and order'. Those in London, however, saw it 'as the very foundation of British presence in the country'.[49] Meanwhile, the British army had to maintain peace and stability, locally and in the region. The hostility to Zionism of British officials in Palestine was intensified by the Zionists' ability to bypass OETA and exert pressure on the government in London. Moreover, administrators in the territory knew that there was far more to the business of colonial government than providing for a Jewish homeland. Throughout the British Empire at this time, constitutional and administrative structures had to be put in place and the whole agenda of 'development' undertaken: provision of infrastructure, social and welfare services. The endorsement of Zionism distracted officials from that broader agenda. Here was a further contradiction. On the one hand, by fuelling inter-communal tension, Jewish immigration rendered the Balfour Declaration unattainable in practice. This is what the men on the spot witnessed. On the other hand, Zionist enterprise helped greatly to subsidise colonial rule. That is what London thought was needed.

Enough members of the British government continued to believe that there was a strategic case for Palestine to remain in British hands. But there was no consensus here. The case against keeping Palestine remained strong, too. The army general staff were confident, as in the past, that British forces stationed in Egypt were sufficient to defend the Suez Canal and would only be financially drained by the need to defend Palestine as well. In this light it is interesting to learn that by 1933 two British regular army battalions were deployed in Palestine, in addition to the six in Egypt. There being none in Mesopotamia, we may suppose that their role was either to defend Palestine itself against external aggression or to maintain domestic order there: in either case (or both), a burden for the empire to carry.[50] In the wake of the First World War, a fear of General Congreve was that, if the British did not withdraw their support of Zionism, a Jewish majority in Palestine would one day crush the Arabs, expel them from the land and get rid of the British as well.[51] The events of subsequent decades show that these fears were not entirely fanciful.

As it became clearer that the country could prove ungovernable, Palestine looked less like an asset than a liability. The contemporary observations of Sir John Shuckburgh reflect this sad conclusion. It is revealing, if not astonishing, that this very high-ranking metropolitan official should in late 1922 tell a colleague that 'he saw no purpose to the mandate, and no way out'. The Arabs were embittered, the Jews were dissatisfied. Overall, Shuckburgh 'was inclined to think that the Balfour Declaration had not been worth it'.[52]

Nonetheless, in spite of all such misgivings, policy-makers retained a balance-tipping, ingrained fear of the French. This persisted even though there were dwindling grounds for it, especially when Lloyd George and his French counterpart, Clemenceau, concluded 'a secret oral bargain' in December 1918 whereby France conceded to Britain the government of Palestine.[53] French apprehensions in Europe regarding a resurgent Germany far outweighed any ambitions they harboured for more territory in the Middle East. Frictions would be many, but the agreed spheres of influence were to hold, largely through shared Anglo-French contempt for, and fear of, the Arabs. Though not a very credible threat, the French were still rivals. In 1918–19 it would indeed have been surprising if the British – especially in the person of the Francophobe Lloyd George – had handed Palestine, overloaded with significance as it was, to France. The British had won it by force of arms and occupied it. There was more to remaining than the habit of clinging on. Meanwhile, there was also a perceived need, initially at least, to confront any revitalised Turkey.

Subsequently, the British discovered – or rediscovered – a primary strategic justification other than the security of Suez for retention of the territory: Haifa. As we have seen, this port had attracted the attention of British policy-makers in 1915 and 1916 as a potential railway link with Mesopotamia. Now it was to become the British terminal of a pipeline from Iraq. James Barr comments: 'Acquired by Britain in 1920 as an eastern bulwark to the Suez Canal, Palestine now gained a new strategic importance as the outlet for Iraq's oil.' The pipeline finally came into service in 1934. It was this asset 'that made the British determined to cling on there – amid mounting opposition to their presence – seemingly at almost any cost'.[54]

Even so, to retain Palestine the British did not have to commit themselves to the Jewish national home there. They did not need a justification such as securing 'national self-determination' for the Jewish people. There was no equivalent cloak for, say, the British acquisition of Mosul. And Lloyd George personally insisted on securing that prize, despite its having been 'promised' to France in the Sykes-Picot agreement. Similarly, the French, the other mandated power in the region, had no compunction in dismissing Arab 'self-determination' when they drove Faisal out of Damascus in 1920.

Moreover, romance played its part, and perhaps carried more influence in some cases, than reasoned calculation. There was a mystique about Zionism. British decision-makers were in awe of it. Sykes probably wrote for many in declaring that when 'we bump into a thing like Zionism, which is atmospheric, international, cosmopolitan, subconscious, and unwritten – nay often unspoken – it is not possible to work and think on ordinary lines'.[55]

◆

Serving to confirm British policy was a disregard of Arabs. This was in line with Weizmann's contempt. In a letter to Balfour in May 1918 he had ascribed to the Arabs a 'treacherous nature', adding that while they 'are superficially clever and quick-witted ... they worship only power and success'. He went on: 'The Arab ... screams as often as he can and blackmails as often as he can... The *fellah* is at least four centuries behind the times, and the *effendi* ... is dishonest, uneducated, greedy and as unpatriotic as he is inefficient.'[56] Weizmann saw Arab concerns as something the Jews had to live with, 'just as they had to live with the mosquitoes'.[57] In this correspondence with Balfour, he was preaching to the converted. By contrast, he and his British patrons agreed, Jewish immigrants to Palestine carried European civilisation into the backwaters of the Middle East.

Elements of anti-Semitism and nimbyism also persisted. The Israeli journalist Ari Shavit recalls the dream of his grandfather and other Herzl Zionists: 'They want the West to tame this part of the orient. They want this Arab land to be confiscated by Europeans, so that a European problem will be solved outside the boundaries of Europe.'[58] The British obliged. And the Arabs noticed. From their reply to the 1922 White Paper comes this passage: 'The immigrants dumped upon the country from different parts of the world are ignorant of the language, customs and character of the Arabs, and enter Palestine by the might of England against the will of the people who are convinced that they have come to strangle them.' These were relatively early days, but the number of immigrants to be so 'dumped', by the 'might' of England and others, was to rise steeply in the later years of the mandate.

Meanwhile there was British pride in adhering to a pledge. Cabinet minutes of the meeting of 18 August 1921 – the one at which Churchill confessed his doubts – record that, although the pro-Zionist policy might involve Britain in great difficulties, nevertheless 'the honour of the Government was involved'. Now that Balfour had issued his Declaration, 'to go back on our pledges would seriously reduce the prestige of this country in the eyes of Jews throughout the world'. Breaking promises to Arabs was one thing, but world Jewry (still) had to be appeased.

The British kept their promise; but this episode was not characterised by honour. Balfour himself admitted later: 'So far as Palestine is concerned, the Powers have made no statement of fact which is not admittedly wrong, and no declaration of policy which, at least in the letter, they have not always intended to violate.'[59]

The potential and influence of Zionism

There were politicians in the British establishment, Lloyd George foremost among them, who resisted having imperial policy decided by the army's analysis of strategic interest. They had visions of their own, imbued with Christian Zionism. The Jews and their capital would develop Palestine and secure it as a friendly presence in a region of strategic value. Some may have been moved, when reading *Daniel Deronda*, by the words of Ezra Mordecai Cohen, Eliot's proto-Zionist visionary: 'The Jews have wealth enough to redeem the soil from debauched and pauper conquerors... And the world will gain as Israel gains. For there will be a community in the van of the East which carries the culture and the sympathies of every great nation in its bosom.' Before the Balfour Declaration, Lloyd George had spoken to Sykes, in April 1917. There is understatement in the official memo of the meeting, but he could not have expressed himself more succinctly. 'The Prime Minister suggested that the Jews might be able to render us more assistance than the Arabs.'[60]

In 1919, the King-Crane commission had reported that 'the people repeatedly showed honest fear that in British hands the mandatory power would become simply a colonising power of the old kind'. The fear was well founded, but this was to be two-tier colonising of a new kind. Here, the British in effect combined two models in place in contemporary East Africa. Palestine was to be both a 'protectorate' (like Uganda), administered by the British, and a 'colony' (like Kenya), settled by Jews in the name of Zionism.

Zionism offered much to British policy-makers bent on imperial expansion. To be sure, its advocates had a reputation for being arrogant, provocative and ungrateful. But Zionism represented manpower, enterprise and above all capital: the Jews could pay for this colonial adventure. The British parliament and government were always loath to spend money on empire – especially on policing empire – but investment in Palestine of Jewish capital and enterprise would reduce the burden.

Article 11 of the British mandate is very revealing.

> The Administration of Palestine ... shall have full power to provide for public ownership or control of any of the natural resources of the country or of the public works, services and utilities established or to be established therein. The Administration may arrange with the Jewish Agency ... to construct or operate ... any public works, services and utilities, and to develop any of the natural resources of the country.

The Rutenberg affair of 1921, pre-mandate as it was, provides a remarkable illustration of the close association of British imperial aims and Zionist aspirations. Pinhas Rutenberg was a prominent Russian Jew who had fled his homeland in 1917. In Palestine he was close to the right-wing Zionist leader Ze'ev Jabotinsky. During the 1921 disturbances they co-ordinated the defence of Jews in Jerusalem. In September 1921 it was announced that Churchill, as Colonial Secretary, had awarded Rutenberg concessions for two major hydro-electric schemes. A number of aspects of this case are of interest. For example, the award was made in London, not by the administration in Palestine itself. It was, moreover, evidently illegal. There was as yet no international approval of the British mandate, which was still in draft. As Joseph Jeffries put it, 'The Government was perfectly aware that there was no authorisation, no warrant for what it intended to accomplish in the interests of Zionism... It was moonshine to talk of subjecting concessions strictly to the terms of a draft document, which, being a draft, therefore had no fixed terms at all.'[61]

But of greater significance than its legal status was the substance of the deal. The purpose of Rutenberg's schemes was not the irrigation of potential farmland for Jewish pioneering settlers pursuing regeneration, but provision of water supplies to factories: in short, the Zionist industrialisation of Palestine. And the key element in all this was funding. Churchill told Parliament in London that Baron Edmond de Rothschild, the founder of pre-war colonies in Palestine, had offered to place at Rutenberg's disposal up to £200,000. Rutenberg became founder and director of the Palestine Electricity Corporation. He had a lasting impact on the territory. Ari Shavit writes with pride and wonder of a power station opened in 1938. 'In only nine months the ingenious engineer Pinhas Rutenberg and his thousand men, working around the clock, managed to build the Reading power station that accelerated the electrification of the land and provided power to the fast-growing Tel Aviv.'[62]

Jewish enterprise devoted to the Zionist goal greatly helped defray the cost of running the British administration in Palestine. In 1928 – that is, before the mass immigration of the early 1930s – the *yishuv*, the Jewish community in Palestine comprising 17 per cent of the population, contributed 44 per cent of the government's revenue. By 1935, harnessed to Zionism, the administration could be described as 'a little dazzled by its mounting revenues and impressive surplus'.[63]

With the characteristic assurance of a ruler who had not actually consulted his subjects but was nonetheless confident that he knew what was best for them, Churchill had told critics of the Balfour Declaration, whom he met on his 1921 visit to the territory, that Zionism would be 'good for the Arabs who dwell in Palestine'. This was a fine example of seeing like a state.[64] In fact, Arabs saw British rule in Palestine very differently. In his report on the May 1921 disturbances, Haycraft offered the following judgement. 'We feel bound to express the opinion ... that the Zionist Commission ... has failed to carry conviction to the Arabs on the point of the National Home benefiting Arabs as much as Jews.'

Meanwhile, further steps were being taken to bring about the Jewish national home. Thanks to the drive and initiative of Weizmann, Zionist influence was intensified in Palestine even before the war ended. In early November 1917, just four days after the issue of the Balfour Declaration, Weizmann proposed a 'Zionist Commission': the sending of a Jewish delegation to Palestine. The British were happy to agree with this, though they insisted that the Commission should act as an advisory body only, to liaise between the Jewish community and the British (military) administration.

Weizmann left for Palestine as head of the six-man Commission on 4 March 1918. Such was his eminence that earlier on that same day, through the intercession of Balfour, he was received by King George V at Buckingham Palace. The King wished him well. The date is remarkable for a further reason: his departure preceded, by over two weeks, the Germans' Spring Offensive on the Western Front. There was no indication, even at this time, that the war would end before the end of the year, nor certainty as to who would win it. Even so, Weizmann arrived in Tel Aviv in April, and would stay in Palestine for several months before returning to London in October.

The establishment of the Commission illustrated both the momentum of Zionism and the extent of Weizmann's influence in London. The Commission itself was to remain in Palestine for three and a half years, funded by American Zionists, after which it was succeeded by the Jewish Agency. During this earlier period, all before the award of Britain's mandate, it exceeded its brief to the extent that it began to function like a government for the *yishuv*.

On his visit, Weizmann had a cordial meeting near Aqaba with Emir Faisal. He set out to charm this leader of the Arab Revolt against the Turks, and he had some success. When they met again in London six months later, Faisal conditionally accepted the Balfour Declaration (though his conditions were not met and, in any case, he could not speak for Palestinians). But Weizmann's relations with the British military administration were less than cordial. General Congreve regarded the Zionist Commission as 'a standing insult to the British administration', its bureaucratic structure precisely mirroring that of the military administration.[65] The military were not alone in finding Weizmann unpalatable. Even William Ormsby-Gore, the pro-Zionist British official who was accompanying the Commission, described Weizmann as 'at times too fanatical and too partisan and uncompromising'. He added: 'He wants all Jews to be 100% Zionist, and few even here can stand quite so strong a dose'.[66] But the Commission stuck to its self-appointed task and became a prime mover in the territory.

At the same time the Zionist voice was heard in London and wherever decisions were being taken. Weizmann remained personally close to the decision-makers. After his visit to Palestine he turned his attention to the victors' peace-making. On 4 January 1919, as part of a delegation which included Nahum Sokolow, he left for Versailles. There, Palestine and Zionism were discussed in the context of the defeat of the Ottoman Empire (and Arab hopes of liberation and self-government). In February, the delegation submitted to the conference their 'first draft for the British mandate', asserting the historic right of Jews to return to Palestine. This document not only insisted that Britain should be the mandatory power, it told the British how to act once they were there. Meanwhile Weizmann wrote to Wilson, brazenly assuring him that 'the Jewries of nearly every country [were] united in favour of a Jewish Commonwealth in Palestine'.[67] Having had an interview with the American President, on 27 February Weizmann appeared in person before the Supreme Council. His speech was later described by Balfour as being 'like the swish of a sword'.[68] The French listened in silence but raised no objection to Britain's being the mandatory power in Palestine.

Weizmann also attended the post-war conference at San Remo in April 1920 where, as we have seen, Britain, France, Italy and Japan formally distributed former Ottoman imperial territories.[69] Though the French voiced some reservations about the inclusion of the Balfour Declaration in the draft mandate wording, Zionist pressure on the British ensured that the commitment to establish a Jewish national home was incorporated. By July the British military administration in

Palestine, which had shown little sympathy to the Zionists, was replaced by a civilian one in which British Zionists were prominent.

Weizmann exploited his continuing proximity to Lloyd George and Balfour. In July 1922 he was among Balfour's guests at the Foreign Secretary's home, along with Lloyd George and Churchill. He could not have been nearer the heart of British policy making. He criticised the British administration in Jerusalem and insisted that the British continue to favour the Zionist project by, for instance, allowing unhindered Jewish immigration into Palestine. Afterwards, Balfour spoke to him. He assured Weizmann that he had Lloyd George's support and high regard, asking if there was 'anything else' he could do. At the same meeting, Weizmann admitted that Zionists were smuggling rifles into Palestine to defend Jewish settlements. Churchill replied: 'We won't mind, but don't speak of it.'[70]

Weizmann was a passionate, eloquent, tireless advocate. It is somewhat ironic that his recently constructed brand of Jewish nationalist messianism seems to have appealed more strongly to British susceptibilities than to the great majority of his own people. He was ubiquitous. He was entirely at ease with British decision-makers: at home with them in London, away with them at Versailles and at San Remo. When empires were coming under critical attack, he played on the hearts and minds of British policy-makers with unflinching purpose and considerable skill. He offered a colonialism that appeared respectable – 'national self-determination' – while at the same time providing a faraway location and 'return' to their ancient homeland for Jewish refugees from Central and Eastern Europe who could thus be diverted from inconveniencing the societies and states of the West.

And he had to compete with no comparable advocate of Palestinian aspirations.

◆

In the period 1917 to 1922, a Jewish national home was not necessary. Chronology is very important here. So, too, is suspension of hindsight, insofar as that is possible. At this time, the British did not have to take account of any moral imperative in relation to Nazism, say, or any concern that persecuted Jews from Europe had nowhere else to go.

British policy towards Palestine conflicted with self-interest. In that age, it was not to be expected that Great Power policy-making would be guided by principles of justice. But in this case the British defied common sense and experience. Their policy was incapable of implementation and bound to produce ever more conflict and disorder. It has to be emphasised that this is no retrospective judgement. Josef Chaim Bren was a Zionist. A writer and journalist, he was killed in the events of Jaffa 1921. Shortly beforehand, he had written: 'Living in tiny Palestine are no fewer than six or seven hundred thousand Arabs who are, despite all their degeneracy and savagery, masters of the land, in practice and in feeling, and we have come to insert ourselves and live among them... There is already hatred between us – there must be, and there will be.'[71]

In the event, the British did from time to time attempt to introduce restrictions on both immigration and land purchase; from time to time, they issued new formulations of what the Balfour Declaration 'meant'. But what they did was always reactive; and it was never enough. We can never know if any interpretation of the Declaration would have assuaged Arab anxieties or forestalled their opposition. A fully thought-through, minimalist interpretation of the Balfour Declaration – to challenge the Zionists' preferred, maximalist, interpretation – was not formulated as British imperial strategy until 1939, by which time it was too late.

Policy-making comes across as casual. Regarding the issuing of the Balfour Declaration in wartime, that was understandable; regarding its confirmation and elaboration in the mandate, it was reckless. Lloyd George was the prime minister responsible. Neither he nor Balfour studied the subject from afar, to compensate for lack of first-hand experience. Lloyd George hated reading Foreign Office memoranda, while Balfour was a man who 'kept himself determinedly innocent of everything concerning Palestine'.[72] A colleague, Curzon, gave a contemporary assessment of Balfour which was a less than glowing testimonial for a man who could influence the fate of millions: 'He never studied his papers, he never knew the facts, at the Cabinet he had seldom read the morning's Foreign Office telegrams, and he never looked ahead. He trusted to his unequalled powers of improvisation to take him through any trouble and enable him to leap lightly from one crisis to another.' Curzon himself, on the other hand, knew Palestine; and it was he who asked the awkward question: 'What is to become of the people of the country?'[73]

Meanwhile, the British authorities had only a cursory grasp of Zionism. They were quick, like Lloyd George, to see moral and material value in its vision of a Jewish homeland in Palestine but appeared to have no further interest in Zionism as an ideology. They did not question the Jewish claim to nationhood, its claim to be a secular rather than a religious movement, or its version of Jewish history. It was enough, it seems, for Weizmann to speak of 'a people who had suffered martyrdom for eighteen centuries'; and for him to say of the Jews' right to Palestine, 'Memory is right.'[74]

What the decision-makers lacked above all was sympathetic imagination. The journalist and Arabic scholar Nevill Barbour later highlighted this when he observed that British policy 'entirely ruled out' the effect of Jewish immigration 'on the Arab mind'. Yet, he goes on, 'the state of mind of the Arab population can easily be imagined'. By 1935, 'the prospect of the complete subordination of the Arabic population, language and culture became in their minds ... an immediate practical possibility'.[75] Revolt followed. Barbour's 1946 verdict on the mandate was withering. 'The British Government ... is forced into attempting the impossible. The result is great inconvenience to itself ... and a grave injustice to the Arab population of Palestine, which is absolutely innocent of any responsibility for the situation brought about by the action of Jewish and English Zionists'.[76]

5

PALESTINE IN 1922

'If the growth of Jewish influence were accompanied by Arab degradation, or even by neglect of Arab advancement, it would fail in one of its essential purposes.' Herbert Samuel[1]

Overview

Palestine underwent some changes in the nineteenth century, but it remained in many respects underdeveloped at the beginning of the British mandate. This was certainly how the British perceived it.

In his introduction to the 1922 'Handbook of Palestine', Sir Herbert Samuel, first British High Commissioner for the mandated territory, offered a number of impressions of his own:

> If I were called upon to express in a single word the distinguishing characteristic of Palestine, I should say Diversity – diversity of religions, diversity of civilisations, diversity of climate, diversity of physical characteristics.

> The Arab villages are, for the most part, still under medieval conditions.

> The new arrivals from Eastern and Central Europe, and from America, bring with them the activities of the twentieth century, and sometimes, perhaps, the ideas of the twenty-first.

These conditions are found in a country so small that it is easy to motor in a single day from the northernmost town to the southernmost, and in a morning from the eastern boundary to the sea.[2]

An era of new development opens widely before her. A multitude of new problems arise.

These are sober observations from an accomplished British politician, as he took on responsibility for a distant, newly acquired, imperial possession. A Zionist himself, Samuel appears to be aware of both the potential and challenges which an on-going meeting of peoples and cultures must bring. And in describing the livelihoods of the Arab majority as 'medieval', he detects what contemporaries and also some later writers have described as backwardness.

◆

But this remote corner of the Ottoman Empire had undergone recent change.

Following Palestine's seventh-century conquest by Muslim armies, Arabs settled in the region and intermarried with a local population who largely adopted Arabic and Islam. From 1516 Palestine was governed – for the most part, with a light touch – by the Ottoman Turks, under sultans whose dynastic legitimacy rested on their commitment to Islam.

Despite the empire having been dubbed in the 1850s 'the sick man of Europe', the later nineteenth century saw both the expansion of the Ottoman state – exemplified by public works and the routine administration of conscription and taxation – and also the beginning of the integration of Palestine into the world economy, through the production of cash crops.

The second half of the nineteenth century was an age of reform. The Ottoman top-down *Tanzimat* ('Reorganisation') was primarily concerned with security, order and efficiency. And it resulted in significant steps towards what the British colonial establishment of the time would have termed 'good government' in the region later known as Palestine. New garrisons improved security on the fertile coastal plains, allowing farmers from the hills to reside where previously they had only cultivated. Urban landowners settled tenant farmers there. The draining of swamps improved living conditions. Main roads were upgraded. Railways followed: a line linking Jaffa and Jerusalem was constructed in 1892, and the Hijaz line, for Muslim pilgrims travelling from Damascus to Mecca, was completed in 1905, with its headquarters in Haifa.

Meanwhile, the upsurge of European interest in Palestine from the mid-century, along with modern means of travel, brought not only more pilgrims (to Jerusalem especially) but also more immigrants. These included Protestant Christians, as well as Jews emigrating from Russia under Zionist auspices. Such groups, though small in number, stimulated local economies where they settled, and, in the case of the Christian Templars of Wurttemberg, for example, introduced the use of fertilisers and machines on farms. This was a low-import, high-export economy. Exports were almost all agricultural products such as grain and barley, sesame and olive oil; the demand for Galilee cotton fell as soon as mid-century hostilities in the Crimea and in America came to an end. Remarkably, water from Jordan was being exported to the USA from 1906.[3] By this time the most conspicuously successful product was citrus, the export of tough-skinned oranges boosting the significance of the port of Jaffa.

Population growth marked this period and underlines impressions of economic progress. It is estimated that the majority Muslim population doubled through natural increase, between 1850 and 1914, while the Christians – around 10 per cent of the Arab population by that later date, and living mostly in the urban areas – tripled in number.[4] Although two-thirds of Palestine's population lived in the rural areas in 1922, we should recall that in the towns there was an accomplished urban elite, among which were the articulate spokesmen of incipient Palestinian Arab nationalism. As for overall numbers, when David Ben-Gurion first arrived in Palestine in 1906, 'the country consisted of 700,000 inhabitants, 55,000 of which were Jews, and only 550 could be defined as Zionist pioneers'.[5] We may add that, like the numerically comparable Christian minority, Jews here were free from persecution, representing no threat to this mainly Bedouin/Arab Muslim region.

Even so, these developments were relative, and limited. The main impulse for growth came from outside.

◆

It is not surprising that the British colonial 'Handbook of Palestine', 1922, paints a somewhat bleak picture of Palestine at the start of the mandate period. Though it is silent on inter-communal rivalries and in particular on Arab opposition to the imminent implementation of the Balfour Declaration, we may learn from it much of interest, and something of value. Edited by two senior British administrators in Palestine, this was a 280-page volume: part-Domesday, part introductory guide for colonial service personnel. It included chapters on (for example) Geography and History, Peoples and Religions, Places of Interest, Government, Geology, Mining and Natural History. It is an impressive publication, a typical testament to the diligence, curiosity and bureaucratic efficiency of the British Colonial Service. The stated objective of British rule was standard, too. 'Peace, order and good government' was the professed purpose of, for example, the British administration in Uganda at this time. A formula, perhaps; but it should not be dismissed as empty rhetoric.

There is more than a trace of world-weariness in these pages: an awareness that this would be a costly, albeit noble, imperial assignment. There are echoes of Rudyard Kipling's poem 'The White Man's Burden', written in 1899 on the USA's acquisition of the Philippines but retaining a resonance for Britain and its own increasingly numerous responsibilities. References to the prevalence of disease, for example, recall his lines: 'fill full the mouth of famine, and bid the sickness cease'. We see in the extracts that follow some incidental references to the economy and to the anticipation of tourists; there are also several mentions of the Jews (as ancient colonisers and as recent immigrants). What is most striking and sobering, though, from the colonial power's point of view, is 'backwardness' (in part the fault of neglectful or 'oppressive' Ottoman rule) along with the characteristically slight presence of British personnel and officialdom charged with administering the territory.

According to the Handbook:

The Holy Land abounds in mineral springs.

The importation of the following articles into Palestine is prohibited: arms and ammunition ... shaving brushes exported from Japan, China, Manchuria and Korea.

Principal imports: cotton fabrics. Principal exports: oranges.

The most important fruit-tree in the hill country is the olive.

The coast-line is bordered by dunes, much of the sand of which is suitable for glass-making. The limestone beds of Cenomanian and Turonian age furnish the principal building stones of Jerusalem and other towns. One of the greatest mineral assets of Palestine is the salt of the Dead Sea.

By the quickest route, under normal conditions, Palestine is reached from London in six to seven days.

Tourists may land and proceed immediately on their tour, except in cases where plague or cholera has occurred on board the ship during the voyage.

In the winter months, clothes suitable for a cold English winter – tweeds, thick overcoats etc – are required; in the summer, white ducks and helmets are desirable, but warmer clothing should be worn in the hills at sun-down.

The Canaanitish [*sic*] immigration is the oldest of which we know with certainty.

The leader of the Israelites, to whom they owe the basis of their religious development, was Moses. Their settlement in the country west of the Jordan was effected very slowly, partly by force of arms, partly by peaceful assimilation with the Canaanites who at that time occupied a much higher plane of culture than the Israelites.

In 1921, on the invitation of the Government, the Jews of Palestine established an elective Rabbinical Council ... under the presidency of two joint Chief Rabbis, the one representing the Ashkenazim, the other the Sephardim.

The Jewish agricultural colonies have grown up in the course of the last forty years and show a level of agricultural and scientific development far in advance of anything else of the kind in Palestine. There are at present 61 of these colonies, large and small, with a population of about 17,000.

The total number of immigrants who entered Palestine from 3 June 1921, when immigration was re-opened, to 31 December 1921, was 4,861 of whom 4,784 were Jews.

Palestinians of all classes were not slow to remark that the Turks, after an occupation which had lasted over four hundred years, had left Jerusalem, as regards the water supply, slightly worse than they found it.

Olive oil is reckoned in Jerusalem and Jaffa by the *jarra*, which equals

6 *rotls* or 17.5 kilos. In Nazareth it is measured by the *rotl*, which equals 2 *okkas* or 2.5 kilos.

The present Administration has maintained the Ottoman Government's system of taxation, in some cases ... abolishing the more vexatious and oppressive.

There is no Palestinian currency.

The geographical situation of the frontiers of Palestine makes the provision of an adequate customs control a matter of some difficulty. From the earliest ages in history the people inhabiting Palestine acted as the middlemen of the East.

Few bridges of any length exist in Palestine.

The coast of Palestine is a coast without harbours; on the 140 miles of coastline there are only three ports of any size and all three are open roadsteads.

There was no telephone service during the Turkish regime. No person is entitled to use a trunk line continuously for more than six minutes.

To find the year of the Christian era corresponding to any Mohammedan (*Hejra*) date, deduct 3 per cent from the Mohammedan year and add 621.54 to the result.

The provisions of the Ottoman Press Law of 1327 apply to all publications.

The usual means of transport when motor-cars are not available is by diligence or victorias drawn by two or three horses and, in the absence of carriage roads, by donkeys and camels.

Camels used solely for the purpose of ploughing are exempted from the animal tax.

[From] a census of animals in Palestine, 1920–21: 57,785 ploughing oxen; 3,934 mules; 325,512 goats; 8,846 camels.

Notifiable diseases [include]: cholera, dengue, leprosy, plague, small-pox, tubercle of lung, typhus and malaria. Owing to the considerable incidence of rabies amongst dogs, jackals and wolves throughout Palestine, poisoning of dogs is carried out on a large scale.

Several carnivorous mammals are still far from rare, such as the jungle cat, the wild cat [and] the striped hyena. The European house mouse and various races of the black rat have been imported and are abundant in the towns.

A plague of mice and rats, affecting all edible crops, waxes and wanes.

The British population (exclusive of the garrison) is estimated at 1,100 souls.

Under the Governors and District Officers are the *mukhtars*, or headmen of villages. Their powers and duties have not yet been codified but included among them are:
- to keep the peace within the village
- to send information to the nearest Police Station of any serious offence or accident occurring in the village
- to assist Government Officers in the collection of revenue
- to publish in the village any Public Notices or Proclamations sent to them by the Governors
- to keep a register of all births and deaths within the village and to send a copy to the Principal Medical Officer once a quarter.

The Legislative Council will have full power and authority ... to establish such Ordinances as may be necessary for the peace, order and good government of Palestine.[6]

Arabic is the normal language of pleading in the Magistrates' Courts. Summonses and other legal processes are issued in English and Hebrew according to the character of the person to whom they are addressed.

Police: in 1920 a separate cadre of British officers was sanctioned, and at present the force consists of 16 British and 55 Palestinian officers, and 1,144 other ranks of whom 395 are mounted.

Addendum. The Peel Commission Report was later to mention, regarding the challenge of providing a judicial system in mandated Palestine, 'the existence of three official languages, three weekly days of rest, three sets of official holidays and three systems of law'. This was a land, moreover, 'where perjury is common, and evidence in many cases, particularly in times of crisis, unobtainable'.

◆

This portrait of Palestine in 1922 may come across as somewhat jaundiced. But there is reality here too. Thus, the Handbook helps to explain why so many aspiring immigrant Jews, especially before the First World War, decided not to stay.

It also shows why the British sought Jews and Jewish capital to help them to develop and fund the mandated territory. It appeared to be a happy coincidence that, just when the British needed men and resources to make newly acquired Palestine pay, Chaim Weizmann and the Zionists were needing a Great Power to enable them to colonise Palestine and bring into being a Jewish national home there.

6

ZIONISM AND BRITAIN
IN PALESTINE, 1922–1939

'Should we be unable to find a way to honest cooperation and
honest pacts with the Arabs, then we have learned absolutely
nothing during our 2,000 years of suffering.' Albert Einstein[1]

Overview

Everything in the past looks inevitable afterwards; but what happened
in Palestine after 1922–1923 is what people at the time expected would
happen, whether they longed for it or dreaded it.

Sir Herbert Samuel's attempts to steer an impartial course did
little more than bring to the fore the contradictions that lay within
his brief. It can be argued that by the end of 1923 – months before he
left Palestine – all the ingredients for irreversible antagonism were in
place. In the 1920s Jewish immigration, land purchase and settlement
remained at modest levels compared with what was to follow, but they
were concrete steps towards building the Jewish national home. Some
Arabs collaborated with this hybrid colonialism, many working with
the British administration, some selling land to Jews. However, the two
communities grew separately and, in terms of political voice, unequally.

It was not so much a steady accumulation of grievance but a highly
sensitive religious conflict in Jerusalem that sparked the countrywide
violence and disturbances of 1929. In their shadow, the third British
High Commissioner, Sir John Chancellor, was prompted to conclude
that the Balfour Declaration had been a blunder. Under Chancellor,

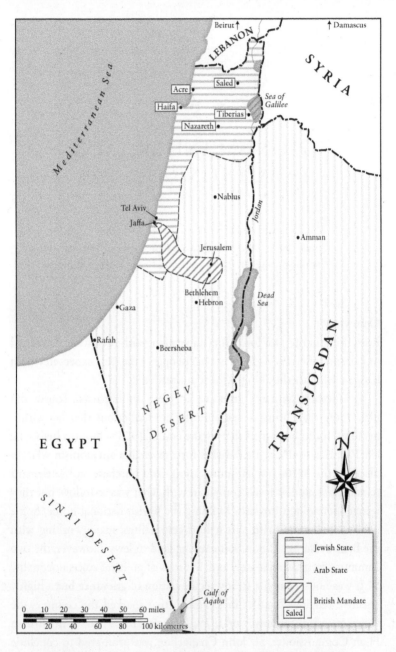

THE 1937 PEEL COMMISSION PARTITION PROPOSAL

and in the wake of the troubles of 1929, the land question became a central issue in Palestinian politics. For a while, a major shift in British policy seemed possible. On the back of six official reports on the land question, the British threatened to delineate the Jewish national home; but Zionist pressure prevented them from doing so.

Renewed and intensified anti-Semitism in Hitler's Germany and Poland, along with the ending of America's open-door policy, led to marked increases of Jewish immigration and land purchase in the early 1930s. This Jewish influx of manpower, capital and enterprise served British economic and financial interests as they had hoped; but it fuelled Arab opposition at unprecedented levels.

For the first fifteen years of the mandate, the Palestinian political elite tried to mediate between the British authorities and the majority Arab population, and to mitigate the effects of Britain's continuing endorsement of Zionism. However, as the career of the Mufti of Jerusalem, Amin al-Husayni, most clearly illustrates, all efforts failed. Arab acquiescence yielded to radicalised opposition, general strike and revolt.

The Arab Revolt that began in 1936 was of a significance to compare with the contemporary Spanish Civil War. It led to yet another British commission of enquiry. The Report of the Peel Commission, however, was singular: vast in scope, unparalleled in its dispassionate thoroughness, it was potentially transformative in its conclusions. These were, in short, that the pledges of the Balfour Declaration were irreconcilable; the British had failed; and Palestine should be partitioned.

Palestine's Arabs rejected Peel and resumed their revolt with renewed intensity and, for a while, some success. In the event, however, it was crushed by British (and Zionist) force. Even so, a new British White Paper, in 1939, formally abandoned the partition proposal and envisaged a unitary self-governing state for a Palestinian population in which the Arabs remained a majority. But the British had lost control of events, while the Arabs were demoralised and effectively leaderless. In the wake of the Second World War – and the unutterably awful suffering of Jews

in Nazi-occupied Europe – in Palestine a battle-hardened Zionism
would triumph.

1922–1928: SIR HERBERT SAMUEL; 1923 AND AFTER

Herbert Samuel's appointment as first British High Commissioner
for mandated Palestine piled contradiction on contradiction. The
Balfour Declaration embodied a contradiction. Samuel was himself
a contradiction, at least from the Zionist perspective. Theodor Herzl
and others in the late nineteenth century had insisted that for Europe's
innumerable, vulnerable, Jews there were only two options – assimilation
or emigration – and that, of these, assimilation did not work. Samuel
was from a Jewish banking family. After education at University College
School, Hampstead, and then Balliol, Oxford, he went into politics and
in 1909 became the first non-baptised Jew to sit in the British Cabinet.
His case illustrated that assimilation *could* work, spectacularly. However,
by 1914 he had adopted Zionism. It was at his insistence that the Cabinet
in early 1915 explored proposals for a post-war Jewish homeland in
a British Palestine. At the time, this initiative came to nothing but, at
what proved to be a significant moment, Samuel had raised the profile
of Zionism among the British ruling class.

At San Remo in 1920, Samuel told Lloyd George that he was
interested in the Zionist idea and willing to promote it – but that he
thought a Christian in charge of Palestine was likely to have more sway
over the non-Jewish population. But close associates (among whom
was Chaim Weizmann, also present at San Remo) persuaded him to
overcome his reservations and to take the job.

Samuel hoped to realise the Zionist goal through a cautious policy
of gradual, orchestrated demographic change. A fortnight before he left
for Jerusalem in 1920, he wrote: 'In fifty years there may be a Jewish
majority in the population. Then the government will be predominantly
Jewish and, in the generation after that, there may be that which might

rightly be called a Jewish country with a Jewish state. It is that prospect which rightly evokes a fine enthusiasm.'[2] In 1915 he had warned that 'to attempt to realise the aspiration of a Jewish state one century too soon might throw back its actual realisation for many centuries more'. Visiting Palestine a few months before taking up the post, he was concerned by what he saw, and complained in a letter to Weizmann that the Zionist Commission had 'the irritating effect of an alien body in living flesh'.[3] A future leader of the British Liberal Party, Samuel could see that Arab opposition to Zionism was genuine and that the Arabs needed some protection from Zionist excess. He once wrote: 'Nothing could be worse than if it were to appear that the one thing the Jewish people had learnt from the centuries of their own oppression was to oppress others.'[4] Gradualism offered Samuel his only chance of inter-communal harmony, and the avoidance of the disorder that every colonial administrator dreaded.

Samuel was to have alongside him in Palestine, as attorney-general, Norman Bentwich. Educated at St Paul's School in London, and Trinity College, Cambridge, he too was an English Jewish Zionist for whom assimilation had worked. Bentwich, though, was less of a gradualist, and his measures in law to 'facilitate' the project made him a more controversial, adversarial, figure than Samuel.

Notwithstanding the prominent position of Zionists in its ranks, British administrators under Samuel sought to be accepted by both the main communities in Palestine. They hoped that the Arabs would welcome the economic benefits of Jewish immigration, while the Jews would be grateful for a haven and a homeland. But they were to be disappointed, in both respects. Historian Kenneth Stein has analysed the Arab-Israeli conflict in depth; it is fitting that he should describe the high commissioner as possessing 'absolute executive, judicial and legislative *authority*' in mandate Palestine, since he certainly could not exercise absolute *power*.[5] He had the right to take whatever initiatives he chose; but his ability to achieve the results he sought was, in these problematical circumstances, close to non-existent.

1923, the end of the beginning

Looking back in 1939, Joseph Jeffries described then-recent dramatic events as 'the mere consequences of what had been schemed and accomplished by the political Zionists and by our own governments' in earlier years. 'It is not consequences but causes which cry out for examination.' And, he concluded, 'the causes, which have been kept concealed, or as far out of sight as possible, are all to be sought within the period from the war to 1923'.[6]

There are firm grounds, in at least four respects, for agreeing with Jeffries that 1923 ended the formative chapter in Palestine's history as a British mandated territory. After that year came consequences rather than change: differences in degree rather than in kind. First, in the middle of 1923, attempts to create a representative legislative council, advocated in the 1922 White Paper, ended in failure (as did subsequent attempts). Second, the Cabinet suggested a reform of the administrative structure, designed to appeal to the indigenous population: the creation of an Arab Agency, to mirror the Jewish Agency. But this was rejected by the Arabs, just as they rejected the legislative council: both were still-born. Third, at around this time in London, the British Cabinet did reconsider the mandate ... only to confirm it as it was. Last, before the end of the same year, Ze'ev Jabotinsky wrote a seminal article, *The Iron Wall*. This was a militant, uncompromising, version of Zionism. It led shortly to the formation of the breakaway Revisionist party. In the long run, it would have great influence on the movement as a whole.

◆

The best illustration of Samuel's essential dilemma as high commissioner lay in his attempt to introduce a legislative council.

It was standard practice at this time, in Africa for example, for a British colonial governor to be advised by an executive council (of officials), and a legislative council (as in Egypt, for example, before 1914). This latter body (typically of nominated members initially, elected members later) gave representation and voice to leaders of the various substantial communities in the colony (so, for example, in Kenya to white settlers and Asians and, belatedly, to Africans). As advisory bodies, they provided contact between rulers and ruled. At best, these were forums for mutual understanding and practical collaboration. And they provided the means, through the gradual widening of membership and the introduction of elections, of piecemeal constitutional progress towards – and preparatory schooling for – eventual self-government. For British authorities, meanwhile, they were valued as a means of appearing less dictatorial – and of actually listening to and responding to a range of opinions in such a way as to make policy-making better informed and policy-taking more likely.

When Samuel proposed this conventional step, he was confronted by the unconventional reality of Palestine. With Jews being a numerical minority throughout the inter-war period and into the late 1940s, Zionists were always fearful of representative institutions. They were understandably wary of Samuel's proposal, under which allocations for the proposed twenty-seat legislative council were: British (10), Muslim Palestinian (4), Christian Palestinian (3), and Jewish (3). Zionists opposed Arab representation – and its potential influence on the administration – of any kind. In the event, they had nothing to worry about. Arabs were consistent in refusing to participate in any institution, such as this proposed council, which would signify acceptance of the Balfour Declaration and the mandate.

Arab leaders organised a campaign: first, to boycott the census on which registration for the voting would be based; and second, to boycott the elections themselves. The ensuing election was a fiasco. The legislative council scheme was suspended. Thereafter, the demographic fault-line became so pronounced that, although two subsequent high commissioners resurrected the proposal in the early 1930s, no elected assembly of Arab and Jewish representatives ever met in mandatory Palestine. The doomed 1923 election was accompanied by a chilling proclamation from the triumphant Palestine Arab Executive: 'Today the limbs of our enemies will tremble with sadness and vexation... Long live free Palestine that it may stand independent!'[7] However, such a response may have been a sign of weakness rather than strength. The price of prioritising principle over pragmatism was exclusion. Without a legislative council, Arabs were to have no constitutional forum in Palestine in which either to air grievances or to take gradual steps towards eventual self-government.

Even so, the primary inflexibility lay elsewhere. The British had already, repeatedly, committed themselves to a non-negotiable transformation of Palestine, in favour of Zionism and in disregard of Arab opposition. It is difficult to see how Arab nationalists could have shed the key condition of their cooperation (suspension of the mandate), in order to participate in constitutional arrangements that focused on the creation of a Jewish national home in their country. Arab leaders had defined their position. As the Peel Report would eventually put it, 'With the British Government holding authority by an occupying force, and using that authority to impose upon the people against their wishes a great immigration of alien Jews ... no constitution which would fall short of giving the people of Palestine full control of their own affairs could be acceptable.'[8]

The fact that no such legislative council came into being in Palestine is significant both in substance and in symbolism. The potential benefits for both government and governed were lost. The losers were the British and the Arabs – not the Zionists or the *yishuv*. This was a major instance of British policy setback and of principled Arab intransigence. In the 1920s and 1930s, the British made repeated attempts to bring a legislative council into being, but it did not and could not happen. While Zionists quibbled about details, Arab nationalists rejected it because cooperation would have implied acceptance of a British administration hitched to the uncircumscribed Jewish national home.

Lines were firmly drawn in Palestine long before Herbert Samuel's term as high commissioner ran out in 1925. In the absence of a legislative council, which would have been inclusive, Palestine's Jewish and Arab communities and their leaderships grew increasingly apart.

♦

Although Samuel as high commissioner favoured a degree of even-handedness, from the early 1920s official British relationships with the two communities, Jewish and Arab, were unequal.

The Jewish Agency had a unique status. It was mentioned in Articles 4, 6 and 11 of the mandate. The 'appropriate Jewish Agency' in 1922 was the World Zionist Organisation, based in London and represented in Palestine by the Zionist Executive (which had replaced the *ad hoc* Zionist Commission); by 1929, the latter had developed into the Jewish Agency by name, representing all Palestine's Jews, Zionist and non-Zionist (except Jabotinsky's Revisionists, and the Orthodox).

The Agency enjoyed huge influence and powers. It negotiated with the British administration on all matters concerning Palestine's Jews; it controlled Jewish colonisation and settlement activities, and oversaw the Jewish National Fund which financed them; it decided how many Jewish immigrants Palestine's economy could 'absorb' (interpreting, as it chose, the criterion of the 1922 White Paper). Through its offices in Europe, it selected the immigrants (prioritising the young, the hard-working and the educated Hebrew speakers); and it founded schools and hospitals for Jews, in Palestine.

Other Jewish organisations were helping to build, and to defend, the homeland. Notable among these were the Histadrut, the labour organisation, and the Haganah, the militia. Thus empowered locally – and retaining extraordinary access to, and influence over, the British government in London – Zionists made significant progress in Palestine, even in the 1920s when immigration levels remained modest. Irreversible progress was made towards the homeland, even before the *yishuv* was much strengthened by the growing wave of immigration from Europe in the early 1930s.

As early as 1920, the Zionist Commission had the character of a cabinet with personnel listed according to their specific departmental brief, such as 'Immigration', 'Trade and Industry', and 'Finance'. Another eight men were listed as district commissioners, in a direct imitation of British colonial nomenclature, in Jaffa, Haifa and Galilee, for example. There was more to the Commission than this administrative arm, for it also established courts for the trial of ordinary civil cases. It was the Commission, too, that provocatively insisted on the installation of Hebrew as an official language of the mandate. By 1923, the Zionist Commission/Jewish Agency was well rooted, its chairman enjoying easy, regular access to the High Commissioner.

As the Peel Commission Report of 1937 put it, somewhat mildly, the Zionist Commission's presence 'was a source of irritation to the Arab inhabitants of the country'. Regarding its successor, the Jewish Agency, the Report is more forthright: this 'constitutes a kind of parallel government existing side by side with the mandatory government, and its privileged position intensifies Arab antagonism'. This privileged embryonic Jewish state within a state – for which the Arabs had no equivalent in their existing homeland – provided considerable capacity for securing, and subsequently fighting for, the Zionist cause.

Authorised to offer the Arabs an Arab Agency, comparable to the well-established Jewish Agency, Samuel failed again. The offer fell short of anything acceptable to Arab leaders. For one thing, Arab Agency members would be nominated by Herbert Samuel, though he did not nominate members of the Jewish Agency. But that was detail. The offer itself was regarded as an offence – and not only by Palestinians. An independent member of the League of Nations' Mandate Commission subsequently delivered a telling judgement: 'The High Commissioner was proposing to organise a Jewish and an Arab Agency with equal rights. In my opinion, the Arabs will find it difficult to accept such an organisation, for the role of the Jewish Agency is defined in Article 4 of the Mandate, which contemplates that it shall assist in the administration of the country... The Arabs, however, *who are in their own country*, must feel that they have the right to exercise more influence in administrative affairs than newcomers. In this I cannot say that they are wrong.'[9]

Joseph Jeffries was later to express his own disdain for the Arab

Agency proposal: 'To this offer the Arabs gave the reception which we would give to an offer of a British Agency in Britain. They dismissed it without thanks.'[10]

Time and again, Palestinian Arab nationalists refused to make political compromises, and it appears that they suffered as a result. But they had initially adopted a principled objection, and they defiantly clung to it. No legislative council; no Arab Agency. Samuel had failed to establish any constitutional forum for the Arabs that might have served in time to legitimise British rule. For the rest of the mandate period, Palestine was governed by a foreign high commissioner in consultation with his executive and advisory councils, composed entirely of officials. There was no constitution, inclusive representative body, or commitment to the civil and political rights of all, to serve as restraints on social breakdown when inter-communal relations deteriorated.

◆

In June 1923, a cabinet sub-committee was established to reconsider British policy in Palestine. By this time the Prime Minister was Stanley Baldwin. He had been among those Conservatives who had voted a year earlier to end the wartime coalition and bring down David Lloyd George. The Cabinet review was an opportunity to evaluate British commitment to Zionism in Palestine in the light of the problems it had created, and even recommend reversal, or at least substantial qualification, of the 1917 pledge made by Arthur Balfour and Lloyd George. Weizmann, always well informed, was alarmed. He feared that the presence on the committee of a number of known anti-Zionists would lead it to withdraw support for the Jewish national home.

However, Samuel travelled from Palestine to London and appealed to the committee in person. His address appears to have been crucial in ensuring that Weizmann's fears were dispelled. The committee reported in July that Britain should *not* reverse her policy. Reversal would tear up the mandate. This could not be countenanced, because Palestine would be occupied by another, rival, power such as France. Moreover, the committee concluded, the British government could not extricate itself 'without a substantial sacrifice of consistency and self-respect, if not honour'.[11]

There was no acknowledgement that erstwhile 'consistency' lay in dogged commitment to an impracticable goal, nor that 'honour' lay in fulfilling overarching League of Nations commitments to the majority people of the territory. Instead, the Balfour Declaration was to be honoured still, and the articles of the mandate left intact. Instead of changing course, the Palestine administration was merely to take new steps to try to reassure the majority population (the Arab Agency offer being one of them). Samuel's reluctance at a personal and professional level to admit failure was understandable. For the British government to persist with contradictory policy goals in Palestine was error of a far higher order.

Was this the only opportunity missed? Menachem Klein (an academic and author who has also been an advisor in Israeli-Palestinian peace negotiations) has suggested two other occasions before 1923 when the British could have re-interpreted the Balfour Declaration and presented Palestine with alternative prospects. First, in 1918–19, they could have established an Arab kingdom in Palestine under Faisal Hussein which would have provided the Jews with autonomy. Second, in 1921, instead of detaching the territory of Palestine east of the river Jordan (to create Transjordan), they could have allowed Faisal, or his brother Abdullah, to rule over the undivided country, again providing autonomy for the Jews within an Arab kingdom under British tutelage. In either event, an Arab-Jewish identity – of which there was some evidence in major Palestinian towns – would have had a chance to grow. As we know, neither of these options was tried. And it is hard to see how either would in fact have been viable. Faisal did not speak for Palestinian Arabs who had been so critical of orchestrated Jewish immigration since well before the recent war. Moreover, as Klein himself acknowledges, Zionists had 'an endless list of demands', and 'Jewish nationalists were never satisfied and always demanded more'.[12] We may infer that no variant of such a compromise – 'Jewish autonomy', undefined, within an Arab kingdom – would have won general acceptance.

◆

Last, 1923 also saw Zionism unveiled. Vladimir (Ze'ev) Jabotinsky was born in Odessa in 1880. There he founded a Jewish self-defence organisation. In Palestine, in 1920, he helped to organise the defence of the Jews of Jerusalem during the disturbances (after which he was briefly jailed by the British authorities for illegal bearing of arms). In 1923 he resigned from the Zionist Executive, in opposition to Weizmann's pragmatism and acceptance of the British 1922 White Paper; and he wrote his seminal article, 'The Iron Wall'.[13] This statement of Zionism in its purest form was remarkably frank and, in the long run, influential. There could be no clearer, unembarrassed, statement that Zionism was settler colonisation and that, as such, it must overcome opposition by force.

For Jabotinsky there were no contradictions, and there were to be no compromises. He wrote:

There can be no voluntary agreement between ourselves and the Palestine Arabs.

My readers have a general idea of the history of colonisation in other countries. I suggest they consider all the precedents with which they are acquainted and see whether there is one solitary instance of any colonisation being carried out with the consent of the native population. There is no such precedent.

Every native population, civilised or not, regards its lands as its national home, of which it is the sole master, and it wants to retain mastery always.

Ze'ev Jabotinsky (1880–1940)
Zionist founder of the Revisionist Party, 1925.

Jabotinsky continued: 'This is also true of the Arabs.' These Arabs
are 'culturally ... 500 years behind us'. But they are not to be deceived
or bribed into acquiescence. Jabotinsky summarised the view of an
anonymous Arab editor, that 'the Zionists want only one thing, Jewish
immigration; and this Jewish immigration is what the Arabs do not
want'. He went on, 'this statement of the position by the Arab editor is
so logical, so indisputable, that everyone ought to know it by heart'.

One day, in the future, there can be agreement with the Arabs, but
only *after* their resistance has been crushed. 'When that happens ... we
Jews will be found ready to give them satisfactory guarantees... In other
words, the only way to reach an agreement in the future is to abandon all
idea of seeking an agreement at present.'

Two somewhat condescending comments provide his assessment of the British: of their usefulness, and of their wishful thinking. First:

> Zionist colonisation can proceed and develop only under the protection of a power that is independent of the native population – behind an iron wall which the native population cannot breach... That is our Arab policy... What need otherwise of the Balfour Declaration? Or of the Mandate? Their value to us is that an outside Power has undertaken to create in the country such conditions of administration and security that if the native population should desire to hinder our work, they will find it impossible.

Second:

> To imagine, as our Arabophiles do, that they will voluntarily consent to the realisation of Zionism in return for the moral and material conveniences which the Jewish colonist brings with him is a childish notion.

The Arab race, he said, is not 'a corrupt mob ... willing to give up their fatherland for a good railway system'.

In the same year, Jabotinsky founded Betar, a right-wing nationalist youth group that resembled those being founded in Europe at this time. There followed in 1925 the formation of his separate political party, the Revisionists. Under its auspices the Irgun militia came into being, breaking from Haganah in 1931 after the 1929 disturbances. But Jabotinsky's impact was far greater and longer-lasting than this. His views confronted the then-dominant Labour Zionism, by stressing the necessity of the use of force. In the words of Avi Shlaim, 'Labour Zionists wanted to proceed toward statehood by immigration and settlement and accorded a lower priority to the building up of a military capability.' By contrast, 'Jabotinsky never wavered in his conviction that Jewish military power was the key factor in the struggle for a state.'[14] And in due course, others in the movement came around to his point of view.

By the end of 1923, there was no mistaking the militancy of the movement to which the British imperial government was wedded.

After 1923

Palestinian responses to British rule in this period were shaped by three main factors. First, that 'Palestine' had been detached from 'Greater Syria' (to Arabs of the region, a most unwelcome colonial contrivance). Second, that this entity, comprising two Ottoman-era regions, coincided with the territory on which Zionist immigration and land purchase were focused. And, third, that Britain's mode of rule was a kind of 'indirect rule'.[15] There was nothing typical about Britain 'facilitating' colonisation of one of its possessions by a third party. But its twin-track overall administrative approach was familiar: 'indirect rule', the recognition and use of existing authorities as junior partners in power; and 'divide and rule', the manipulation of existing differences in native society.

Palestine offered the British opportunities in both respects. A prosperous and influential urban class of 'notables' existed – its members accustomed to playing an intermediary role during the Ottoman period. And within this class was competition between eminent families that any competent incoming successor government could expect to exploit. The disturbances of 1920 in Jerusalem and 1921 in Jaffa had demonstrated that order could not be taken for granted. But for most of that first decade, in contrast to the following one, the British enjoyed two benefits: the Jewish national home was as yet only a commitment and prospect, rather than a burgeoning reality; and prominent Arabs still believed that through cooperation they would persuade their new masters to orientate their political strategy towards eventual Arab self-government in the whole of Palestine.

Working with and through such notables, the British could hope for political stability. These great families relished the posts, the renewed status, and access to policy-making that the British provided. Yet there was a degree of interdependence in these relationships. The British needed the notables to contain or divert local grievances, so as to avoid disruption. In turn, the notables had to cooperate with government, while articulating their own and their followers' interests. This balancing act was challenging, and the stakes were high. The notables' position was always vulnerable in two respects. If they lost credibility over time as guardians of local interests, they could be bypassed by other, perhaps younger or more radical, figures. And if a notable from one eminent family in Jerusalem failed to provide his British masters with social order, he could be replaced by a nominee from a rival family.

Competition for positions under the British was especially marked between the Husayni and the Nashashibi dynasties. The Mufti of Jerusalem was an expert in Islamic law and in charge of Jerusalem's Muslim holy places. This post was held in succession by Tahir al-Husayni (to 1908), and two sons: Kamil (to 1921) and then Amin. Haj Muhammad Amin al-Husayni was to be the most prominent of all Palestinian notables in the mandate period, his career embodying the perils of the dual role of intermediary between the government and the governed. This being the case, it is important to note that his elevation to the post of mufti was initially engineered by Herbert Samuel and his colleagues. As was customary, a small number of eminent Muslims met to select a successor to Kamil: but Amin was not the man they chose. Amin owed his elevation to the British mandate authorities who calculated, not without reason, that he would serve them well. For many years he did.

'Divide and rule' – as applied to the other top post in Jerusalem, that of Mayor – also appeared for a while to serve Britain well. Another member of the Husayni clan, Musa Kazim, had been appointed Mayor in 1918, by Ronald Storrs, the newly arrived British military governor of the city. What Storrs gave he could also take back. When Musa Kazim participated prominently in the 1920 Nabi Musa disturbances, having earlier refused to accept Hebrew as an official tongue in his department, Storrs removed him. Exploiting the most intense dynastic rivalry in Jerusalem, Storrs then replaced Musa Kazim with Raghib al-Nashashibi. In 1923, Raghib formed a Palestinian National Party. Prepared to accept

Amin al-Husayni (1893–1974)
Mufti of Jerusalem, 1921–1948, and President of the Supreme
Muslim Council, 1922–1937.

British mandatory rule – and even to have close, if covert, relations with
the Zionists – its hallmark was hostility towards any policies adopted by
the Husayni family.

For his part, Musa Kazim, free from the restraint expected of him (by
the British) as Mayor, became active in the Palestinian Arab Executive
(PAE). This had emerged from the first meeting of the Palestine National
Congress in Haifa, 1919. From 1920 he was its leader. Though openly
nationalist in its goals, the PAE sought to represent Arab Palestinian
opinion in a working relationship with the British administration. The

PAE remained outside the government structure and it had no officially sanctioned powers; but it was more than tolerated. It was permitted to make representations to British authorities in Palestine and also in London. In early 1921, for example, Kazim met Churchill, and took the opportunity to demand the revocation of the Balfour Declaration and an end to Jewish immigration.

After the May troubles, Kazim met Samuel and again demanded an end to Jewish immigration, thereby increasing the pressure on the High Commissioner, which led Samuel to declare a temporary suspension. Then, in November 1921, Kazim led the first of several delegations to London where, once more, he demanded the abandonment of the Balfour Declaration. On this occasion – at the insistence of the British who were in pursuit of inter-communal cooperation – he met Weizmann. There could be no agreement, however, between the advocate of the Jewish homeland and one of its fiercest critics. They were, after all, on opposite sides of a colonial relationship. One British observer described Weizmann's attitude as that of 'a conqueror handing to beaten forces the terms of peace'.[16]

No match for Zionism, the PAE was crippled by two weaknesses: the refusal of the British officially to recognise it, and its own lack of unity. Inner divisions and rivalries reduced the PAE to irrelevance by the early 1930s. From the start, the PAE included both Nashashibi and Husayni members (and its 1930 delegation to London was to include Raghib al-Nashashibi as well as Amin and Musa Kazim al-Husayni). But, relying on little more than negotiation and petition, it never convinced the British that it was a force that needed to be attended to. It did not stop the League of Nations ratifying the mandate in 1922; though it blocked Britain's legislative council, it did not persuade the British to introduce a constitution for Arab self-government; and it did not influence British policy on the Jewish national home. Rather, the PAE 'seemed to pass from one failure to another'.[17] The Palestine National Congress from which it first derived its authority withered, too, incapable of even an annual meeting through the mid-1920s.

Raghib al-Nashashibi (1881–1951)
Mayor of Jerusalem, 1920–1934.

Meanwhile, conscious no doubt that Christian-Muslim associations had given birth to the PAE, the British took steps to divert all classes of Muslim Palestinian Arabs away from such inter-denominational nationalist political activity and towards the particular concerns of their religious community. After the May 1921 riots, the British established a new body, a Supreme Muslim Council (SMC). This was to exercise – for one religious community – a degree of self-rule in Palestine. However, not democratically elected, it could not claim to be fully representative. Nor was that the intention: the British wished only to conciliate Muslim Arabs by offering them a middle-man of status between the community and the administration. Even so, reflecting the size of the Muslim Arab majority, the SMC came to enjoy much influence over its own people. It had considerable autonomy in the exercise of (sharia) law and justice, in particular, though also in spheres such as education, health and even the press. By 1924 it had over 1,100 office-holders.

Indirect rule had always involved seeking indigenous authorities and adapting (or creating) administrative devices through which to work with them. The SMC exemplified this. The British choice as chairman was Amin al-Husayni who, a few months earlier, had been appointed by Samuel as Mufti of Jerusalem. In some respects, Amin was a bold choice. He was motivated not only by hostility to Zionism but also by the cause of Arab self-rule for Palestine within a Greater Syria. Like his kinsman, Musa Kazim, he had been involved in Nabi Musa. In the wake of those disturbances, he fled Palestine to work with Faisal Hussein in Damascus ... though he had to flee Syria, in turn, when the French killed off Faisal's new kingdom. Samuel seems to have supposed that Amin, chastened by his experiences, would be prepared to cooperate with a high commissioner who acknowledged that the Balfour Declaration bore more than one commitment, and who had his own criticisms of the Zionists. Moreover, Samuel needed Amin to deploy his family's considerable prestige and influence to keep the peace – specifically to avoid further spontaneous protests such as had occurred in 1920 and 1921 – and thus provide stable conditions for 'good government'.

The SMC under Amin al-Husayni was the only spokesman of the Arab population recognised by the authorities. But it should be stressed that, while the British had adapted the pre-existing role of mufti (to extend its religious authority, under Amin, across the whole territory), the SMC was novel. If its chairman failed to provide the British with the effective collaboration for which they had appointed Amin, they could remove him. Similarly, they could dismantle the SMC, whose officials were paid out of the public purse. In the event, for much of the 1920s this fabricated agency of indirect rule thrived and worked well for the British; and Amin remained on good terms with the administration.

Though the SMC is described by Gudrun Krämer as enjoying 'a status similar to the Jewish Agency', the differences between the two are striking.[18] The terms of the mandate illustrated this most clearly. As we have seen, a Jewish Agency was referred to in three separate Articles. There was no such mention of the SMC or any other Arab agency – indeed, no mention at all of the Arabs as a people. The British administration in Palestine was indelibly marked by treatment of Jews and Arabs that was separate and unequal.

Yet there was in practice one similarity. In the absence of a legislative council, and of equivalent Jewish and Arab agencies, the British worked closely with two remarkable individuals: Amin al-Husayni, Mufti and chair of the Supreme Muslim Council, and also with David Ben-Gurion, the powerful leader of the Zionists' Histadrut labour federation. Hoping to hold Palestine's main communities in some sort of balance, the administration came to recognise Amin and Ben-Gurion as legitimate leaders of their respective communities – if only because they might keep at bay, in each case, more extreme elements. The two leaders grew stronger as a result. But there was no shared vision; nor did they seek common ground or partnership. Rather, the Mufti used Islam to promote Arab nationalism, while Ben-Gurion used socialism to push the Zionist agenda. The two men never met. They could not be peacemakers.

◆

The two communities, Arab and Jew, grew apart. Not totally: unpoliticised neighbours could remain neighbours, and Jews and Arabs worked side by side in government offices and in the police, for example. But communities as a whole became primarily inward looking and preoccupied with their own problems. Jews and Arabs might visit the same doctors or hire the same craftsmen, but their knowledge of each other was limited. In the absence of a shared language, prejudice and anxiety grew unchecked.

By the end of the 1920s, Arabs were increasingly conscious of the separate economic development of the *yishuv*. The Arab economy was overshadowed by the rapidly expanding Jewish sector, which benefited from a steady influx of financial and human capital that the Arabs could not match.

Trade union issues in one industry illustrate the general trend. The first railway TU in Palestine was formed in 1919: the Jewish Railway Workers' Association. Among Zionists, some socialists believed that accepting Arab members would serve the common good in shared pursuit of improved pay and conditions. There was clearly tension here, as articulated by one Histadrut official in 1920: 'From the humanitarian standpoint, it is clear that we must organise them ... but from the national standpoint, when we organise them, we will be arousing them against us. They will receive the good that is in organisation and use it against us.'[19] In the event a new, inclusive union was launched in late 1924, involving around 25 per cent of the railway work force. But it unravelled the following year when the Palestine Arab Workers' Society came into being as a counter to the Jewish union.

Jews and Arabs were educated in separate schools. One instance of Jewish ascendancy in this field, during the Samuel period, stands out. A Jewish Iraqi millionaire made a huge financial bequest to the British government, for the development of education in Palestine. Zionists energetically campaigned against the administration's inclusive suggestion: that the money should fund an elite school for both Jewish and Arab boys (in which lower grades would study in Hebrew or Arabic as appropriate, while the upper grades would study in English). In the event, the administration gave way, and an academic high school was established for Jews exclusively. Later, a proposal to set up a joint-venture agricultural school was vetoed by the Zionists; instead, two, neighbouring, agricultural schools were established, one for Jews and one for Arabs. Segregation was taking root. Gathering Jewish ascendancy had another dimension: by 1931, though they constituted only 18 per cent of the population, there were more literate Jews in Palestine than literate Muslims and Christians combined.[20] In higher education the Jews had a top-quality university; the Arabs had none.

Perhaps the most visible illustration of separation lies in the story of Jaffa and Tel Aviv. Jaffa was a historic town, with a majority Arab population. At the start of the mandate period it had a marginal Jewish neighbourhood, Tel Aviv, founded by Zionist immigrants in 1909. After the May 1921 disturbances, Jewish residents fled Jaffa for Tel Aviv, where they initially lived in tents on the beach. Herbert Samuel then granted Tel Aviv status as a separate, autonomous, municipality. In 1923 the daily Hebrew newspaper, *Ha'aretz,* moved its offices from Jerusalem to Tel Aviv, marking the latter's standing as the centre of a new Hebrew culture. In short, even in the period of its first high commissioner, there was a trend towards the internal partition of Palestine. The trend accelerated after Samuel's departure.

Zionist and Arabs were separate and unequal in one further respect: their *voices*, where decisions were made. The Arabs were allowed to send delegations to London from time to time, but no spokesman emerged to match the status and influence of Weizmann.

The land issue in the 1920s

There could be no doubt that land was the central matter in creating Zionist-Arab Palestinian tensions.[21] Zionism initially pursued colonisation by land purchase, not by force of arms. It was through such transactions in the 1920s that Jews and Arabs came increasingly into contact. In 1920, Samuel had confirmed his readiness 'to facilitate' the creation of the Jewish national home by reopening the Land Registries, which had been closed during the war and in the OETA period. Zionists were free again to buy land.

In this first decade of the British mandate, more than 60 per cent of the land purchased by Jews was bought from Arab absentee landlords. For the most part residing outside Palestine, these were town dwellers, not farmers or agricultural entrepreneurs. Many were happy to shed estates from which they were cut off by the newly drawn Anglo-French boundaries for Syria and Palestine. Much property sold at this time was surplus land – in large estates, relatively empty and uncultivated

– so there were relatively few victims when landlords, absentee *effendi*, chose to sell. There were notable exceptions, however. Many families were evicted in the Jezreel valley in 1925, when the American Zionist Committee purchased land from Elias Sursuq, a prosperous Arab businessman who lived in Beirut. The Hope-Simpson Report of 1930 was to observe that the British administration had, in this instance, given 'insufficient consideration' to the terms of the mandate which required them to ensure that the rights and position of the Arabs were not prejudiced by Jewish immigration.

Hillel Cohen, a Jerusalem-born scholar of Arab-Israeli relations, highlights a remarkable fact: among the well-placed Arabs seizing the opportunity of escalating land prices were a quarter of the members of the PAE. They included the PAE's president. 'Individual Palestinians,' Cohen writes, 'took a range of practical attitudes toward the Zionists, from active resistance through passivity to accommodation and collaboration.'[22] We may add that such a spectrum of responses towards settlers was not unusual. It was visible among Africans in contemporary British Kenya, for example. But in Palestine, as elsewhere, the often covert collaboration of a minority did not of itself either nullify the overall impact of colonialism or significantly inhibit the emergence of nationalist political forces.

Nonetheless, the Jewish purchase of land during the 1920s was on a relatively small scale and consequently not an issue of general concern to the Arab population. According to official British estimates, Palestine had 8,250,000 *dunams* of cultivable land (one *dunam* being roughly a quarter of an acre); in the 1920s, Jews legally purchased only 116,000 *dunams*.[23]

Given the real and symbolic value of land, however, statistics relating to sales and evictions came to count for less than perception – especially, and increasingly, among Arab Palestinians. The gravest problem resulted less from land sales as such, which could make sense for individual sellers, than from their political significance in a country dedicated to the Jewish national home. Thus Al-Fula, the Arab village sold by Sursuq, became an Arab nationalist symbol, as proof of relentless Zionist ambition. But it was only after 1929 that land and dispossession came to rival immigration as the focus of Palestinian national resistance to Zionism in the territory.

1929–1932: WHITE PAPER AND BLACK LETTER; SIR JOHN CHANCELLOR

On 23 September 1928, a number of Jews in Jerusalem erected a screen to separate men from women at the Western Wall. Local Muslims were alarmed. They were proprietors of the site – for them, al-Buraq – and this unprecedented act appeared to be a step towards turning the site into a synagogue.[24] In order to pacify the Muslims and restore the status quo, British police requested the perpetrators to remove the screen and, when they refused, took it down themselves. But the episode did not end there. The Mufti initiated a campaign that included building a provocative new construction next to and on top of the Wall. In response, Zionists began to demand total control of the site.

1929, the beginning of the end

No rapprochement was reached, and in the following summer the issue caught light. On 14 August 1929 around 6,000 Jews held a march in Tel Aviv, chanting 'The Wall is ours'. In Jerusalem there were Jewish gatherings and demonstrations at the site, sparking a sequence of Arab/Muslim responses and Zionist counter-responses. After a week of rising tension, Arabs rioted and attacked Jews – not just in Jerusalem, but in other towns and in the countryside too. On 26 August, the acting high commissioner telegrammed London: 'Attacks, threats of attacks and assaults have taken place and are continuing throughout the length and breadth of the country from moment to moment.'[25] The administration was powerless. Hebron witnessed particular brutality when Arabs attacked a Jewish community that had resided there for generations (though many Jews were saved by their Arab neighbours). By the end of a week of violence, casualties were over 800 in total: 133 Jews killed, 339 wounded; 116 Arabs killed, 232 wounded.

At one level it seems odd that a modern, essentially secular, territory-wide conflict – between colonisers and colonised and/or between two competing nationalisms – should incorporate an ancient religious argument over access to holy sites. Yet this was a time when both Arab and Jewish politics exploited religious symbols. An incident on 15 August illustrates the close association, under perceived Islamic pressure, of non-Zionist and Zionist Jews. That evening, large numbers of religious Jews gathered to pray near the Wall – and they were joined by baton-wielding young men of Betar, the extreme nationalist youth group affiliated to Jabotinsky's Revisionist party.

There are no contradictions here. The clash between the two communities and cultures was all-embracing. A Jewish witness gives terse but telling testimony. Chaim Halevi, a twenty-one-year-old office worker who had arrived from Vilna three years previously, was a fervent Revisionist Zionist who had already told his parents, 'I have thrown off the defilement of the diaspora.' He now explained to them the events of the summer of 1929. Of relations between Arabs and Jews he wrote: 'They hate us and they are right, because we hate them too.' There could be no doubt, he insisted; and he forecast that the accomplishment of the Zionist goal would push the Arabs out of the country, and 'nothing will be left of them'.[26] Nor were the more perceptive British in much doubt. On his return to the country after leave, Sir John Chancellor saw that there was far more to the crisis than a religious dispute in Jerusalem. He judged in September 1929 that 'the origin and character of the present disturbances are essentially racial'.[27]

After 1929

Following the disturbances, British investigators were unanimous in identifying the causes of rising inter-communal tension. These unwelcome realities were a direct result of policy derived from the

Balfour Declaration. The first report on 1929 was that of Sir Walter Shaw, a former chief justice. He was instructed by the Colonial Secretary to focus only on the immediate troubles; but he did not neglect the context. In March 1930, his commission of enquiry blamed the Arabs for the violence; but it blamed the British mandate for creating the conditions from which the violence arose. 'The fundamental cause' of the disturbances was 'the Arab feeling of animosity and hostility towards the Jews consequent upon the disappointment of their political and national aspirations and fear for their economic future'.[28] The administration should review management of the Western Wall; but the major issues, according to Shaw, were Jewish immigration and land purchases. 'Excessive' immigration had to be halted; and Arabs had to be protected from eviction.

There was potentially more at stake than the eviction of individual Arabs from their land. Shortly before Shaw's report was published, Chaim Weizmann presented to senior officials in London a scheme for the future wholesale transfer of Arabs from Palestine to a neighbouring country. According to Weizmann, Sir Thomas Drummond Shiels, the Parliamentary Under-Secretary for the Colonies, was sympathetic: he did not see why 'one should not really make Palestine a national home for the Jews, and tell it frankly to the Arabs – pointing out that in Transjordan and Mesopotamia they had vast territories where they could work without let or hindrance'.[29] The implication in these reported remarks by a senior British imperial official is that, for Arabs, working 'without let or hindrance' could no longer be taken for granted in their own country.

Prompted by Shaw, the British government in London sent a retired colonial official, Sir John Hope Simpson, to investigate the central issues further. There were, of course, no statistics on which all could agree. There was specific controversy over the extent of Arab landlessness, and the degree to which Jewish land purchases were to blame for it. But Hope Simpson did not doubt that the British should restrict further Jewish immigration for land purchase and settlement.

His lack of personal sympathy with the projected Jewish national home emerges in a letter he wrote in August 1930. 'All British officials tend to become pro-Arab... The helplessness of the *fellah* appeals to the British official with whom he comes in touch. The offensive self-assertion of the Jewish immigrant is, on the other hand, repellent.'[30] What had moved so many British officials, military and civilian, since 1917 appears to have been not so much an inherent anti-Semitism as their witnessing of on-going injustice, inseparable from the implementation of the Zionist project. In a secret annexe, never published, Hope Simpson wrote that the Zionists were 'consciously trying to buy up all of Palestine, leaving the Arab masses without a living'.[31]

Hope Simpson's report was published on 21 October, the same day as the 1930 White Paper.

The 1930 White Paper

The opening lines of the Passfield White Paper promised a 'full and clear statement of policy' in the aftermath of the 'unhappy events' of August 1929 (and following the Shaw and Hope Simpson Reports).[32] Its core message was that nothing significant had changed or would change.[33]

What it delivered was little more than a reminder – urged on the British government by Sir John Chancellor, their own high commissioner in Palestine – that in the Balfour Declaration and mandate the British had made undertakings to *two* communities, not only one.

In summary, this is what the White Paper contains. An 'impartial and progressive administration' will hereafter 'promote the essential interests of both races'. His Majesty's Government must 'emphasise in the strongest manner possible' that 'a double undertaking is involved, to the Jewish people on the one hand and to the non-Jewish population of Palestine on the other'. The Prime Minister has insisted, the White Paper continues, that Britain continues to administer Palestine 'in accordance with the terms of the mandate'.

The British recognise the 'mutual suspicions and hostilities' of the two peoples and that they can only succeed if they have the 'willing cooperation' of both. Mistrust among the peoples of Palestine has arisen from their forgetting that the mandate committed Britain to the interests of both communities. 'What is required is that both races should consent to live together and to respect each other's needs and claims.' It is 'useless' for Jewish leaders to press London on immigration and land issues in accord with 'the more uncompromising sections of Zionist opinion'; similarly, it is 'useless' for Arab leaders to seek a constitution that would effectively block London's obligations to the Jews.

The Paper does acknowledge problems, but they can be overcome. 'However difficult the task may be, it would ... be impossible, consistently with the plain intention of the mandate, to attempt to solve the problem by subordinating one of these obligations to the other.' Meanwhile, the Council of the League of Nations has insisted that 'the two obligations imposed on the Mandatory are in no sense irreconcilable'. We may note that this endorsement was absurd: first, because they clearly *were* irreconcilable and, second, because Britain itself influenced the pronouncements of the Council of the League. The White Paper concludes by looking forward to 'the Arab and Jewish communities developing in harmony and contentment'.

Throughout the Paper, clarification amounted largely to repetition – repetition not only of the Declaration and the terms of the mandate but also of large extracts from its own 1922 predecessor. In three respects, however, it alarmed the Zionists, albeit again by re-statement. First, the Jewish national home would come about as an organic development of the existing community. Second, levels of Jewish immigration would continue to reflect the country's 'economic capacity'. Third, the Jewish Agency should recognise that its autonomy was circumscribed.

Horrified Zionists immediately condemned the White Paper as pro-Arab. That is why they set about challenging it. But it was not 'pro-Arab'. It did not reverse the Balfour Declaration or the mandate. Far from it: the explicit commitment to Zionism and the Jewish homeland remained. Rather, by repeating the Declaration and articles of the mandate (as well as excerpts from the 1922 White Paper) it reminded all concerned that the British had indeed taken on a *dual* obligation. They were officially committed to acting in the interests and well-being of both Jews and Arabs. It could have seemed 'pro-Arab' only because British policy and sympathies thus far, in the eight years or so since the military occupation, had leaned towards Zionism.

At one level there was little more to the White Paper than a headmasterly appeal to both communities to be sensible, be realistic, behave and cooperate with an administration that had only their separate and aggregate interests at heart. But it was disingenuous of the British government to claim impartiality. The Zionists sought a Jewish state; the Arabs were resisting colonisation. In Palestine, the British were seen as foisting one people on another. There was no chance of compromise or 'willing cooperation'. For the British to call for it may have been well intentioned, but it was desperate and unrealistic.

The White Paper did not explain *how* Britain's twin aspirations could be fulfilled. The government could only restate the contradiction (the dual obligation) and profess even-handedness in managing what was, quite evidently, already an unmanageable task. An admission that the Balfour Declaration had been a folly, and adherence a mistake, was not to be expected, of course. But the British government may have missed another opportunity to significantly define and delimit 'the Jewish national home'.

It was also disingenuous of the British to criticise, as the White Paper did, Zionists who claimed that 'the *principal* feature' and 'primary object' of the mandate was the Jewish national home and that the passages designed to safeguard the rights of the non-Jewish community 'are merely *secondary* considerations'. 'This is totally erroneous,' trumpeted the White Paper. But it was not at all erroneous. The 'primary object' of the mandate, arising from the original 1917 Declaration, was not to administer even-handedly, but to 'facilitate' the creation of the Jewish national home. The government denied this in public, but not in private. Chancellor noted what Ramsay MacDonald said to him shortly before the issue of the White Paper: 'In our policy we must come down on the

Jewish side or the Arab side.' MacDonald 'favoured the Jewish side.'[34]

The Zionists were right. The obligations undertaken in the Declaration and the mandate were not equal. That is why public advocacy of equality, several years later, aroused their anger. They set out to have the White Paper annulled.

The Black Letter

The subsequent 'Black Letter', written by the Prime Minister to Weizmann, showed in February 1931 that Zionism did indeed retain its hold over British policy-making in Palestine.[35]

Considering the bureaucratic blandness of much of its content, and that its restating of Britain's commitment to Zionism in the Balfour Declaration and the mandate could not have been more explicit, the Passfield White Paper had provoked an extraordinary storm of protest. The truth had hurt. From Wales, Lloyd George thundered that the British people were not 'scuttlers!'[36] In London, Weizmann stepped forward to play a key role in winning the day for the Zionists.

To be sure, the Labour Prime Minister, Ramsay MacDonald, was less sympathetic to Zionism than his Liberal predecessor, Lloyd George, had been. In mid-June 1930 he had written of the Zionists in a private letter: 'They know perfectly well what we are trying to do in the face of great difficulty, much of which they have created.'[37] But later that year the Prime Minister was under huge pressure, especially in the face of the global economic crisis. On 6 November he met Weizmann for lunch, having reassured him beforehand that any difficulties were minor. Even so, they were significant enough for MacDonald to establish a Cabinet sub-committee to discuss, with Jewish leaders, the situation in Palestine. This Anglo-Zionist group met from mid-November until the end of January 1931. Their final report took public shape as 'the MacDonald Letter' – an echo of Balfour's 1917 letter to Lord Rothschild – though only after Weizmann had persuaded MacDonald to deliver it in the House of Commons as a re-re-definition of the same British policy.

Coolly examined today, the White Paper and the Black Letter (as the latter was soon labelled by the opponents of Zionism) are remarkable for what they have in common. It was not merely diplomatic coinage for MacDonald to insist that British policy towards Palestine, as expressed in the White Paper, had not substantially changed.

As the following extracts illustrate, for the most part the letter restated the British position of 1917 and since.

> It is the intention of HMG to continue to administer Palestine in accordance with the terms of the mandate as approved by the Council of the League of Nations.

This is what the White Paper had maintained.

> Under the terms of the Mandate HMG are responsible for promoting the establishment of a national home for the Jewish people, it being clearly understood that nothing shall be done which might prejudice the civil and religious rights of existing non-Jewish communities in Palestine.

This is the Balfour Declaration again.

> A double undertaking is involved... It is the firm resolve of HMG to give effect, in equal measure, to both parts of the declaration and to do equal justice to all sections of the population of Palestine.

This repeats the White Paper.

> [In the face of] differing interests and viewpoints ... the full solution of the problem depends upon an understanding between the Jews and the Arabs.

This desperate appeal echoes that of the White Paper.

The obligation to facilitate Jewish immigration and to encourage close settlement by Jews on the land remains.

The effect of the policy of immigration and settlement on the economic position of the non-Jewish community cannot be excluded from consideration.

On the one hand, on the other hand: here are the two obligations.

Control of immigration ... is not in any sense a departure from previous policy... HMG have felt bound to emphasise the necessity of the proper application of the absorptive principle... HMG ... do not contemplate any stoppage or prohibition of Jewish immigration though government immigration regulations must be properly applied.

This is another echo of the 1922 White Paper.

The principle of preferential and indeed exclusive employment of Jewish labour by Jewish organisations is a principle which the Jewish Agency are entitled to affirm.

If in consequence of this policy Arab labour is displaced or existing unemployment becomes aggravated, that is a factor in the situation to which the mandatory is bound to have regard.

On the one hand, on the other hand: here are the two obligations again.

HMG have set their hand and they will not withdraw it. But if their efforts are to be successful there is need for cooperation, confidence, readiness on all sides to appreciate the difficulties and complexities of the problem and ... recognition that no solution can be satisfactory or permanent which is not based upon justice, both to the Jewish people and to the non-Jewish communities of Palestine.

In short, His Majesty's Government will continue to support the Zionist colonisation of Palestine, and urges 'the non-Jewish communities' to acquiesce in being colonised.

Michael Cohen describes the letter as 'negating' the White Paper; but Norman Rose, historian and biographer (of Weizmann, among others), was surely correct in judging that it did not 'abrogate' it.[38] There were indeed genuflections towards the Zionists. There was, for example, an explicit statement that HMG would not restrict land purchases. In fact they had not previously restricted them, nor did the White Paper say that they would in future. In practice, the British found that restricting land purchase was as hard to achieve as controlling immigration. There were shifts of wording, too: 'promote' rather than 'facilitate' the Jewish national home (though realistically, to facilitate *was* to promote). And there were soothing sentiments, such as apologies for any criticism, in the White Paper, of the Jewish Agency and Histadrut.

Even so, one is left wondering how there could have been such a furore. The reality was that, at heart, British policy had not changed. Both the White Paper and the Black Letter had essentially restated and endorsed commitment to the Balfour Declaration of 1917 and the mandate. British governments doggedly held firm, in the light of ever-increasing evidence that policy thus inspired could only end in disorder and failure, most spectacularly just a year earlier in 1929. Since 1917 they had been trying to reconcile two competing pledges. Commissions of enquiry had repeatedly identified uncomfortable truths, but London could only implore the colonisers to move less provocatively towards their goal and implore the colonised to acquiesce.

Weizmann's had been a histrionic overreaction (including his resigning as president of the Jewish Agency). Overall, certainly, the *tone* of the Black Letter was different from that of the White Paper. The latter had appeared to blame the Jews for the problems of Palestine; MacDonald's letter countered this with sympathetic reassurance and brought fresh clarity as to where British loyalties continued to lie. Surface calm was restored. Chancellor, who had so strongly influenced the White Paper, was replaced as British high commissioner in November 1931 by General Sir Arthur Wauchope, far more sympathetic towards the Zionists (though ignorant of Palestine). Under his stewardship, the passing of the crisis over the White Paper brought a period of unprecedented growth and expansion. Immigrants and capital flowed into Palestine; the future of the Zionist project was secured.

The Passfield White Paper was never implemented. The British had evidently considered diluting their commitment to the Jewish national home – but Zionists had acted swiftly to obstruct any such move. For their part, Arabs noted how easily the findings of an independent commission could be reversed by Zionist pressure in London. The verdict of the PAE was particularly passionate and uncompromising: 'Mr MacDonald's new document has destroyed the last vestiges of respect every Arab had cherished towards the British Government.'[39] Chancellor, who had done everything he could to persuade London to adjust policy in line with Arab sensibilities, confided to his son that the Prime Minister's letter to Weizmann 'has had even a worse effect [*sic*] than I anticipated. Feeling among the Arabs v HMG and the Jews is boiling.'[40] Five years later it boiled over.

British decision-makers were simply not prepared to respond to appeals for justice or reason, whether they came from their own officials on the spot or from Arab spokesmen. They had nailed their colours to the Zionist mast in 1917, and again in 1922, and they appeared determined to sail on towards the rocks.

Sir John Chancellor

Sir John Chancellor was Britain's third high commissioner to mandated Palestine, spending three years in the country, from late 1928 to late 1931. His background was typical – military, with administrative experience overseas – but his response to Palestine, and his acute sense of responsibility for all its peoples, was exceptional. His views were shaped

Sir John Chancellor (1870–1952)
British High Commissioner of Palestine, 1928–1931.

partly by the August 1929 disturbances, though he was on leave at the time. His stand-in, Sir Harry Luke, attributed British failure in Palestine to the Balfour Declaration. For his part, on his return Chancellor was appalled when he heard details of murders and massacres carried out by Arabs. But this high commissioner's views were shaped, also, by his uncluttered reading of the Balfour Declaration. This, he repeatedly insisted, contained *two* commitments: one to Zionism, the other to the country's indigenous inhabitants. Though these were, he also sadly insisted, irreconcilable, the British administration had to do its best to serve Arabs as well as Jews. His perspective clearly influenced the 1930 White Paper.

In this personalised, top-down administration, differing personalities and views mattered. The other inter-war high commissioners prioritised – by sympathy, default or design – Balfour's *first* pledge, to Jewish immigrants. Herbert Samuel was Jewish and a Zionist. His successor (1925–28), Field Marshal Plumer, took a 'non-political' approach, blandly declaring that antagonism between Arabs and Jews must be replaced by goodwill. But his detachment had the effect of favouring the Zionists. Plumer was fortunate, in that his years saw low levels of Jewish immigration, and there was surface inter-communal calm. Chancellor's replacement, Sir Arthur Wauchope (in office 1931–38), openly favoured Zionism. 'I am a whole-hearted believer in the success of the National Home,' he wrote; and he expressed his 'deepest sympathy' with the Jews who settled in Palestine.[41] He could light-heartedly compare himself, as high commissioner, to 'a circus performer, trying to ride two horses at the same time'; but he knew which horse he preferred to cling to, and there was to be nothing jocular about the consequences of his choice.

Chancellor, on the other hand, focused his attention on the *second* of Balfour's pledges in the Declaration: protection of the rights of Palestine's existing inhabitants. He did not, however, 'go native'. His analysis was legalistic and coolly constitutional. He could be highly critical of Arab leaders. For example, when they could not agree which of them should go on a mission to London, Chancellor commented: 'they are like children and very difficult to help'.[42] Nonetheless, he recognised the force and validity of Arab objections to the mandate and, without adopting them wholesale, he consistently articulated them. Chancellor gave the Arabs the voice they had lacked. In the interests of order as much as justice, he urged his masters in London to recognise the need for a Palestine policy that was even-handed, in reality as well as on paper. But it did not take him long to recognise the obtuseness of the British government, its on-going ties to Zionism, and the hopeless outlook for

Palestine's indigenous majority. His own exasperation and despair grew profound.

The clearest record of Chancellor's analysis of the situation in Palestine is to be found in his confidential despatch of 17 January 1930, six months after the August 1929 disturbances, to the Colonial Secretary. He knew Sidney Webb, Lord Passfield, to be relatively sympathetic; perhaps this encouraged Chancellor to write such a frank commentary on the Balfour Declaration and the mandate. It was bold too. Sir Walter Shaw's enquiry into 'the recent outbreaks' had been instructed to avoid contextual and strategic issues. Free from any such injunction, Chancellor stepped forward and confronted them.

In his despatch, Chancellor recalls that Palestine's inhabitants received news of the Balfour Declaration 'with incredulity'. During the following two years, 'Arab incredulity ... was changed into hostility'. As to the present, 'the Arabs have not accepted the Palestine mandate'. It was invalid, the Arabs argued, for two reasons. First, in giving 'direct power' to the British administration – enabling it to promote the Jewish national home, rather than some measure of self-government to all the people – it violated the terms of Article 22 of the League of Nations Covenant. Second, in providing explicit preferential treatment for the Jews, a number of mandate articles broke the commitment in the Balfour Declaration not to prejudice the civil rights of the existing inhabitants. The Balfour Declaration as a whole, with its commitment to a Jewish homeland, was unacceptable to the Arabs; so, in consequence, were the mandate and the White Paper of 1922.

The Arab peoples had never forgotten their 'pride of race and empire', Chancellor continued. And while they saw political progress for Arabs elsewhere in the region – in Iraq and Transjordan – in Palestine valuable concessions had been awarded to the Jews (such as mineral resources of the Dead Sea), and mass Jewish immigration had, the Arabs believed, brought 'grievous' unemployment among their own people. Whether this was the case or not, Palestine's Arab majority was now 'acutely conscious of the presence among them of an alien population'.

Antagonism towards the policy of the British in Palestine was by now both 'deep' and 'general'.

At the end of August 1929, Chancellor had chosen to forward to Passfield a message from the executive committee of the Nablus Arab Congress: 'The time has come when this Holy Land and its people must be saved from the difficulties and misfortunes brought upon it by the application of an unnatural and unjust policy.'[43] Then, in November, he had forwarded the resolutions of an economic congress of Palestinian Arab businessmen in Haifa. These called for 'checking Zionist immigration which brought misery to the country' and described the Balfour Declaration as the cause of their 'lamentable condition'.[44] By insistently presenting the Arabs' case, Chancellor appeared to agree that Britain's policy towards them was 'unnatural and unjust'.

As for the Jews, in his despatch and at other times, Chancellor repeatedly distinguished between Zionists, whom he lambasted, and non-Zionists – 'wiser Jews' – whom he respected. 'Many Zionists do not conceal the fact that their policy is not only to create a Jewish national home but also to convert Palestine into a Jewish National State... As a consequence of Zionism, latent hostility has been the distinguishing feature of the relations between Arabs and Jews.' Zionist colonisers in Palestine, he wrote elsewhere, were 'aggressive and offensive' to Arabs – while other Jews were 'kindly and friendly'.[45]

Chancellor referred in his despatch to resolutions of the Sixteenth Zionist Congress, held in Zurich the previous summer. These stated that 'the most important task of the Jewish National Fund was the creation of land reserves'. In particular, 'a land reserve of irrigable lands in accordance with a definite plan for colonisation ... Colonisation is to be the basic policy of the Jewish Agency for all time.' There was no room for ambiguity here. In his own comment, Chancellor identified the inevitable outcome of consolidating a colonial relationship in Palestine: 'the interests of the indigenous population and the interests of the Jews as regards agricultural land are in direct conflict'.

The despatch throws light on Chancellor's relations with the Arabs.

No doubt with the Jewish Agency in mind as a contrast, he laments the absence of contact between the British administration and the Arab leadership (though he refers to his own talks with the PAE). He informs Passfield that he has himself accused Arab leaders of 'extreme folly' in refusing to accept the 1922 White Paper or to participate in a legislative council. Such stubbornness had led to their 'isolation and impotence' and brought them no nearer to the fulfilment of their aspirations. And yet... Chancellor understands *why* the Arabs have not cooperated with the government or participated in it. To do so would have signalled acceptance of Declaration, mandate and White Paper.

Chancellor told Arab leaders that it would be 'vain', now in 1930, to ask that Britain *abandon* the Balfour Declaration. But 'the *manner in which the policy of the Balfour Declaration was given effect to* was another matter, which might be open to discussion and argument'.[46] Chancellor's stand was quite remarkable. The most eminent British official in Palestine was challenging his own government's commitment to the territory's largely unhampered colonisation. This was the bishop questioning Christianity, the general questioning war, the king questioning monarchy. Chancellor was listening to Arab leaders and, though not adopting their position wholesale, recognising the strength of their case and seeking to persuade his masters in London, through the Colonial Secretary, that in the interests of justice as well as order British policy had to change.

The mandate had not only confirmed the Balfour Declaration, Chancellor insisted, but, in its articles regarding the Jews, misguidedly reinforced it. He was politically wise enough to state that the Declaration itself had to remain 'the basis of British policy in Palestine'. But in his despatch, he now formally proposed to Passfield the removal of the several articles in the mandate that went beyond it. The mandate was 'an authoritative constitutional document governing the status of Palestine'. But in its terms, Chancellor continued, in phrasing of diplomatic understatement, 'the second part of the Balfour Declaration appears to have been relegated to a second place'. Articles 2, 4, 6 and 11 all had to be amended. In this way Britain should 'withdraw from the Jews the specially privileged position, as compared with the Arab inhabitants of the country, which has been given to them under the mandate, but which is not justified by the terms of the Balfour Declaration'.

Alongside this constitutional change, Chancellor sought restrictions on the immigration of Jewish settlers, and legislation to protect the indigenous population from 'dispossession of its land'. These were familiar recommendations which other critics had made. What distinguishes Chancellor's despatch is the novelty of a British high commissioner seeking to change the constitution.[47]

Chancellor's deeply pessimistic opinion was that, even if the mandate were purged of the offending articles, nothing substantial would change. Indeed, levelling the playing field, by amending the mandate as he proposed, would only highlight the contradiction and the impossibility.

Every dilemma could be traced back to 1917. As early as October 1929, Chancellor told his son, 'I feel a rankling sense of injustice on account of the Balfour Declaration and I do not know what can be done'.[48] In June 1930, he raised this central concern with Ramsay MacDonald, in person. He told the Prime Minister that 'the difficulty of our position arose from the fact that in dire straits in the war we had made promises to Arabs and Jews which were irreconcilable'.[49] A dozen years after Balfour's Declaration, Chancellor now emphasised 'the difficulties of our task in attempting to carry out irreconcilable promises'. Shortly before he departed by ship from Palestine for the last time, Chancellor returned to this theme. Addressing fellow British officials, he surmised that Palestine was the most difficult territory to govern of any in the British Empire. No administration could succeed in shouldering such dual responsibilities. In a measured critique of the policy adopted by Britain towards Jews and Arabs in Palestine since 1917, Chancellor explained that it was 'natural that each people consider its interests should have precedence over the other'.[50]

In his interview, Chancellor was frustrated. He found the beleaguered Prime Minister incapable of tempering Britain's commitment to Zionism.

He was told that Britain had financial concerns in Palestine and thus had to inspire confidence among Jews for the raising of further funds for the development of the country. Moreover, the Jews 'were bringing pressure to bear upon the government from all quarters', added MacDonald, via 'highly organised propaganda'. Following the most recent temporary suspension of Jewish immigration, the Prime Minister continued, 'false announcements as to what has been done were telephoned all over the world by the Jews within 24 hours'. He had 'ticked off' Weizmann for those distortions. Meanwhile, Jews were 'strongly represented in the House of Commons'. In response, Chancellor warned MacDonald of the danger of alienating world Muslim opinion, not least in India. But he realised that no Arab voice could be as 'immediate and imminent as that of the Jews who were constantly in Downing Street'. Chancellor had previously lamented that 'Zionists [*sic*] influence in Jerusalem and London has outgrown all reasonable dimensions'.[51]

MacDonald had numerous other political challenges at this time. Chancellor's responsibility was Palestine alone, and he felt alone in bearing it. Just a month after his January 1930 despatch to Passfield, he wrote some rough pencilled jottings on a Government House notelet under the heading 'Reasons for Retiring'.[52] Addressed to no one (other than to himself), they provide a precious insight into his personal and professional situation. 'I dislike the policy of the Balfour Declaration and consider that we have broken our word to the Arabs. I cannot therefore whole-heartedly carry out the policy of HMG'. He did not feel he could rely on London. His seventh point reads: 'Distrust of Zionists and their intrigues and want of confidence in the intention of HMG and CO to support me against them.' This was not just a single moment of despair. He had written to his son in October the previous year: 'I am so tired and so disgusted with this country and everything connected with it, that I only want to leave it, as soon as can do so without failing in my duty.'[53]

Chancellor had privately told the Prime Minister that 'it was necessary for HMG to be fully informed of the facts of the situation', but he found only that Weizmann carried more sway than he did.[54] His response, after the disturbances, to the Arab Executive's declaration that he was not fit to be high commissioner, was light-hearted on the surface, yet essentially grim. 'I said that I was not disposed to contradict them as to that; but that I was of the opinion that under present conditions I knew of no-one who would be a good High Commissioner of Palestine except God.'[55]

Nothing immediately followed his 1930 episode of anguished introspection. It was not until July of the following year that the official *Gazette* carried news of Chancellor's forthcoming departure from Palestine.[56] On the point of his leaving, he spoke to the Mayor and Municipality of Jerusalem. 'Three years ago ... I was full of hopes and plans ... to make the people of Palestine more prosperous and more happy. But that was not to be. Life is full of disappointments. My three years in Palestine have alas been full of trouble.'[57]

By the 1930s, 'empire' had come under increasingly potent criticism – at least to the extent that administrations in mandated territories were publicly committed to promoting the economic development of indigenous peoples, and their political progress towards self-government. Yet the British in Palestine were backing, instead, settler colonialism by Zionists who were dedicated to transforming the territory into a Jewish state and, by provoking the resident Arab population, were rendering 'peace, order and good government' quite unattainable. This is what drove Chancellor towards despair and resignation.

What concerns us historically is not Chancellor's personal disillusionment, but the force of his case for revision of British policy and his awareness of the need for change without delay. There is something tragically prophetic in the letter he wrote to his son on hearing that the Shaw Commission was on its way to investigate the events of 1929. 'If the Report does not make concessions to the Arabs (such as fulfil some of the promises that have been made to them) and curb the ambitions of the Zionist Jews, there will I fear be a real rebellion against the government which is becoming every day more unpopular owing to the Balfour Declaration and the mandate policy.'[58]

Chancellor's carefully argued case was rejected. Within five years of his departure, the Great Revolt had begun.

1933–1936: IMMIGRATION; LAND; PALESTINIAN POLITICS; ARAB REVOLT

The ingredients for heightened tension and open conflict were all in place. The distinguishing feature of the early 1930s was an upsurge in Jewish immigration from Central Europe, especially Nazi Germany. No Zionists – not Herzl, nor Jabotinsky – had claimed that Palestine could absorb all Jews. But in the 1920s foundations had been laid for the future settlement of hundreds of thousands. Now the momentum of colonisation towards the Jewish homeland markedly intensified. Arab perception of rapidly growing immigration, settlement, land sales and dispossession was a primary underlying cause of the violent disturbances of the later 1930s.

Jewish immigration and the land issue in the 1930s
The British administration had long recognised that immigration was the most controversial of issues. Though devolving much responsibility for its management to the Jewish Agency, it insisted on its right to exercise overall regulation. Thus, a temporary suspension of immigration had followed previous disturbances. The military administration halted Jewish immigration in April 1920, in response to the Nabi Musa disturbances in Jerusalem; restrictions were lifted by Herbert Samuel soon after his arrival in July. The more serious turmoil in Jaffa, in May 1921, led Samuel himself first to turn away ships carrying Jews who were fleeing persecution, and then formally to suspend immigration. A month later immigration resumed. Prompted by the unprecedented troubles of 1929, the British again imposed temporary restrictions, in May 1930.

The Passfield White Paper returned to the issue. It claimed consistency of immigration policy with its forerunner of 1922, in that the 'economic capacity' of Palestine should continue to determine immigration levels; consistency of policy, too, with Article 6 of the mandate insofar as 'the rights and position of the other sections of the population shall not be prejudiced by Jewish immigration'. It acknowledged that there had been a range of problems: 'many cases of persons being admitted who ... should not have received visas'; around 8,000 arrivals, over three years, who had stayed on 'without sanction'; and a large number of illegal immigrants who evaded frontier control. In this context, the White Paper went on, the administration would more closely scrutinise the work of the Jewish Agency.

The British gamely sought to present a balanced policy. On the one hand, the Arabs had to recognise 'the facts of the situation'. Jewish leaders, on the other hand, had to recognise the need for 'some concessions'. It was only in 'a peaceful and prosperous Palestine' that the ideals of the Jewish national home could be realised; it was only by 'cordial cooperation' between the Jews, the Arabs and the government that prosperity could be secured. In short, the Jews had to accept that immigration would be monitored; the Arabs had to accept that immigration would continue.

MacDonald's mollifying Black Letter assured the Zionists that the British still had a 'positive obligation ... to facilitate Jewish immigration'; and claimed that regulation of immigration was 'not in any sense a departure from previous policy'. Even so, it continued, the effect of immigration and settlement on the economic position of the non-Jewish community 'cannot be excluded from consideration'. Admitting an 'apparent conflict of obligation' – not admitting that the conflict was *real* – it insisted that the 'absorptive principle' was 'vital', according to purely economic criteria. Yet continued immigration, albeit regulated, was in the interests of all.

What mattered, as ever, was not textual analysis but what occurred in practice. In the early 1930s, Jewish immigration and settlement soared to an unprecedented extent.

Jewish Immigration (and Emigration), 1920–1936[59]

1920 (Sept–Dec)	5,514	(0 registered)
1921	9,149	(0 registered)
1922	7,844	(1,451)
1923	7,421	(3,466)
1924	12,856	(507: July–Dec)
1925	33,801	(2,151)
1926	13,081	(7,365)
1927	2,713	(5,071)
1928	2,178	(2,168)
1929	5,249	(1,746)
1930	4,944	(1,679)
1931	4,075	(666)
1932	9,553	(0 reg'd)
1933	30,327	(0 reg'd)
1934	42,359	(0 reg'd)
1935	61,854	(396)
1936	29,727	(773)

As we have seen, there had been a Jewish community in Palestine long before Zionism. Adding to their numbers after the First World War, most settlers of the 1920s were searching for a better life. Many were 'Zionist' not so much in belief as in effect. Four-fifths of Jewish immigrants spurned rural 'regeneration' and settled in the towns: so, in the 1920s at least, it was the presence of growing numbers in the territory rather than sizeable land purchases that brought the homeland nearer and alarmed Arab witnesses. Whenever Arabs rose against the increasing Jewish presence, they made no distinction between Zionist and non-Zionist – a reality that tended to drive all Jews together, dependent on newly formed Zionist militias to defend them.

In the 1920s the *yishuv* expanded unspectacularly. Around a quarter of newcomers left. Compared with that of the 1930s, the level of net immigration remained low, no more than 20,000 Jewish immigrants arriving in the years 1927 to 1931. As the 1929 disturbances were to demonstrate, however, this was a question not only of numbers but of relationships and perceptions. After the White Paper and Black Letter came a marked deterioration of Arab-Jewish relations: accelerating Jewish immigration and more extensive, and more disruptive, Jewish land purchases, made the Arab community feel ever more threatened.

Numbers mattered; demographic statistics were political. At the time of the 1931 census, tension was manifest at every level. When the British administration tried to create a committee to advise how best to secure accurate figures for the census, they failed to get agreement from respective community leaders as to its composition. It had to form two committees, one Arab, the other Jewish. These were hard to handle. Chancellor remarked: 'their ingenuity and malevolence in imagining base motives which they impute to the government are hardly credible'.[60]

Snapshots – of population figures (absolute, and relative), along with the changing percentage of land in Palestine owned by Jews – capture something of the evolving significance of Jewish immigration.[61]

1920 Arab population: 542,000 (89.9 per cent)
1920 Jewish population: 61,000 (10.1%) 2.04% land

1929 Arab population: 744,250 (82.4%)
1929 Jewish population: 156,840 (17.6%) 4.4% land

1935 Arab population: 886,402 (71.4%)
1935 Jewish population: 355,157 (28.6%) 5.3% land

In the mandate years before the Second World War – indeed, before the Arab Revolt – the direction of change is clear: a steep rise in the number and proportion of Jewish inhabitants of Palestine; a significant percentage increase, albeit from a very low base, in land alienation. A final snapshot, from the end of the mandate period, illustrates continuation of these trends:

1946 Arab population: 1,237,334 (64.9%)
1946 Jewish population: 608,225 (35.1%) 7.0% land

As the Peel Commission later observed, immigration was 'aggravated' in the 1930s by three factors: the coming to power of Hitler and the Nazis in Germany; increasing economic pressure on Jews in Poland; and the 'drastic restrictions imposed on immigration in the United States'. Regarding the last of these, commissioners clearly had in mind the Johnson-Reed Act of 1924. This did not take aim solely at Jews: in fact, it discriminated most harshly against Asians and all immigrants from East and Southern Europe (such as Italians).[62] Nor was its impact on Jews immediate. But it was huge – 'drastic', indeed – in the long run. American nimbyism qualifies as one of the most significant contingencies in the story of the Jewish national home.

Comparative figures for the mid-1930s are striking. In 1934, for example, we see that 42,359 Jews migrated to Palestine. In this same year, the US accepted just 4,100, and Britain 1,882. By 1937 there was more parity – there were 10,536 Jewish immigrants into Palestine, 11,352 to the US (2,584 to Britain) – but only in 1938 and 1939 (years of the Arab Revolt in Palestine) did the US figure clearly exceed that for the British mandate.[63] Meanwhile, Zionism appears to have remained of relatively little interest to the millions of Jews in the USA. During the interwar period, American Jewry gave for the relief of European Jews 15 times the amount they gave to the *yishuv*.[64]

In the early 1930s the Jewish population of Palestine more than doubled, to the point where it was approaching 400,000. This was an increase, and a total, which British policy-makers of the first mandate years, such as Herbert Samuel, had neither advocated nor envisaged. Now it was welcomed, if only in part. The growth of the population of Tel Aviv from 46,000 to 140,000 was associated with a boom in the urban economy; meanwhile, the Jewish population of Haifa more than doubled. But, in addition to legal entry, illegal immigration rose sharply. The British were to estimate that 40,000 Jews entered Palestine without legal certificates between 1920 and 1939.[65] 'Economic absorptive capacity' had always been impossible to calculate, let alone act on. British administrators were not really in control.

But were there (yet) 'enough' Jews in Palestine? Albert Viton, a Jewish academic, offered in 1938 a sobering comment. Reflecting on Zionism's 'ideological confusion', he agreed with nineteenth-century Jewish critics who had realised from the start that Zionists did not provide the answer to the Jewish Question. 'They saw clearly,' he wrote, 'that while the purely mystical longing for Zion could be realised in the form it had taken for centuries, and while the modern nationalist ideal could also be realised if a suitable territory were found, together they were impossible of realisation, for Palestine could not possibly solve the Jewish problem.' He went on: 'after half a century of effort, Zionism can show less than 400,000 Jews in Palestine... The Jewish problem remains unsolved, for Palestine has not even absorbed the natural increase of European Jewry.'[66] Viton himself, born in Lithuania in 1913, emigrated, like so many, to the USA.

How the figure of 400,000 was viewed depended of course on the viewer. In Palestine, the mid-1930s saw economic growth providing not only the British administration with the financial surplus it craved but also Arabs with jobs, improved wages and a standard of living perhaps higher than anywhere else in the Middle East. Even so, and at the same time, Arabs became more afraid of becoming a minority in their own country; and, notwithstanding land sales by individuals, Arab political organisations continued to be united in opposing Zionism.

Before the great revolt broke out in 1936, there were clear signs of growing Arab resentment, and of a slowly escalating breakdown of social order. So, for example, in Jaffa in January 1932 a National Congress of Arab Youth came into being. Its members patrolled the beaches to prevent illegal immigration. In October the following year, an anti-Zionist demonstration in Jaffa led to violence and ended with the deaths of twenty-six demonstrators, and of a policeman. The PAE responded with a week-long strike and more demonstrations. But the immigration of Jews, seeking refuge from intolerable persecution in Central Europe, continued to increase.

◆

In the 1930s, as Jewish immigration grew sharply, the inflow of Jewish capital into Palestine reached a new level. Land sales took on a pattern different from the 1920s. Now, the land changing hands was typically in smaller plots, cultivated, occupied and owned by the inhabitants. In growing numbers, poor *fellahin*, indebted to money-lenders, had no choice but to sell. Entire Palestinian Arab villages disappeared through land sales. Chancellor noted that 'distressingly poor' peasants had 'no alternative' but to sell their land; and the Arab sellers, or their tenants, were usually evicted by the Jewish purchasers.[67] Even by 1931 'Zionist land purchases' had led to the expulsion of around 20,000 peasant families from their lands.[68]

A key institution here was the Jewish Agency. It contributed to the drafting of the administration's policy statements, and when it needed to act retrospectively it exercised considerable influence by lobbying investigative commissions. In this context, Zionist agents were generally at an advantage. They were more accustomed than Arabs to verbal negotiations and to producing written evidence for the defence of their status in Palestine. By 1931, moreover, over 2,000 Jews could read and use Arabic; just twenty-one Muslims and Christians in all Palestine knew Hebrew.[69] Most importantly, Arab offers to sell land always exceeded Jewish ability to buy. This was the case even around Jaffa, the city at the heart of the Arab nationalist movement. Nearly a fifth of the land bought by Jews in the first half of the 1930s was here. Among Palestinians who put 'the pursuit of financial gain over the communal interest and national ideology' were the Nashashibis – who were thus singled out as culprits by Arab critics of the notables.[70]

The British gave the land issue an unprecedented profile when they investigated the disturbances of 1929, but the administration acted as no more than a somewhat vacillating umpire. It might have tackled Arab rural poverty – for example, through providing credit facilities and sponsoring more effective farming methods – but instead it passed laws and issued rules. The countryside remained in thrall to the market, and responses to it.

Although the Jewish National Fund had a strategic master plan for land purchasing, deals were usually improvised *ad hoc*. In the event, the Zionists bought far less than they had set out to buy; but it was enough. At the end of the mandatory period, 1948, they owned less than 10 per cent of the country as a whole, but this was around 25 per cent of the land, mainly in valley and coastal areas, which was considered fit for cultivation and habitation. This was a formidable, irreversible and historic achievement, largely accomplished before the Second World War. Kenneth Stein, whose meticulous study covers the inter-war period, presents a striking conclusion: 'an analysis of Jewish land acquisition and Arab land sales makes it seem quite evident that a formidable Jewish national territory ... was already present in Palestine in 1939'.[71]

These land transactions had a big political impact. Evictions alarmed the British, who valued social order over everything else. Diligent British investigations into causes, and their recommendations, produced not only vigorous Zionist counter-arguments but also growing Arab awareness of a disturbing countrywide phenomenon. Inter-communal tensions – and Arab criticism of the British – rose, alongside the growing expropriation, evictions and unemployment. Social unrest contributed to the radicalisation of the Palestinian nationalist movement, and eventually to revolt. Neither the precise extent of land purchase nor the precise number of evictions – both keenly contested – really mattered. Arabs sensed that the Zionists wanted a state in Palestine and were, with the British standing by, on course to achieve that goal. By the mid-1930s, many Arabs who might previously have known of Zionism only as an abstraction were increasingly aware of a menacing reality: a menace, moreover, which their political elite had failed to check.

Palestinian Arab politics

From before the First World War, leaders of the Palestine Arab majority had made it clear that they were opposed to Britain's sponsorship of the Zionist colonisation of their homeland. Nonetheless, the hallmark of Arab nationalist political activity in the 1920s had been acquiescence, albeit conditional. This was in the hope that their imperial masters would in due course turn the Balfour Declaration on its head, rescind offending items of the mandate and prepare the way for Arab self-government for the whole country, as was required for Class-A mandated territories by the League of Nations Covenant.

But – like the violent disturbances of 1920 and 1921 – conversations, petitions and delegations achieved nothing of substance. The far greater disorders of 1929 exposed the depth of growing inter-communal antagonism. Cooperation began to be recognised as ineffectual. Then the stakes rose. Jewish immigration and land purchases occurred from 1933 on a scale not previously seen. The British were, as ever, responsive to Zionist pressure. By contrast, though aware of and attentive to Arab grievances over land, the British were apparently incapable of acting effectively to address them. Above all, they gave no reliable indication that steps towards the Jewish national home, indirectly quickened by Nazi persecution in Germany, would be blocked. In this unfolding context – and still without any legitimate constitutional arena for opposition – Arab acquiescence in Palestine would shortly yield to revolt.

•

There were repeated illustrations of the futility of initiatives taken by increasingly frustrated Palestinian Arab Nationalists. We may now look briefly at the demise of the Palestine Arab Executive (PAE), marked by the failure of the notables' 1930 delegation to London; the fruitlessness for Palestine of the 1931 General Islamic Conference; and, lastly, the rise and fall of the Arab Independence Party.

We noted earlier the emergence of the PAE and Musa Kazim al-

Palestine Arab Executive Delegation to London, 1929–1930
Front row, from the left: Raghib al-Nashashibi (second); Amin al-Husayni
(fourth); Musa Kazim al-Husayni (fifth).

Husayni's role as its head in the 1920s. But its interventions repeatedly
proved fruitless. In March 1930, Amin al-Husayni, the Mufti, was a
leading figure in the PAE delegation that visited London. It carried High
Commissioner Chancellor's approval. It sought to persuade the British to
adapt their policies in Palestine in the wake of the 1929 events that had
illustrated the seriousness of the situation. But it was to achieve nothing.

Amin, having resisted Zionist provocations and successfully urged
the British to respect historic Muslim rights (and to retain the status
quo regarding access to the holy sites), had emerged from 1929 with
an even higher profile as an Arab spokesman. His delegation was
remarkable in two respects. First, there was a show of unity. Rivalries
between and within notable clans were suspended, enabling Amin to

travel in the company of Raghib al-Nashashibi, Mayor of Jerusalem, as well as his elder kinsman, Musa Kazim (who still led the PAE and was officially leader of this party). Second, it was restrained in its main constitutional proposal. These prominent notables requested not full independence or majority rule, but an elected legislative assembly, proportionally representing Arabs and Jews, subject to a British high commissioner who could veto any legislation. Here was a notable new flexibility: in advocating this step forward, the delegation appeared to register acceptance of the mandate.

But still the British would not – or could not – ignore Zionist opinion. The particular stumbling block in this instance was the proposed electoral system. The British knew that the Zionists would not accept a democratically elected legislature based on proportional representation while Jews formed only around 18 per cent of the population. When the delegation returned to Palestine in June 1930, it was empty-handed and disillusioned. The October White Paper essentially reiterated existing British policy. The attitude of the British towards Arab supplications remained patronising and dismissive. For instance, Ramsay MacDonald, the Prime Minister, was soon to complain that he could not find 'a suitable Arab' to negotiate with – even though this delegation had included Amin al-Husayni, the Mufti of Jerusalem and Britain's own choice as head of the Supreme Muslim Council.[72]

In the wake of this setback, and after the British unambiguously restated their commitment to the Jewish national home in the Black Letter of February 1931, Amin chose to seek wider, international, Muslim and Arab support for Palestinian opposition to Zionism. To this end, he helped to convene in Jerusalem a General Muslim Conference. He had assembled something similar three years earlier, to focus on urgent issues relating to holy sites in Jerusalem. The later meeting, of 145 delegates from twenty-two countries, for ten days in December 1931, had a wider brief.

In terms of its public utterances this conference fulfilled Amin's hopes; and the Mufti himself, for so long discreet, was now associated with internationally endorsed, full-blown, criticism of British policy-makers. The Conference condemned Jewish immigration and land purchase (as well as Zionist designs on Muslim holy places). Interestingly, it also affirmed solidarity with Christian Arab Palestinians – an echo of the interfaith solidarity seen in the formation of Christian-Muslim associations at an earlier stage in the rise of Palestinian nationalism. Though still seeking to persuade, rather than confront, his British masters, the Mufti did not prevent delegates from launching 'a furious attack on the colonisers of the Muslim world'. [73]

This episode thus strengthened Amin's pan-Arab and pan-Islamic credentials. British imperial strategic interests were not served by alienating, through their policies in Palestine, the wider Islamic and Arab worlds. But once again nothing changed those policies.

In August the following a year, 1932, a secular political party emerged which was both anti-Zionist and anti-British. Istiqlal, the Arab Independence Party, sought a mass base for a boycott of the British administration. Many founding members had attended the recent Conference. The new party's stance was not mediation but confrontation. It criticised the moderation of the Mufti and of the PAE. It distanced itself from the established notables, castigating them for their infighting; for their intimate yet vain cooperation with the British; and (aware of a number of cases of substantial land sales to Jewish buyers) for their self-serving compromises with Zionism. Istiqlal maintained that Palestinian identity was part of Greater Syria's; and it called for the full independence of, and for unity among, all Arab countries.

But this political firework soon fell back to earth. Independent and articulate, it won some support among the younger, educated middle-class Palestinian elite. However, partly perhaps because it was secular and declined to rally Islamic sensibilities, it could not marshal a mass following. In a further indication of Arab political disunity, Amin, who rightly saw this party as a challenge to his authority and his role, was able to mobilise his own considerable support to oppose it. The British administration was able to ignore it.

Protests and rioting in Jaffa, Haifa and Nablus in October 1933 confirmed a general loss of faith both in Jerusalem-based notables riven by dynastic rivalries, and in political parties incapable of checking accelerating colonisation. These outbreaks did not threaten the existence of British rule; but they did herald the radicalism and direct action – and disorder – that was to break out far more widely in the near future. In one, personal, respect they symbolised a generational and imminent strategic shift in Arab resistance. On 27 October, twenty-two demonstrators were killed by security forces. Among the estimated 137 wounded was Musa Kazim, by now eighty years old, struck by a police baton. He died shortly afterwards. By 1936, his son, Abd al-Qadir al-Husayni, had emerged as a prominent exponent of armed resistance to Britain, and Zionism.

•

As mentioned earlier, the judgement of the British reporter Joseph Jeffries was that 1923 was the decisive year in the history of the mandate, and that everything that followed should be regarded as consequential. The dramatic impact on events, ten years later, of the Syrian-born Muslim preacher Izz ad-din al-Qassam may be seen as a consequence of the growing resilience of Zionism under British rule and of the failure of the Palestinian Arab notables as intermediaries to prevent it.

Al-Qassam's primary commitment was to Islamic revivalism. His gospel was social and puritanical. Only a purified Islam could survive and thrive in the modern world. He was a fighter too – against Italian forces in Libya before the First World War, and against French forces in Syria after it – but we find him in 1928 heading the new Young Men's Muslim Association in Haifa, a non-political organisation devoted to the spread of Islamic values and morality. At this time, he enjoyed generally good relations with Amin al-Husayni and accepted his authority as Mufti and head of the Supreme Muslim Council. But the events of 1929 prompted him to recruit peasants and urban labourers who would, when the time was right, follow him into battle. By 1933 he was falling out with Amin, insisting that there was no longer any alternative to armed resistance (a view that Amin was himself to adopt, but not yet).

In 1935, provoked by the discovery in Jaffa of a cache of arms for the Haganah, the Jewish militia, al-Qassam called for *jihad* against Zionism and British rule. He had several hundred recruits by now, organised in cells, zealous, disciplined and armed. But his was a very short-lived campaign. The killing of a Jewish police sergeant in November prompted a major manhunt, and two weeks later he and his followers were ambushed by British troops. Al-Qassam was killed.

But this was more a beginning than an end. Al-Qassam's funeral in Haifa attracted an unprecedented number of people, around 3,000. This was as much a political as a social gathering, grief expressed alongside calls for revenge. This one man's influence was profound and long-lasting. 'A man of integrity, social concern and eloquence', he had displayed bravery and defiance at his death.[74] Indeed, his death did much to inspire the outbreak of anti-British and anti-Zionist violence in Palestine the following year. Meanwhile, his campaign exemplified the radicalisation of Arab politics at this time – both in its ideological militancy and in its grassroots social base – and the generational shift from established figures to a somewhat younger leadership. Eminent notables were not among those who attended his funeral.

And the trajectory of al-Qassam's life has significance in one further respect. The British had begun the mandate years keen to divert political aspirations into religious activity. It is thus somewhat ironic that they were confronted a dozen years later by a call for *jihad*. In addition, we may ask what hope there was for a quiescent Islamic response to British promotion of a Zionist movement which, though avowedly secular, had challenged Islam at its sensitive heart, over the holy sites of Jerusalem, in 1928/29. When, shortly afterwards, the Jewish national home turned from a possibility into an imminent reality, urgent radicalism was the all but inevitable result. Al-Qassam was a product of British/Zionist colonisation.

So, too, was the belated radicalisation of the Mufti, Amin al-Husayni, himself. *Primus inter pares* among Palestinian Arab notables, throughout the 1920s he had been a model of moderation, adopting and maintaining a mediating role. After all, his prominence under the mandate depended on his continuing service to the British. The early 1930s, however, brought fresh choices; and in due course, hesitantly at first and reluctantly, he chose principle over privilege. He was to play a final role as a go-between during 1936, trying to restrain popular radicalism while keeping in touch with the British administration. But the evidence was already accumulating that he would no longer be able to serve two masters. The years of 'entangling connections' with the British – and, by association, with the Zionist colonisers of his people – were coming to an end.[75]

But confrontation was to prove no more fruitful. And the main reasons for this are to be found not so much in weaknesses among the Arab political class – in the account, for example, that Raghib al-Nashashibi once told a friend that he would oppose any position that Amin al-Husayni took[76] – as in the capabilities of the British state. Its armed forces had defeated the Ottomans in 1917. Alongside the patronage of prominent individuals, by the mid-1930s the British administration employed over 30,000 Arabs. Meanwhile, its powers of coercion were many, including the banning of meetings and demonstrations, censorship, detention and exile. And underpinning the whole was a barely deviating commitment to Zionism. This was in large part an incubus; but the *yishuv* substantially funded the British administration, and Zionist paramilitary forces were to work in partnership with the British to suppress the coming revolt.

For the Arabs, no form of opposition or resistance worked; all options failed, because nothing could have succeeded. We may come to a comparable conclusion regarding the British. They had initially committed themselves to the Jewish national home with a gusto paired with complacency. But from the early 1930s they were no longer in control of events. The evidence was accumulating that, in launching this hybrid colonialism, David Lloyd George had been too clever by half.

Meanwhile, the on-going potential of Zionism in Palestine owed much, albeit tragically, to events elsewhere. Adolf Hitler came to power in Germany in January 1933. Public attacks on German Jews by his Nazi storm troopers, and a boycott of Jewish shops and businesses, soon followed. Throughout Germany, the isolation, humiliation and persecution of Jews became persistent and intense. In September 1935 – two months, that is, before the martyrdom in Palestine of al-Qassam – the Nuremberg Laws deprived Jews in Germany of their citizenship. Many fled, to more than thirty countries. Tens of thousands fled to Palestine, seeking safety. Here, in the long term, they helped secure the Jewish national home.

In the short term, though, they posed a challenge for the British and a provocation to politically conscious Arabs.

The Arab Revolt (1)

If the death of al-Qassam provided smouldering fuel for the 1936 disturbances, there was an encouraging stimulus from outside, too. In Egypt and Syria, demonstrations and strikes persuaded Britain and France respectively to negotiate the future of their colonial relationships. There being no such prospect in Palestine, the tension broke on 15 April. Arab followers of al-Qassam ambushed a bus and killed two Jews. In revenge, two Arabs were killed by members of a Zionist militia. Those deaths set off riots in Jaffa. The spontaneity and range of local incidents displayed a widespread frustration at the failure of nationalist leaders and parties, up to that point, to resist the advances of Zionism.

Only after a week, in which acts of violence succeeded each other on the ground, did political leadership come into being. The Arab Higher Committee (AHC) was a *de facto* successor of the Arab Executive. It was headed by Amin al-Husayni. It contained personnel of both the Husayni and Nashashibi clans. It included Muslims and Christians, moderates and radicals. Here was a rare show of national unity. But these leaders had not led. Committees had already sprung up in almost every Arab

The Arab Higher Committee, 1936
Front row, from the left: Raghib al-Nashashibi, Amin al-Husayni.

town to organise strikes and boycotts, their members acting on their own initiative. So, the AHC 'was the child of the spontaneous revolt', to quote the Palestinian-American historian Philip Mattar.[77]

Nonetheless, the AHC did what it could to articulate popular concerns and to put pressure on the administration. On 26 April the Mufti, who had sought in vain for many years to persuade the British to alter their course, wrote a letter to the High Commissioner. It may be read as a last heartfelt appeal for the British to give precedence to the principles of the League of Nations Covenant over the terms of their Palestine mandate. The letter conveys his exasperation. 'The British government has always ignored Arab rights, Arab national existence, and Arab demands; instead it administers Palestine under direct colonial rule and facilitates Jewish immigration and the usurpation of Arab lands.'[78] At the same time, the AHC submitted three demands: an end to Jewish immigration; an end to Jewish land purchases; and Arab national self-government.

In response, and recognising that immigration was a central issue, on 18 May 1936 the British administration announced that Jewish immigration would be restricted to 4,500 for the coming six months. But this limited act of appeasement achieved nothing. Small arms were imported illegally to Arab groups from Transjordan, Syria and Iraq. Urban terrorism increased. The Jewish population of Hebron had to be evacuated. Arab revolt in the countryside took a number of forms, among them the uprooting of around 200,000 'Jewish' trees. Meanwhile the Mufti – the prime intermediary of the earlier mandate years – seems finally to have abandoned any hope of a middle way. High Commissioner Wauchope wrote of him in September: 'There are many factors that weigh with that astute mind, but his chief fear is to be left alone in the open, liable to be accused by friend and foe of treachery to the Arab cause.'[79] Such was the fate of compromise and cooperation.

Nonetheless, by the end of September both sides sought a truce. The British army had not performed with distinction. It was initially overwhelmed. If the contemporary comment of the Chief of the General Staff is a guide, the loyalties of the high command were as divided as before: the Arabs were 'only fighting to keep the land which they consider is theirs'.[80] Thereafter, the armed forces of the mandatory power regained the upper hand. Measures such as house searches without warrants, night raids, preventive detention, and the destruction of the homes of actual or presumed rebels had a debilitating effect. On 16 June 1936, the British blew up between 220 and 240 buildings in Jaffa – officially 'to improve health and sanitation', though primarily to allow military access and control. Six thousand Arabs were rendered homeless by this single act of destruction. On this occasion it was not just an Arab city but Britain's reputation that suffered. When the British

Chief Justice condemned his own government's action, and was sacked, the Arab press feasted. *Filastin* – the newspaper which, we recall, was founded in Jaffa in 1911 to highlight the then-remote threat posed by Zionism – now carried the details of this case in its edition of 19 June. 'The operation of making the city [Jaffa] more beautiful,' it observed with scornful sarcasm, 'is carried out through boxes of dynamite.'[81]

For its part, the Palestinian opposition recognised economic and military reality; it was exhausted and losing hope. After six months around 200 Arabs, eighty Jews and thirty British had been killed, and another 1,300 had been injured. Moreover, by now there was pressure from Arab rulers in neighbouring Iraq, Saudi Arabia and Transjordan to suspend the strike. The strike was called off but not before it had proved, in one respect, not so much in vain as counter-productive. The strikes and boycotts of Jewish businesses may have helped the Zionist cause by pushing the Jewish economy towards the separation and self-reliance its more zealous advocates wanted. Meanwhile, it prompted the British recognition of Tel Aviv as a separate 'Jewish' port in May 1936, to free the *yishuv* from dependence on 'Arab' Jaffa.

The suffering, especially of the Palestinian Arabs, had been in vain. To achieve a truce, the British had not had to concede any of the three demands. Instead they merely promised yet another independent commission of enquiry into Arab complaints. But this one, the Peel Commission, was to be of great historic significance in two respects, one long-term, the other immediate. The commissioners came to the reluctant, if unavoidable, conclusion that the only practicable political way ahead was a division of Palestine: there should be a Jewish state and an Arab state. But the Palestinian Arab leadership rejected it. There ensued a renewal of disturbances, this time a full-scale revolt against British rule, British policies and, in particular, the imminent prospect of partition: of the Zionist goal being, at least in part, realised.

1937–1939: PEEL COMMISSION AND REPORT; REVOLT AND REPRESSION; WHITE PAPER

The commissioners arrived in Palestine in November 1936 to investigate the causes of the most recent disturbances and to make recommendations. Their report was a measured yet devastating indictment of British rule in Palestine. Taken as a whole, it may be read also as a lament. It is a sad acknowledgment that the origins of what it terms 'the present antagonism between the races' lay in obligations which the British had first undertaken twenty years earlier, and then incorporated into the mandate. Thus, the mandate was the problem and, in the judgement of the commissioners, termination of the mandate presented the only chance of a solution.

'Under the stress of the World War, the British Government made promises to Arabs and Jews in order to obtain their support. On the strength of those promises both parties formed certain expectations.' Twenty years on, the British would not wish to repudiate the obligations. 'The trouble is that they have proved irreconcilable.' The mandate was doomed at the outset. It had embodied two contradictory aspirations. The inevitable result had been separation, inequality, and growing, increasingly violent, discord. A drastic reversal of British policy was now the only rational course.

The Peel Commission

The members of this commission of enquiry were men who might be expected, collectively, to make discerning judgements and firmly grounded recommendations.[82] They were chaired by Lord William Peel, a former Secretary of State for India and the grandson of Prime Minister Sir Robert Peel. The ceasefire in Palestine held while they diligently went about their work. They published their report in July 1937.[83] It was a model of discernment and lucidity. Its diagnosis and prescription are indicated by the following summary and extracts:

Nothing had changed since the early 1920s. The early outbreaks of

1920 and 1921 were caused by 'the demand of the Arabs for national independence and their antagonism to the National Home'. The demand, and the antagonism, remained 'unmodified'. Increased Jewish immigration, and the growth of Arab nationalism in Palestine and the wider region, intensified the contest – hence the protests of 1929 and later. The disturbances of 1936 were thus 'similar in character' to the previous outbreaks, only 'more serious and more prolonged'. Also contributing by now was Arab alarm at the extent of Jewish land purchases, and a creeping distrust of the British administration and its intentions. But, the Report repeats, there was no change regarding the underlying causes. To be sure, the Jewish national home 'is no longer an experiment'; and by 1937, 'Arab nationalism is as intense a force as Jewish'. But the Arab leaders' demand for national self-government and 'the shutting down' of the Jewish national home was unchanged. 'Arab antagonism to the National Home, so far from weakening, has grown stronger.'

The development of the two peoples had been uneven to the extent that the condition of Palestine had become all but irreparable. According to the Report 'the gulf between the races is thus already wide and will continue to widen if the present Mandate is maintained'. It was too late to seek inter-communal harmony, since 'there can be no question of fusion or assimilation between Jewish and Arab cultures'.

Lest there be any ambiguity: 'conciliation is useless'; there is 'no hope of compromise'.

Again, under the heading, 'The Possibility of a Lasting Settlement', the Report states that 'an irrepressible conflict has arisen between two national communities within the narrow bounds of one small country. There is no common ground between them. Their national aspirations are incompatible.' The trend was irreversible: 'the conflict has grown steadily more bitter since 1920 and the process will continue'.

Therefore, each community should be prepared, separately, for self-government. The Arabs of Palestine were as fit to govern themselves as the Arabs of Iraq or Syria.[84] The Jews of Palestine were as fit to govern themselves as any organised and educated community in Europe. Yet 'associated as they are under the Mandate, self-government is impracticable for both peoples'. The condition of contemporary Palestine was brought about by the 'impact of a highly intelligent and enterprising race backed by large financial resources, on a comparatively poor, indigenous community on a different cultural level'. In this light, it was no surprise that the Christian Arabs had thrown in their lot with the Muslims.

Partition was now the only possible solution. Arab and Jewish aims were unattainable in a continuing unitary state. On the one hand, the Arabs wanted self-rule. But Britain could not abandon the Jewish national home to an Arab majority government. As the Report puts it, in masterly understatement, 'belief in British good faith would not be strengthened anywhere in the world if the National Home were now surrendered to Arab rule'. On the other hand, what the Zionists demanded – a Jewish state – could only be imposed on a million Arabs by force.

The British administration in Palestine is 'unable to dispel the conflicting grievances of the two dissatisfied ... communities it governs'. The Report observes: 'The difficulties have steadily become greater till now they seem almost insuperable. Partition offers a possibility of finding a way through them ... to the fullest extent that is practicable in the circumstances of the present time.' Adopting a somewhat unbureaucratic metaphor, the Report states its conclusion with some passion:

> The disease [from which Palestine is suffering] is so deep-rooted, in the Commission's firm conviction, the only hope of a cure lies in a surgical operation.

There was no guarantee that even partition would work, but it was the best hope:

Partition ... offers a chance of ultimate peace. No other plan does.

The unitary alternative would merely continue the current contradiction and feed the same grievances. A third option, cantonisation or some form of federalism, was attractive at first sight, but it would be impracticable and, anyway, neither Jews nor Arabs would accept it. To be sure, neither Arabs nor Jews would welcome partition either but, the commissioners concluded, the two communities might come to agree that it was the only possible way ahead. After all, 'while neither race can fairly rule all Palestine, each race might justly rule part of it'.

The proposed partition:

- Jews to have all Galilee, plus the coastal strip south to beyond Jaffa*
- Arabs to have the hill country north of Jerusalem, including Nablus; and the whole territory south of Bethlehem, including Hebron, Gaza, the Negev.

* Jaffa to be linked by a pear-shaped strip of territory inland to Jerusalem and Bethlehem, all of which was to remain a British mandate.

This proposal was based on the existing distribution of Jewish land ownership and population. By judicious land purchases, the Zionists had sought in the early 1930s to create contiguous Jewish areas. Meanwhile migratory patterns took Arabs increasingly away from Jewish settlements, a trend underscored by the administration's policy of resettling landless Arabs of the coastal areas in central hill regions. Arabs who worked in urban areas or on Jewish settlements resided far from the Jewish concentrations. A considerable degree of 'partition' had already come about.

But the demographic developments of recent years had not been tidy enough to offer simple lines of demarcation. Partition would 'sooner or later' have to be accompanied by 'an exchange of land and population'.

Within the area allocated by the Peel Commission to the Jewish state, there were about 225,000 Arabs; and there were Jewish minorities in the areas allocated to the Arab State.[85] 'The existence of these minorities clearly constitutes the most serious hindrance to the smooth and successful operation of partition.'[86] Zionists, a number of whom had advocated 'transfer' many years earlier, welcomed the prospect of the relocation of resident Muslim communities. Ben-Gurion noted in his diary on 12 July 1937: 'the compulsory transfer of Arabs from the valleys of the proposed Jewish state could give us something which we never had... We are being given an opportunity which we never dared to dream of in our wildest imaginings.'[87]

Herbert Samuel was appalled by the Peel recommendation. But partition was the all-but-inevitable outcome of dogged British commitment to the Balfour Declaration and the mandate articles which they had written for themselves and to which he had been tied. The *de facto* irreversible process of separation which followed the collapse, by 1923, of Samuel's efforts to create a unified political community, embracing both Jews and Arabs, was now on the verge of formal, legal, recognition.

Aside from their core analysis, two passing observations by the commissioners are revealing. First, their Report is tactfully generous to the British authorities in suggesting that, when the two conflicting obligations were incorporated in the mandate, 'they did not fully realise the difficulties of the task it laid upon them'. But the truth is rather different: there is extensive evidence that 'the difficulties of the task' were evident even before the First World War, and that they had been proclaimed from many quarters immediately after the war. Moreover, the British had several subsequent opportunities – long before Chancellor's late challenge – to write themselves a mandate which was more just (if not deliverable).

Second, and more significantly, these commissioners were prey to a persistent and highly influential nimbyism, as can be seen in one remarkable passage. 'The Jewish Problem is not the least of the many problems which are disturbing international relations at this critical time and obstructing the path to peace and prosperity. *If the Arabs at some sacrifice could help to solve that problem*, they would earn the gratitude not of the Jews alone but of all the Western World.'[88] 'At some sacrifice' proved to be something of an understatement. Taken overall, this seemingly casual afterthought betrayed a profound, continuing, nimbyist and arguably anti-Semitic reluctance to fully re-open *British* doors to Central European Jews. The British continued to act as if it was not their own responsibility but that of the Arabs to solve the Jewish Question – by giving the Jews a substantial portion of Palestine.

The Report of the Peel Commission anticipated the findings of the United Nations' own 1947 commission, both in its analysis and in its conclusion that partition of Palestine into an Arab state and a Jewish state was the only possible way ahead. Implicitly, the Peel Report also confirmed that the British inter-war administration of Palestine had been quite extraordinary and transformative. Zionism had been of little consequence to Jewry, let alone the world at large, before 1914; just twenty years after 1917, with the uneven yet perennial backing of Britain, it was on the verge of concrete, if partial, realisation.

Above all, the Peel commissioners concluded that in 1937 antagonism was already irreconcilable: that 'irrepressible conflict' existed between two communities, Jewish and Arab, who would continue in close proximity to inhabit a vehemently disputed territory, whatever the status and definition accorded that land by statesmen, for their own purposes, in remote parts of the outside world.

That 'irrepressible conflict' would be the British bequest to Israel in 1948.

The Arab Revolt (2) and its repression

Weizmann was initially horrified by the Peel Report, but the Seventeenth Zionist Congress in Zurich eventually accepted the principle of partition-with-transfer and voted, 299–160, in qualified acceptance of the Peel plan. The Arab Higher Committee, on the other hand, immediately rejected the Report. Any other response to partition and transfer would have been astonishing, given the Arab leaders' perennial opposition to the Jewish national home and determined defence of their own national rights in their own homeland.

On 26 September 1937, just two months after the publication of the Peel Report, Lewis Andrews, Acting District Commissioner of Galilee, was murdered by four Arabs. Known as a friend of Zionists, he was ambushed when on his way to evensong at the Anglican church in Nazareth. This act marked the resumption of the disturbances, shortly to become a revolt of far larger scale and impact than the previous year's. During the summer and autumn of the following year, 1938, much of the countryside and many of the towns in Palestine were briefly under rebel Arab control, including Jaffa and the Old City of Jerusalem.

Against this renewed challenge, the British adopted extreme counter-insurgency measures. For example: the death penalty for unauthorised possession of arms; and collective punishments for entire villages. Such measures were legal.[89] The Manual of Military Law, 1929 – a timely updating of British military regulations – stated that 'the existence of an armed insurrection would justify the use of any degree of force necessary effectually to meet and cope with the insurrection'.[90] Group punishments and reprisals were thereby legitimised, even if they inflicted suffering on innocent individuals.

The suppression of the revolt, thus licensed, came to involve the systematic destruction of Arab property across both urban and rural areas of Palestine. Sometimes, British troops told Palestinians to demolish their own houses. Such coercive methods carried political risks, however. Though he was covered by an indulgent legal code, General Bernard Montgomery was aware of the danger of self-inflicted reputational wounds. He banned newspaper reporters from his area of northern Palestine, so that his soldiers could carry on their repressive work without inhibition.

The revolt strengthened the *de facto* partnership of British and Jewish authorities. Reaction to the revolt confirmed where British loyalties lay *in extremis* and so fulfilled the worst fears of countless Palestinian Arabs. The Haganah cooperated with the British, who in turn employed thousands of Jewish police auxiliaries and provided them with armoured vehicles.[91] Moshe Shertok of the Jewish Agency negotiated directly with the new British High Commissioner, who had taken up his post in a Palestine already in revolt. Harold MacMichael was neither particularly pro-Arab nor pro-Jewish. 'He was British,' observed Ben-Gurion, 'and acted in accordance with the interests of his administration.'[92] For MacMichael this entailed calling upon the Jews to help restore British control. For its part, the Jewish Agency was ready to join forces and to share the costs of repression: it paid the salaries of Jewish police auxiliaries, while the British provided arms and uniforms.

By that time, special night squads were carrying out counter-insurgency operations in Galilee under British command. These squads, incorporating British and Jewish personnel in roughly equal measure, were the creation of Orde Wingate, a young British officer. Brought up among the Plymouth Brethren – an evangelical, non-conformist group of Christians who took the Bible as their supreme guide – he regarded as a religious duty the establishment of a Jewish state in Palestine. This was Christian Zionism in military uniform, and ready for a fight. Wingate, like Montgomery, is more widely known as a British military hero of the Second World War, when he won fame for his exploits in Burma, leading missions deep into Japanese-held territory. But he was awarded the DSO (Distinguished Service Order) in 1938, for his operations in Palestine. Wingate's squads humiliated Arab villagers, whipping the bare backs of some, forcing others to smear their faces with mud and oil. In revenge for an Arab massacre of fifteen Jews in Tiberias, Wingate entered the Arab village suspected of involvement, selected ten men, and shot them.

Meanwhile the Irgun militia, which had broken from the Haganah, adopted its own terrorist tactics against Arab civilians. In July 1938 bombs placed in the Haifa fruit market killed seventy-four and injured 129. To be sure, not all Zionists approved of such methods. According to Shertok, they were inconsistent with Jewish values – and would make

The Arab Revolt: British troops round up Arabs in Jerusalem, 1938.

it even more difficult in future for Jews and Arabs to find ways of living together.

After the signing of the Munich Agreement in September 1938 the British were free to send more troops and police to Palestine to complete the quashing of the revolt. Once 25,000 troops were engaged, the inevitable outcome was secured. Estimates of the Arab dead range from 3,000 to 6,000; by contrast Jewish losses were several hundred. Over 10 per cent of the adult male Arab population may have been killed, wounded, imprisoned or exiled.[93] Many fled; among them, Amin al-Husayni. This symbolic act, along with the banning of the Arab Higher Committee, marked the death of Britain's erstwhile policy of ruling in Palestine, indirectly, by consent, through notable intermediaries. It marked the failure of the notables, too, while the revolt itself – devoid of unified leadership, strategy or programme – also failed. It never had the potential to overthrow British rule.

A large proportion of the Arab casualties came from internecine, Arab-on-Arab, violence. The British impact on Palestine since 1917 had been destabilising in a number of ways, and 'collaboration' appeared to have taken many forms. Arabs in the hill country, especially, took measures against not only the British and the Zionists, or the Jews more generally, but also against members of the Arab urban elite, rural landowners and rival clans. Such a trauma had its counterparts elsewhere. A dozen years later, for example, during the African nationalist revolt (known as Mau Mau) against British settler colonialism in Kenya, numerous 'Loyalist' Kikuyu were killed by Kikuyu 'Freedom Fighters' – while losses among British settlers were few.

Terrible violence was adopted by all sides: Arabs, the British, and some Zionist forces. Destruction, too: on 25 August 1938, the day after a British assistant district commissioner was assassinated in his office in Samaria, British forces bombed nearby Jenin and demolished a quarter of the town. Perhaps the main point about this rebellion and its suppression, however, is not to weigh one side's perpetration of brutality against another's, but to recognise that it was the British who, beguiled by Zionism and what it offered them, had inexorably brought this conflict upon the peoples of Palestine.

The British were for a while humiliated. The scale of this mass popular revolt against their rule, the setbacks they suffered at its height, and the methods they had to use to regain control, led to a huge loss of prestige across the Middle East. Britain was seen to have alienated not only the Arabs of Palestine but Arabs throughout the region. The conference at Bloudan, in Syria, in September 1937 – called by Amin al-Husayni in response to the Peel Report – provides evidence of the internationalisation of the Palestine problem. Arab governments were reluctant to send official representatives, but Bloudan attracted around 450 attendees. Among these were young, radical, Muslim Arab graduates of the American University in Beirut and also Christians, including a Greek Orthodox bishop. The purpose of the gathering was to focus Arab attention and to seek Arab consensus on Palestine. The main resolution was a confident assertion, aimed at Britain, that the survival of Anglo-

The Arab Revolt: British retribution in Jenin, 1938.

Arab friendship hinged on the realisation of Arab demands: abrogation of the Balfour Declaration and the mandate, and the establishment in Palestine of an Arab government comparable with those in Iraq and Egypt.

Yet the British government – having earlier accepted the League of Nations Covenant and been mandated by the League to administer Palestine in the interests of all its inhabitants – had responded at times to the widespread insurrection of an alienated people with methods of ruthless retribution and subjugation. Palestine being a mandated territory under the League of Nations, we should note that, around this time, the League had just faced and failed its most severe test. In October 1935, Italy under Benito Mussolini invaded Ethiopia (another League member state). Using methods of exceptional brutality, such as poison gas and the bombing of hospitals, the Italians were able after a few months to claim victory. The League's vacillating in the months before the Italian invasion produced widespread dismay and, from a member of the British public, a trenchant comment of some relevance to what was about to take place in Palestine. 'Let us at least have the courage of our cynicism,' wrote Mr F.L. Lucas in a letter to *The Daily Telegraph*. 'Let us be done with Covenants.'[94]

A little later, the unfolding situation in Palestine provoked Mahatma Gandhi into criticising what Zionists and the British were doing. 'My sympathies are all with the Jews,' he wrote. 'But my sympathy does not blind me to the requirements of justice... Palestine belongs to the Arabs... What is going on in Palestine today cannot be justified by any moral code of conduct. The mandates have no sanction but that of the last war. Surely it would be a crime against humanity to reduce the proud Arabs so that Palestine can be restored to the Jews.'[95]

The events of 1936 to 1939 ended with a triumph for Britain's coercive power, but they amounted to proof of her inability to govern Palestine peaceably. The Balfour Declaration had purported to be even-handed, with promises to two communities. Yet the Americans, King and Crane, it will be recalled, had reported in 1919 that 'no British officer, consulted by the commissioners, believed that the Zionist program could be carried out except by force of arms'. Twenty years on much of what they had predicted, then, had actually occurred with, as they put it, 'a certainty like fate'.

Arthur Balfour died in Surrey, England, in 1930. His legacy in Palestine included severe inter-communal strife and a protracted uprising against British rule. Even so, one hundred years after the event, Balfour's great-great-nephew, the 5th Earl, told *The Daily Telegraph* that the Balfour Declaration had been 'a great humanitarian gesture' for which 'humanity should be eternally grateful'. The majority Arab population of Palestine was not.

The 1939 White Paper

Publication of the Peel Report two years earlier had, far from solving the problem of Palestine, revived and magnified the revolt against British rule which had begun in 1936. The May 1939 White Paper was in one respect even less successful: its proposals were acceptable to neither community.[96] This outcome was not surprising, especially in view of the failure of a London conference in February-March to produce an agreement – and in view of the failure, there, of the Arab and Jewish representatives even to talk directly to each other.

There is in this White Paper wishful thinking on a gargantuan scale. But there is some realism too: partly within its contents, and partly in its overall tone of concession to regional Arab opinion so recently alienated by Britain's response to the revolt in Palestine. Since March, Britain had faced the prospect of a second global war; the mandatory power thus anticipated a heightened need for Middle Eastern oil.

The White Paper jettisoned the Peel partition plan and replaced it with a plan for a unitary state. There was an evident tilt towards Arab interests. It envisaged specified controls on Jewish immigration, and self-government that would recognise the majority which the Arabs enjoyed – though, as always, the policy was wrapped in the language of even-handedness.

> The objective of HMG is the establishment within 10 years of an independent Palestinian state ... in which the two peoples in Palestine, Arabs and Jews, share authority in government in such a way that the essential interests of each are shared.

As we have seen, there were numerous critics, Arab and Zionist, within and beyond Palestine, of British policies, and of assumptions that lay behind them. More surprisingly, at times the British themselves were capable of, if not self-criticism, at least some recognition of error and failure. Thus, much of what had been said by others, repeatedly over time, finds an echo within Britain's own White Paper of 1939.

First, damage arising from former vagueness:

> Previous commissions of enquiry have drawn attention to the ambiguity of certain expressions in the Mandate, such as the expression

'a national home for the Jewish people', and they have found in this ambiguity and the resulting uncertainty as to the objectives of policy a fundamental cause of unrest and hostility between Arabs and Jews.

Second, the vanity of former pious longing:

> It has been the hope of British Governments ever since the Balfour Declaration was issued that in time the Arab population, recognizing the advantages to be derived from Jewish settlement and development in Palestine, would become reconciled to the further growth of the Jewish National Home. This hope has not been fulfilled.

Third, the importance of Palestinian Arab political fears, as well as economic calculation, in relation to rates of Jewish immigration.

> If immigration has an adverse effect on the economic position in the country, it should clearly be restricted; and equally, if it has a seriously damaging effect on the political position in the country, that is a factor that should not be ignored...

> The lamentable disturbances of the past three years are only the latest and most sustained manifestation of this intense Arab apprehension.

Fourth, acknowledgment of the high and continuing level of civil disharmony:

> The bitterness between the Arab and Jewish populations ...

> The establishment of an independent state ... would require such relations between the Arabs and the Jews as would make good government possible.[97]

> As soon as peace and order have been sufficiently restored in Palestine.

Fifth, qualification of the Balfour Declaration and circumscription of the Jewish national home.

Most remarkably, the White Paper contained a definite distancing from Zionism. This was highly significant as an implied admission of error (though not, as it turned out, as an indication of what would happen in the future). Michael Cohen has observed that it 'marked the end of Britain's commitment to the Jews under the Balfour Declaration'.[98] Such a judgement depends, again, on interpretation: what did the Balfour Declaration mean? We see from the following extracts that the British now subtly claimed that the promise of 1917 had already been essentially fulfilled – before explicitly envisaging an end to Jewish immigration in the near future.

> The population of the National Home *has risen* to some 450,000.

> The growth of the Jewish National Home and its achievements *are* a remarkable constructive effort.[99]

To be sure, the British planned to admit, over the following five years, a further 75,000 Jews; but after that time 'no further Jewish immigration will be permitted unless the Arabs of Palestine are prepared to acquiesce in it'.

> His Majesty's Government are satisfied that, when the immigration over five years which is now contemplated has taken place, they will not be ... under any obligation to *facilitate the further development* of the Jewish National Home by immigration regardless of the wishes of the Arab population.[100]

And one further sentence leaves no doubt. From now on 'the High Commissioner will be given general powers to prohibit and regulate transfers of land'.

•

One last aspect of Britain's policy statement catches the eye: the further perpetuation of nimbyism.

The White Paper stated that an immediate cessation of Jewish immigration was out of the question: 'it would damage the whole of the financial and economic system of Palestine' and so affect everyone adversely. But there was another, pressing, consideration. 'His Majesty's Government are conscious of the present unhappy plight of large numbers of Jews who seek refuge from certain European countries, and they believe that Palestine can and should make a further contribution to the solution of this pressing world problem.' So, as we saw in the Peel Report, Palestine's Arabs – not the people of Great Britain – were expected to play their (disproportionate) part in responding to a 'Jewish Question' that was now so much more acute than when Herzl and others had posed it.

The immediate crisis facing Europe's Jews at this particular time, before the outbreak of the Second World War, lay in Germany (and in recently annexed Austria).

In June 1933, the year of Hitler's coming to power, there were, according to that month's census, 505,000 Jews in Germany.[101] By September 1939, 282,000 of these had left. The main destinations of these refugees were, in round figures: 95,000 to the USA, 75,000 to Central and South America, 60,000 to Palestine and 40,000 to Britain. In the USA, the 1924 Act was still in place, effectively restricting Jewish immigration by quotas and also by a difficult, complicated, time-consuming process for visa application. With the onset of the Great Depression, the notion of 'economic absorptive capacity' appeared to apply there, as well as to Britain's Palestine mandate: prospective immigrants had to find an American sponsor who could guarantee that they would not become an economic burden. There was a sudden increase in demand for visas in 1938. The following year, 1939, was the first during the 1930s when the US admitted in full its German-Austrian annual quota (27,000). But by this time there were over 300,000 European Jews on waiting lists to get to the United States.

In their 1939 White Paper the British were now proposing to admit a further 75,000 German Jews into Palestine: that is, far in excess of the number the home country had so far taken in, or were contemplating taking in. Put another way, the British were proposing to admit *to Palestine* around 30 per cent of the Jews now living in Germany (202,000) and annexed Austria (57,000), before the Arab veto on further immigration might come into force.

•

This statement of British imperial government policy came to nothing. It was not endorsed by the League; it was rejected by both Zionists and Palestine's Arab majority; it was soon to be overtaken by events.

The White Paper had ruled out a Jewish state. There is thus no difficulty in explaining the uncompromising Zionist response. Ben-Gurion said of the document, 'a more evil, foolish and short-sighted policy could not be imagined'.[102] Irgun relaunched attacks on British government buildings and Arab civilians.

Why, on the other hand, did the Arab political leadership reject it? Though the Arabs had failed in their revolt, they were now being offered defined limits on further Jewish immigration and the prospect of majority rule in a unitary self-governing state within a few years. There were objections to be found, of course: no immediate cessation of immigration, for example, and future devolution to be dependent on cooperation between Arabs and Jews. In voting 6 to 4 against accepting the new British policy, the AHC may have felt under pressure from so many of its thoroughly alienated Arab fellow countrymen to reject any compromise.

Another interesting question is counterfactual. What if these terms, the most sympathetic ever offered to the Arab inhabitants of Palestine, and containing a clear definition of (and limit to) the Jewish national home, had been British policy at the commencement of the mandate? With such relatively low levels of Jewish immigration at that time, one can imagine the Arab notables acquiescing – though it would have needed the (implied) commitment to Arab majority rule to be more loudly trumpeted (along with the ambitions of more extreme Zionists, less loudly). In short, there might have been scope, in his role as the first high commissioner, for Herbert Samuel.

By 1939, all sides were aware that this White Paper was unlikely to be implemented. But in one respect it was indicative. The British in Palestine were clearly looking for an exit strategy. Indeed, they had already proposed one way out. Meanwhile they had no knowledge of the ways in which another global war, while initially changing little on the ground in Palestine, would transform the wider context and leave no time for further British prevarication.

Adopting once again a headmasterly tone, the British stated in the White Paper that 'the two people in Palestine ... must learn to practise mutual tolerance, good will and cooperation'. This had never been likely. But the British were by now at last capable of balancing wishful thinking with realism and sober prediction. Were Jewish immigration into Palestine to continue up to the absorptive capacity of the country 'regardless of all other considerations', then 'a fatal enmity between the two peoples will be perpetuated and the situation in Palestine may become a permanent source of friction amongst all peoples in the Near and Middle East'.

Britain's achievement in Palestine by 1939

The British record is one of failure. Perhaps some British supporters of Zionism in the period 1917 to 1922 would have regarded as success the emergence by the late 1930s of a national home in Palestine of around 400,000 Jews. But the costs – for example, in money, lives and reputation – had been considerable, and there was every prospect that Britain's legacy would be an ungovernable country. Although for the time being the British remained in power, the government had lost the consent of the governed.

European colonisers liked to wrap their self-interest in protestations of service to others – especially when assuming the constraints of mandated authority – but this myth had been shattered in the case of Palestine by the revolt (and revolt was itself the strongest evidence of political and administrative failure). The British had not been able to provide 'good government', let alone consensual steps towards self-government. The Peel Commission Report and the 1939 White Paper produced differing proposals for the future, but each was an exit strategy. For the British this was a colonial cul-de-sac, and the end – though about to be delayed and configured by another world war – was approaching.

In the 1920s and, especially, the 1930s it was not only the growing antagonism between Arabs and Jews that meant that the British in Palestine were constrained in what they could do. As the mandatory power, they remained answerable to an external authority, the League of Nations. In part because they were respectful of it, international oversight through the League 'narrowed Britain's room for manoeuvre and contributed to the … failure that marked the British mandate'. While their own preferences over time – especially under Chancellor – were to maintain authority in part by curtailing Jewish immigration and conciliating Arabs, by the mid-1930s Zionists were putting increasing pressure on the League in Geneva to find refuges for emigrant persecuted Jews. They were not alone. East European statesmen in particular were, in turn, 'eager to divest themselves of as many Jews as possible' – and thus agreed with Zionists on the need for Britain to uphold the Balfour Declaration.[103]

For their part the Arabs had failed – until the undeliverable assurances contained in the 1939 White Paper – to divert the British from their commitment to the primary pledge of the Balfour Declaration. Though its final dimensions could not yet be known, the Jewish national home was already a reality; and British policy was to admit 75,000 more Jews, not into Britain but into Palestine. Every political tactic from collaboration to resistance had been tried and had failed: the notables had achieved little or nothing as intermediaries; political parties had not been recognised; petitions, deputations and the press had fallen on deaf British ears. Strikes, spontaneous violence and, most recently, territory-wide armed resistance had been repressed so effectively that, within a few years, the Arabs were incapable of effective opposition to the embryonic Zionist state. Much is written about Arab disunity in Palestine between the wars. But, even when the political class did display unity, and when all levels of Arab society combined to an unprecedented extent to confront British and Zionist forces during the revolt, they had no success. Nor did they even have realistic expectation of success, given that this was not an age when settler-colonial states of Europe's imperial powers were being violently overthrown.

For Zionism in Palestine, however, it was a different story. In the early days of the mandate it had been a movement nervously dependent on British patronage. It had emerged by the late 1930s as a formidable and irresistible force on which, in turn, the British depended both economically and latterly even militarily. The *yishuv* was secure and robustly defended. The Peel commissioners had conceded the substance of a Jewish state. The White Paper had withdrawn the offer, but that statement was widely and correctly interpreted as a short-term political ploy, not as a commitment to a practicable new British strategy for the country. Meanwhile, desperate Jews were continuing, as far as they could, to flee from the cruelties inflicted on them in Central Europe. Immigration into Palestine increased – irrespective of British policy and approval.

The inter-war history of the British in Palestine had been such that, when the Jewish state was eventually established, less than ten years later, it was that of a battle-hardened Zionism: a very far cry from the earlier Zionist visions of Yitzhak Epstein and Ahad Ha'am. It was one, moreover, in which there had been no reconciliation. The Arab-Jewish conflict that the British had fostered, irresponsibly if indirectly and unintentionally, had assumed a still more intractable form.

Who was in control of events in Palestine? Not the British. Their colonial adventure was almost over. David Lloyd George's caprice and arch cleverness had resulted in tragic failure and, in the White Paper of 1939, confessions of a kind. From the heart of government and not, this time, just from a single perceptive high commissioner, came admission that the British had indeed blundered and backed the wrong horse. And all this had come about with what King and Crane had termed in 1919 'a certainty like fate'.

7

THE SECOND WORLD WAR
AND AFTER, 1940–1947

'The state idea is not in my heart. I cannot understand why it is needed.' Albert Einstein[1]

Overview

This period saw the death throes of the British mandate and the triumph of Zionism. Palestine remained relatively quiet for much of the war period, though by the end there was an upsurge of Zionist militancy against the British and their partial implementation of the 1939 White Paper. The transformation was in the global context. As knowledge of Jewish suffering in Europe spread, pressure on the British intensified – from Zionists and also from many other countries – to admit innumerable Jewish refugees into Palestine and to prepare for a Jewish state there. In the event, the newly elected Labour government of Clement Attlee had to accept financial and new strategic realities, including the need to align Britain with the USA in the Cold War. In 1947 it announced its intention to abandon the mandated territory.

Palestine in the Second World War

It was clear before the Second World War that the British were eager to leave Palestine. They had good reason to search for a way out. The country had become ungovernable and the contradiction inherent in the Balfour Declaration had by now taken on concrete and unmanageable form. Conflict between two communities was no longer a matter of prophecy.

The irreconcilability of their ever-more deeply held aspirations had left the British with no choice but to plan their own departure – whether through partition (1937) or a fantasy programme (1939).

But when and how would the abdication come about? The answer lay in the association of, on the one hand, what was happening in Palestine and, on the other, what was happening to the Jews of Europe – and the growing global awareness of, and response to, the scarcely imaginable extent of their suffering.

For much of the Second World War, the situation in Palestine was relatively quiet. For Arabs, this was the aftermath of a revolt comprehensively crushed. Most Palestinian political activists were in exile or held in detention. There was no leadership asserting the nationalist cause – the Arab Higher Committee (AHC) had been dissolved – though strangely, now, following the White Paper of 1939, British concessions to nationalist demands appeared to a remarkable extent to have been won. Meanwhile, war conditions brought economic prosperity for many; even the poorest benefited from inflation that reduced their burden of debt. An influx of British troops did far more than deter further disturbances, for it helped to create a considerable demand for products of the Palestinian economy.

There is one particularly vivid and, in some respects, poignant illustration of the extent of conditional Palestinian acquiescence in this particular period of British rule: the complete futility of calls from Amin al-Husayni, the exiled Mufti, for a renewal of resistance. Radicalised beyond reason by the bitterness of his alienation from the British, the Mufti met Adolf Hitler in Berlin, in November 1941. He concluded an agreement with Hitler – albeit secret, and vague – that in the event of an Axis victory the Jewish national home would be abolished, and the Arabs would have Palestine to themselves. That same year, Amin began making broadcasts via the Bari radio station in southern Italy, calling on his fellow Arabs to rise up, on the side of the Axis powers, against Britain and France. But, as his biographer puts it, his wartime initiatives were an 'abysmal failure'.[2]

By contrast, the Zionist response in Palestine to the war in Europe was complicated. What should Zionists do? David Ben-Gurion articulated an adroit formula: the Zionists, he said, should oppose the White Paper as if there were no war, but help the British war effort as if there were no White Paper. But this was scarcely a basis for practical policy. In the event, Jews of the *yishuv* adopted a wide range of strategies calculated to further the cause of the homeland/state. Differences of opinion fostered internal disputes. Moderates were alarmed by the violent actions of extremists, fearing that they would alienate the British and give permanence to the White Paper; extremists, especially when terrible news of extermination camps reached Palestine, acted as if only an immediate removal of the British and their restrictions on the flow of immigrant refugees could rescue the Jews in Europe and save their own cause in Palestine.

Differences of approach were evident within the Zionist defence forces. For much of the war the Haganah – the *yishuv's* primary defence force, which dated back to pre-mandate days – largely cooperated with the British authorities (though it engaged in facilitating illegal immigration). By mid-1945, 30,000 Jewish soldiers in Palestine had enlisted to fight in the British armed forces. By contrast, Irgun's policy changed under pressure of wartime events. Irgun had been founded in 1931 when some members of the Jerusalem Haganah broke away to become, by the later 1930s, the armed wing of the Revisionists. Irgun and the Haganah disagreed over tactics during the Arab Revolt, when Ben-Gurion insisted that all Zionist forces accept Haganah discipline. In the eyes of Haganah, Irgun was an irresponsible and dangerous force.

When Jabotinsky, shortly before his death in 1940, suspended hostility to Britain, there came a further split. Not accepting this ceasefire, a group under Avraham Stern (Fighters for the Freedom of Israel) broke away. They regarded Britain, not Germany and Italy, as the main enemy. They embarked on a campaign marked by the robbing of Jewish banks to fund attempts to assassinate British personnel. Stern himself was killed by British forces in 1942, but the 'Stern Gang' carried on – its leaders including Yitzhak Shamir, a future Prime Minister of Israel – and, though they failed to kill the British High Commissioner, Harold MacMichael, they succeeded in assassinating Lord Moyne, the British minister resident in Cairo, in November 1944.

By this time more was known about the dreadful fate of the Jews on mainland Europe. Irgun, now led by Menachem Begin, another future Prime Minister of Israel, had declared war on the British. In this respect Irgun resembled the Stern Gang. Yet there were ideological differences between the two groups. The context of war led the Stern Gang to adopt an inter-communal socialism: they did not regard the Arabs as a danger, but rather as potential allies in a struggle to free Palestine from the British. This was a prospect somewhat out of harmony with the unambiguous symbol of Irgun at this time: a rifle straddling a map of Palestine, and the words 'Only Thus'.

In other words, during the Second World War, Zionism was no more a monolithic movement than it had been in its infancy or indeed during the inter-war decades of the mandate. Some still had faith in political or diplomatic action: Chaim Weizmann continued to advocate working with the British, not against them. But they were opposed by those who did not; and, among the latter, rivalries emerged that as before were personal as well as ideological or tactical. Yet a composite picture does emerge from the war years: of rising violence against British targets (also a dominant feature of the immediate post-war period); and, among the Zionists responsible, of an evolving closer association between militant forces and national politics.

Even so, for the time being the British had little difficulty maintaining control over Palestine. But the post-war future of Palestine would be shaped by wartime developments far from the territory: the unprecedented and previously unimaginable calamity of the Holocaust, and the impact of this news on the consciences and calculations of the wider world.

In order to understand this change of context, we must consider three meetings that took place at around this time: at Evian in France (1938), in London (1941) and at the Biltmore Hotel in New York (1942). They did much in aggregate to determine, if indirectly, the fate of the British, the Arabs and the Jews in Palestine.

◆

Long after Hitler's rule was established – and with state-sponsored anti-Semitism on the increase in Nazi Germany, Poland and elsewhere – representatives of thirty-two countries gathered in Evian, France, in July 1938 for an International Conference on Political Refugees. As David Vital puts it in *A People Apart*, his history of the Jews in Europe, 'The paramount and most immediate question now as always was whether the Jews had allies ... or whether they were alone.'[3] The Evian conference would provide a startling answer.

The conference had been proposed in March 1938, by the US government of Franklin Roosevelt, in response to growing public awareness of the worsening conditions of the Jews in Europe. It was conceived as a public gesture of sympathy. But terms and conditions applied that strangled its effectiveness at birth. The participants would in due course merely advertise international indifference. They would display their selfishness, confirm their existing prejudices, and produce nothing by way of assistance to a people *in extremis*.

Officially, the delegates were required to discuss not the rapidly deteriorating situation of Jews in their current countries of residence, but only the situation of existing refugees. Germany was not to be criticised. The focus was to be not on Jews, by name, at all, but on 'political refugees'. At Britain's behest, there was to be no mention of Palestine either. And no country's delegation would be asked to modify the (restrictive) immigration and naturalisation policies their respective governments were enforcing.

Britain, France and many others offered a range of excuses for not opening their own doors to Jewish refugees. Only the Dominican Republic volunteered to help.[4] A number of delegates made no attempt to disguise the anti-Semitism that drove their policies. For example, the Prime Minister of Canada, one of the British Empire's (white) dominions, referred to Jews as a people who, if admitted, were bound to pollute Canada's bloodstream. The minister for trade and customs in Australia (another white dominion), who had clearly not noticed the Aborigines in his country, said: 'as we have no real racial problem, we are not desirous of importing one'.[5] At about the same time as the Evian Conference, the Polish government – which had been considering Madagascar as a dumping ground for its Jewish inhabitants – asked if the British government would admit them to Palestine, or perhaps to another part of the British Empire such as Northern Rhodesia, at the rate of 100,000 per annum.

Such attitudes were not far removed from those residing in Britain itself. A few months after Evian, Neville Laski, president of the British Board of Deputies, asked to discuss his concerns with the Prime Minister. He was granted a meeting with Lord Halifax, the Foreign Minister, instead. The minutes of this meeting recorded an unguarded expression of the Foreign Office's view: 'it is extremely doubtful whether it could be said that the position of the Jews in Central Europe is in any way a British interest'.[6]

At the conference, there was no evidence that there were any countries, anywhere, prepared to admit German or other desperate refugee Jews in significant numbers. The US quota – of 27,000 a year – was already filled for a long time ahead.

This was devastating for most of the Jewish delegations. These numbered as many as twenty (of a total of thirty-nine) though this multiplicity indicated weakness: the Jewish voices were diverse and disunited. They were low-powered, too, with no great figures attending (Weizmann, for instance, having decided at the last minute that his travelling to Evian would be futile). They were patronised and allowed to be little more than observers. They were hardly participants. Their only chance to speak for their people in their hour of need was a single afternoon (within a ten-day period), during which each was given just five to ten minutes to address a sub-committee. None was allowed to appeal to the plenary.

But the Zionists among these Jewish spokesmen had a different outlook on the matter. Their fear was that arrangements might indeed be agreed on that would seriously damage their cause – including destinations for Jews other than Palestine. This prospect, though improbable, led Yitzhak Gruenbaum, a veteran Polish Zionist, to warn: 'Palestine might cease totally to be regarded as a country suitable for immigration... There is a danger that in the course of the search for a country of refuge some other, new, territory will be found to which ... Jewish migration will be directed. We for our part must defend the principle that it is *only in Palestine* that Jewish settlement can succeed and that there can be no question at all of an alternative to it'.[7]

Ben-Gurion expressed a similar Zionist position but in a rather different way. He acknowledged that the world was beginning to recognise the severity of the Jewish Question. But his lament was that this recognition – and the Evian conference itself – was unhelpfully timed. This was a period, July 1938, when the Arab Revolt was at its height in Palestine and bringing anarchy to Britain's mandated territory. 'What is in need of exposition is the solution to the Question,' wrote Ben-Gurion, 'and for this the time is not ripe because in the eyes of the wider world Palestine is classed with Spain. You don't solve the problem of refugees (it will be said) in a country in which there are riots, in which bombs and murders are daily affairs, and in which there is unemployment and economic stagnation.'[8] But his, like other Zionists' fears, proved groundless. On the eve of the Second World War, the powers remained paralysed by prejudice.

◆

Eighteen months into the war, a remarkable and revealing meeting occurred in London, in February 1941. Weizmann, President of the World Zionist Organisation, called on Ivan Maisky, the Soviet Union's ambassador to the United Kingdom. He wanted to discuss markets for Palestine's oranges, but conversation ranged far more widely. From Maisky's diary we learn what Weizmann was thinking, at that critical moment, about Zionism, Palestine and world Jewry.[9]

What is striking, from Maisky's record of this impromptu conversation, is the contrast between Weizmann's profound human sympathy regarding the imminent future of his fellow European Jews, now facing an existential threat, and his entrenched contempt towards the Arabs of Palestine.

Weizmann was very pessimistic. 'I cannot think without horror about the fate of the 6 or 7 million Jews who live in Central and South-Eastern Europe,' he told Maisky. He had no confidence that the British would come to their aid. In a concise statement that combined racialism, arrogance and condescension with ignorance and indifference, he went on to paint a frank picture of political Zionism's world view. 'The English – and especially their colonial administrators – don't like Jews.' In Palestine 'they prefer Arabs to the Jews. Why? For one very simple reason. An English colonial administrator will usually get his training in British colonies like Nigeria, the Sudan, Rhodesia and so on. These places have a well-defined pattern of rule: a few roads, some courts, a little missionary activity, a little medical care for the population. It's all so simple, so straightforward, so calm. No serious problems, and no complaints on the part of the governed.'

Palestine was very different. 'It's true that the Palestinian Arabs are the kind of guinea pigs the administrator is used to, but the Jews reduce him to despair. They are dissatisfied with everything, they ask questions, they demand answers.' The Jews are 'a nuisance. But the main thing is that the administrator constantly feels that the Jew is looking at him and thinking to himself: "Are you intelligent? But maybe I'm twice as intelligent as you".'

For their part, the Arabs of Palestine must make way for the Jews – on a scale as yet undeclared. To Weizmann, 'the Arab' was idle and incompetent. 'His laziness and primitivism turn a flourishing garden into a desert.' Weizmann articulated a large-scale transfer plan that displayed a Stalinist ruthlessness towards the Muslim majority who had for hundreds of years before 1917 known Palestine as their home. This was 'to move a million Arabs now living in Palestine to Iraq, and to settle 4 or 5 million Jews from Poland on the land which the Arabs had been occupying'.

♦

World Zionist Congresses had been held roughly every two years since Basel, 1897. But none had been held during the First World War; and circumstances again prevented any such congress during the Second World War. However, there being an urgent need to discuss the future both of Jewry and the movement, 600 delegates from eighteen countries (though primarily from Zionist groups within the USA) gathered for a week in the Biltmore Hotel, New York, in May 1942.

In response to news of terrible events, the Biltmore Programme, put forward by David Ben-Gurion and agreed at this meeting, was both a fierce response to the British White Paper of 1939 and an urgent, ambitious, updating of the Zionist ambition for Palestine.[10] The Basel Programme, forty-five years before, had launched the movement into unknown waters; the Biltmore Programme sought to steer it, through the most ferocious storms, to its destination.

Confirming the tragic ambiguity of wording in Britain's vain appeal for help in the First World War, it referred back to 1917. 'The Conference calls for the fulfilment of the original purpose of the Balfour Declaration and the mandate which, recognising the historical connection of the Jewish people with Palestine, was to afford them the opportunity ... to found there a Jewish Commonwealth.' This was a brazen, if understandably self-serving, interpretation of the Balfour Declaration: its 'original purpose' had in fact been to rally the Jews of Russia and the USA to the Allied war effort; it had made no reference to any 'historical connection' (though the mandate subsequently did); and it had carried two pledges, not just one.

As for the Jewish national home, this was recognised at Biltmore as having been already brought into being: 'the Jewish people have awakened and transformed their ancient homeland [and] have written a notable page in the history of colonisation'. But, unlike the formulators of the White Paper, the assembled Zionists presented this achievement not as nearing completion but only as the preliminary stage for a post-war Jewish state: 'a Jewish Commonwealth integrated in the structure of the new democratic world'.

Democratic? Unlike its 1897 predecessor, the Biltmore Programme did mention the Arabs: first, as 'neighbours' who had shared in 'the new values' and achievements of Zionism in Palestine; second, as 'peoples and states' whose national development was welcome. But taken as a whole this document may be read as a passionate commitment, at a time of struggle 'against the forces of aggression and tyranny', to Palestine's imminent transformation into a Jewish state in which Arabs would play no democratic part. The 'new world order' based on 'peace, justice and equality' would not apply to the Arab majority of Palestine. The final paragraph left no room for ambiguity. The programme 'urges that the gates of Palestine be opened [and] that the Jewish Agency be vested with control of immigration into Palestine and with the necessary authority for up-building the country'.

In Jerusalem, Ben-Gurion won over the *yishuv* to the new programme. By November 1942 there was no denying the existential crisis. News reached Palestine that pogroms and expulsions had given way to the systematic physical extermination of European Jewry. Just a few months earlier, delegates at Biltmore had assumed that there would be millions of refugees at the end of the war; now it was clear that such numbers would not survive. In this light, the Zionist case inevitably assumed a new form: justice for the Jewish people lay no longer in the righting of historic wrongs; it lay now in the immediate, urgent, provision of a refuge which surviving Jews could call their own.

This was the potential of Biltmore. But it was not in itself a turning point. Rather, the Programme reflected the radicalisation of the Zionist movement as a result of the war and of the acute sufferings of the Jewish people. As the war progressed – with execution of the Final Solution on the one hand but increasing certainty of an Allied victory on the other – Biltmore encapsulated an appeal to the world which, for a variety of reasons, it would largely support.

Unlike the 1917 advocacy of a Jewish homeland within Palestine, this unequivocal call was for the transformation of Palestine into a Jewish state without restrictions (though *not* broadcast were Zionist assumptions about population transfer, such as Weizmann had privately expressed to Maisky). In the meantime, Biltmore was followed by an intense advertising and fund-raising campaign. Echoes of earlier times included systematic lobbying among American politicians (which led sixty-two senators and 181 congressmen to urge President Roosevelt to support Zionism in Palestine); and the founding of pro-Zionist Christian organisations, proposing the restoration of the people of Israel to the land of their fathers.

But even now Zionists by no means spoke for all Jews. Their critics, in America and elsewhere, did not regard further immigration of Jews into Palestine for a Jewish state there as the right answer. By 1943 – when there was no denying the unprecedented threat to Jews in Nazi occupied Europe – the American Council of Judaism had come into being, to challenge the Zionists' Biltmore policy and contest several of its key assumptions. 'We oppose the effort to establish a national Jewish state in Palestine, or anywhere else, as a philosophy of defeatism... We dissent from all these related doctrines that stress the racialism, the national and the theoretical homelessness of the Jews. We oppose such doctrines as inimical to the welfare of Jews in Palestine, in America, or wherever Jews may dwell.'[11]

The council had only a few thousand members, though it claimed to represent the majority of American Jews and it included some public figures. It was to submit its views to the United Nations, after the war. The council represented perennial concerns about Zionism's colonising project for Palestine and its claims to speak for World Jewry. It opted for a unitary, Arab-Jewish, state for Palestine. Its views echoed those raised by Jews critical of Zionism before the First World War and then, during it, by Edwin Montagu. He, it will be recalled, had branded Zionism 'mischievous', and the British decision to support it 'anti-Semitic'.

But, thirty years on, it was the Zionist insistence that prevailed: that only the doors of Palestine be opened to Jewish refugees, not those of every country.

◆

As the situation of European Jewry deteriorated towards the war's end, the British found themselves confronted by increasingly convergent responses to that crisis: from, on one hand, the Zionist movement (worldwide, and in Palestine); on the other, many countries with an interest in the Jews' fate. The Zionist response, as seen at the Biltmore Conference, was a heightened determination to present a Jewish state in Palestine as the only means of both assisting survivors of the Holocaust and, in the long term, safeguarding the Jewish people. And the general international response, as seen at the Evian Conference and persisting through the war, was – largely out of self-interest – to endorse this approach. Most significantly, in spite of the Holocaust, politicians in the USA declined to come to the aid of European Jews by increasing immigration quotas. They chose not to open their own doors, but to advocate considerable additional Jewish settlement in Arab Palestine.

To this extent Zionism was a godsend. Governments could adopt once again the position pioneered by the British in 1917: an option that incorporated a degree of anti-Semitic nimbyism yet appeared compassionate and just. As Weizmann had sensed, decades earlier, Zionism excused the selfishness of others and offered them pain-free kudos.

There was tragic irony here, for Britain was now the exception. The hard-pressed British administration in Palestine was committed, at least by the White Paper, to limiting Jewish immigration; curtailing, not extending, the Jewish national home; and steering the territory towards self-government and majority, that is Arab, rule. Other countries were proposing indefinite Jewish immigration to Palestine: that is, the policy that Britain had herself initiated thirty years earlier. But the British themselves, long since responsible for Palestine but now facing the inescapable and unmanageable results of their own policy, were insisting that immigration must stop, and were actually turning away traumatised Jewish refugees.

From 1945

Rather as in 1918, when the end of global war brought matters to a head in Ireland, 1945 brought renewed pressure on Britain in Palestine, where its administration came under renewed attack.

Zionist resistance to British post-war policy – still tied to the pro-Arab White Paper – certainly played its part in bringing about the end of the mandate. When in June 1946 terrorist attacks against them intensified, British military authorities imposed a curfew on the major cities. They deployed more than a 100,000 British soldiers and police to surround Jewish settlements, and made 3,000 arrests. Shortly afterwards there was news of a pogrom in Poland in which forty Jews were killed. This renewed the association, for Zionists, of Jewish suffering in Europe with Britain's continuing immigration restrictions in Palestine. Irgun responded by blowing up the King David Hotel in Jerusalem, headquarters of the British administration, killing ninety-one people and injuring a further forty-five. The British in turn responded with more repression, though by now their cause was lost.

But it was the Labour government in London that had to decide what to do next – in the light of their lack of authority on the ground in Palestine, their own dwindling potential as an imperial power, and increasingly critical world opinion.

At first it fell to the Foreign Secretary, Ernest Bevin, to seek a diplomatic solution, in partnership with the USA. In 1946, a twelve-man Anglo-American committee produced a plan. It allowed for considerable Jewish immigration but advocated a bi-national state under UN auspices. Thus, intended to appeal to each side, it was predictably turned down by both. There followed another Anglo-American enquiry, this one undertaken by just two men. Their proposal was for a four-way partition of Palestine; and it was vetoed by the Zionists. Finally, Bevin produced his own scheme. This did little more than revisit 'cantonisation'. This was one of the options considered by the Peel Commission ten years earlier, only to be rejected by them, then, as impracticable and unacceptable. It came as no surprise that both Arab and Jewish leaders, convened in London in early 1947, rejected it: the former were demanding independence for the whole territory, the latter a separate state of their own. At this point the British gave up and admitted defeat.

The main factor here was that, seriously weakened financially and economically by the global conflict, a struggling British Empire undertook a review of its strategic needs that was free of romance and wishful thinking. The British were about to withdraw from India, their most treasured possession. Independence for India (and Pakistan) in the summer of 1947 was a huge, substantial and symbolic, statement that the days of the British Empire were numbered. In such a context it made no sense at all for the British to be keeping up to 100,000 troops in an ungovernable Palestine, the strategic significance of which (in relation to the Suez Canal), always questionable, was at last discounted.

And overriding every other consideration in the aftermath of the Second World War was the onset of the Cold War. In this new, global confrontation, British interests corresponded to the USA's. But this was an unequal partnership. The USA and the USSR were the two superpowers; Britain and France, yesterday's giants. One aspect of this new relationship was Britain's having to cede to American preferences on Palestine. It was the American President, Harry Truman, under Zionist pressure and inclined politically to appease it, who insisted that the British in Palestine immediately take in 100,000 Jewish refugees, while the British were turning them away.

This being the case the Prime Minister, Clement Attlee, concluded that the British were not the free agents that they had been at the end of the First World War. An intolerable situation on the ground in Palestine, financial constraints and strategic retrenchment: all pointed in the same direction. His government had no option but to announce, in February 1947, that it would shortly leave the territory, handing responsibility for its future to the United Nations.

Long before then, a mood of gloom reminiscent of Sir John Chancellor's had set in among British officials with responsibility for Palestine. During the war the penultimate British High Commissioner, Sir Harold MacMichael, had no illusions. He had served the British Empire elsewhere, for example, as Governor of Tanganyika in the 1930s, but Palestine was different. Perhaps seven attempts on his life brought detachment and despair. A reported conversation with Ben-Gurion provides a fitting obituary for the colonial adventure undertaken by David Lloyd George. 'He had no idea what the British wanted from him,' wrote Ben-Gurion of MacMichael. 'The government's policy was constantly changing... For twenty-five years London had not known what it wanted. He himself had no clue what he was doing in Palestine.'[12]

At the start of the war, the British diplomat Malcolm MacDonald had described Palestine as 'a mill-stone round our necks'.[13] In August 1947, the year of Britain's abdication, Hugh Dalton, Chancellor of the Exchequer, termed the territory 'a wasps' nest'.[14] The metaphors had changed but in its essentials the situation in Palestine had not. The British abandoned the territory. Their legacy was a continuing conflict between the two communities they had done so much to bring to mutual antagonism. The death of the mandate was followed by the triumph of Zionism.

◆

The last word on Britain's responsibility for a conflict without end must go to the Foreign Secretary, Ernest Bevin. His announcement, of the British government's decision to leave Palestine, was a brief but devastating verdict – beyond need of further commentary – on what his predecessor in post, Arthur Balfour, had initiated in 1917 and then seen cemented into the mandate.

On 18 February 1947, Bevin spoke to the House of Commons as follows: 'We have reached the conclusion that the only course now open to us is to submit the problem to the judgement of the United Nations... We shall explain that the mandate has proved to be unworkable in practice, and that the obligations undertaken to the two communities in Palestine have been shown to be irreconcilable'.[15]

8

THE LEGACY

'The colonial context prevailed over romantic ideals.'
Nathan Weinstock[1]

Exodus '47

On 12 July 1947, the steamer *Exodus 1947* set out from southern France. It was heading for a port in Palestine. It carried around 4,500 Jewish survivors of the Holocaust. They could expect a warm welcome from the Zionists – though not from the Arab majority, nor from the British authorities. The journey was organised by Haganah, the Palestine-based Jewish militia. These 'displaced persons' were to be 'illegal immigrants' – if, that is, *Exodus 1947* could break the naval blockade established by the British in Palestine to restrict immigration into a deeply divided land which they struggled to govern. On 18 July the ship was intercepted by British Royal Marines, off the coast of Gaza. The British forces violently seized control of both ship and passengers. Afterwards, they landed dead and wounded in Haifa, transferred the would-be immigrants to three other ships, and took them back to France. The French were no more inclined than others, even at this time, to welcome desperate Jewish immigrants. They embarrassed the British by refusing to accept them. They were taken on to Hamburg. Here they were forcibly disembarked. These desperate victims of Hitler's war and genocide had been landed in, of all places, Germany.

The British had already told the United Nations that they would abandon Palestine the following year. By chance the *Exodus 1947* affair

– an excruciatingly sad comment on the British mandate – was observed in Haifa by the Swedish chairman of the UN's investigatory 'special committee' on Palestine, charged with advising what should replace British rule.

UNSCOP, 1947: The Peel Report revisited

The United Nations Special Committee on Palestine (UNSCOP) convened on 26 May 1947 and reported later that summer.[2] It comprised eleven members, supposedly neutral, drawn from Europe, Central and South America, Iran, the British Dominions and India. India at this time provided a terrifying warning. The British announced Partition on 3 June. Independence for two states, India and Pakistan, followed on 15 August – accompanied by the displacement of 10–12 million people and the deaths of hundreds of thousands.

There was no representative on UNSCOP from an Arab country. What bound the membership was not so much their neutrality but the fact that none of their own countries would pay the price for any 'solution' they arrived at for Palestine. Five Arab states, unsympathetic to the mission and no doubt with the 1939 British White Paper in mind, asked the UN to grant self-government to a unitary post-mandate Palestine. The UN declined to discuss this alternative.

Early in the Report, a representative of the United Kingdom is quoted as saying, 'we have tried for years to solve the problem of Palestine. Having failed so far, we now bring it to the United Nations, in the hope that it can succeed where we have not.'

In Palestine the committee encountered 'profound tension'. During three months of hearings, they found the Jewish Agency willing to cooperate. However, the Arab Higher Committee (AHC) regarded UNSCOP as an agency for Zionism and boycotted it. The commissioners were enthusiastically welcomed by Jewish communities; they met hostility in the Arab areas.

Among their main findings were the following:

- It had long been acknowledged on all sides that the 'Jewish

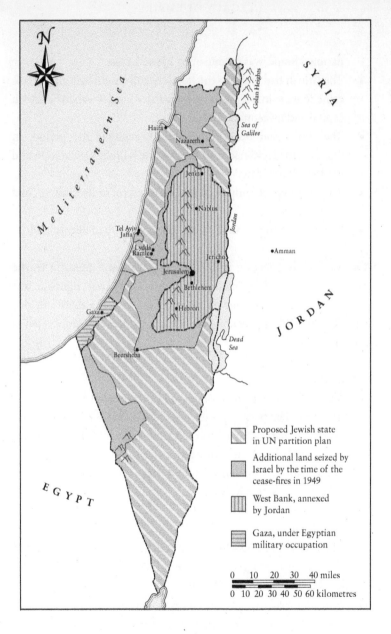

Proposed Jewish state in UN partition plan

Additional land seized by Israel by the time of the cease-fires in 1949

West Bank, annexed by Jordan

Gaza, under Egyptian military occupation

0   10   20   30   40 miles

0 10 20 30 40 50 60 kilometres

THE UN PARTITION OF PALESTINE, NOVEMBER 1947,
AND THE 1949 ARMISTICE LINES

national home' was precursor to a Jewish state.

- The British had clung to the hope that all would be well if Arabs came to share in the prosperity of a Palestine developed by Jewish capital and investment. In vain.
- The Arabs had been consistent, throughout the period, in rejecting the legitimacy of Zionism, the Balfour Declaration and the British mandate.
- The Peel Report, 'impartial and unanimous' in its findings, had been sound.
- The earlier King-Crane Report of 1919, too, had been sound.

Before summarily rejecting it, UNSCOP gave full expression to the Arab case. This rested on 'natural' rights and 'acquired' rights. It was put to them at an early stage by representatives of the AHC. In this résumé, UNSCOP's largely unsympathetic responses are paraphrased in parenthesis:

Natural rights

- The Arabs were the majority people in Palestine [Agreed]
- The Arabs had been in possession of this land for over a thousand years [No 'natural right' accrued from this, since they had never possessed Palestine as a sovereign nation]
- Arab national existence should be free to develop [Arab nationalism is 'relatively new'].

Acquired rights

- The McMahon-Hussein correspondence of 1915 [There existed 'no unequivocal agreement' as to the significance of this – and it was beyond UNSCOP's scope]
- Promises were made to the Arabs in 1916, on the basis of which the Arabs rose in revolt against the Ottomans, on Britain's side [No comment]
- The terms of the mandate for Palestine were illegal, being

inconsistent with Article 22 of the Covenant of the League of Nations [The British had been entitled to write their own terms]
- The right of a people to national self-determination had been withheld [Not applicable to Palestine, because of the Balfour Declaration]
- The Balfour Declaration had no legitimacy, and subsequent immigration of Jews into Palestine was illegal [At the Paris Conference, Faisal Hussein had recognised the special nature of Palestine and in correspondence with Weizmann had accepted the Balfour Declaration].

In relation to this last point, it is worth recalling that Faisal's authority to speak for or negotiate on behalf of Arab Palestinians had been highly questionable. Indeed, Chaim Weizmann himself was to observe of Faisal that 'he is not interested in Palestine' and 'he is contemptuous of the Palestinian Arabs'.[3] At the time of his dialogue with Weizmann, Faisal was seeking British support against the French in Syria. His engineered acceptance of the Balfour Declaration was, moreover, conditional; and his conditions were not met.

Dismissing the Arab case, though recognising the passion with which it was held, UNSCOP concluded as the Peel Commission had done. Palestine had to be partitioned: that two states, one Jewish and one Arab, would inherit the deeply troubled land on Britain's departure.

Only ten years separated these two reports. That was a decade in which the Jews of Europe had been the victims of unprecedented barbarity, and the post-war international world order had changed almost beyond recognition. But the two sets of findings were remarkably similar. UNSCOP's partition plan resembled the Peel Commission's. There were differences, but in essence the 1947 two-state map echoed that of the Peel Report. Moreover UNSCOP, too, concluded that the mandate had been from the start impracticable; that the Arabs had not been appeased by material betterment, as Britain had hoped; and that Arab hostility to Zionism had not eased but intensified.

Finally, some observations on the British mandate, in the words of the UNSCOP Report. The mandate was approved in 1922 in the face of 'opposition ... from the overwhelming Arab majority'. The King-Crane report had already warned in 1919 that 'the Zionist program could not be carried out except by force of arms'.

> The application to Palestine of the mandate system ... implies the belief that the obligations undertaken towards the Arabs and the Jews respectively would prove in course of time to be mutually compatible, owing to the conciliatory effect on the Palestinian Arabs of the material prosperity which Jewish immigration would bring to Palestine as a whole. That belief has not been justified, and there seems to be no hope of its being justified in the future.

> [The British had hoped that] sooner or later the Arab fears would gradually be overcome and that Arab hostility to the terms of the mandate would in turn weaken and disappear... This seems to have been the basic assumption, but it proved to be a false one.

To conclude: the UN vote of November 1947 represents a global act of nimbyism. Shared anti-Semitism brought together the Cold War superpowers, Truman's USA and Stalin's USSR, along with numerous other states who would pay no price for the creation of Israel. It was the neighbouring, mainly Arab, states who voted vainly against this unwelcome transformation of *their* back yard.

1947 to 1949: The First Arab-Israeli War

The First Arab-Israeli War came as a direct consequence of the tensions that the British had brought into being in Palestine. And it gave shape to the longer-term legacy of the thirty years of British rule.

On the Jewish side, David Ben-Gurion had been preparing the *yishuv* for war since the announcement of Britain's imminent departure. It was not clear then, in early 1947, whether they would be fighting Palestine's

Arabs or neighbouring Arab states. In the event, they had to survive the attacks of both in turn. First, from November 1947 to mid-May 1948, they were faced by a guerrilla campaign waged against them by Arabs of Palestine, which they successfully withstood. This stage is sometimes referred to as 'the civil war', though unhelpfully: it was war within a single territory but not war among a single people. Acts of terror and brutality by both sides marked this period. Second, from mid-May 1948 to early 1949, in a more conventional war, they had to confront an array of forces launched against them by neighbouring Arab states.

◆

Arab-on-Jew violence erupted on 30 November 1947. News of the UN General Assembly's historic vote was as divisive as previous partition proposals had been: celebrated by Jewish communities, lamented by Arabs. Each side, Jewish and Arab, suspected the British, still notionally in authority, of favouring the other. But interventions by the mandatory power, more concerned by this time with the safe withdrawal of its own forces from the territory, were of little significance. What counted were the many advantages the *yishuv* enjoyed: in national organisation, training and weaponry, command and control, and funding from the diaspora. Perhaps above everything else came a motivation powered by a sense – in the wake of the Holocaust in Europe – that, as a distinct community, they were fighting for their lives as a people as well as for the very existence of their embryonic state. As before, this contrasted with a Palestinian nationalism that had been for many decades articulated by an urban elite but remained of less compelling appeal to the urban poor and rural communities. Most among the latter, however, saw Zionism as a threat to their homes and homeland, and many were ready, as in the years of revolt in the 1930s, to resist occupation and dispossession.

After a few months of being on the back foot, Haganah was able to go onto the offensive and crush the Palestinian Arab resistance. Indeed, by early April it was clear that for the *yishuv* a war of survival was turning into a war of conquest. Haganah implemented its Plan D, to take over strategic areas as they were evacuated by the British, to gain control of key towns and lines of communication, and to secure borders against any invasion by Arab armies.[4] One such town was Haifa. Though allocated to the Jewish state by the UN, its population numbered about as many Arabs (70,000) as Jews. In the last week of April 1948, Haifa fell to the Haganah. Thousands of Arabs left the city. Overall, by mid-May it was clear that Jewish forces had been victorious in this first stage of the war; and they were well placed for the second. But Arab Palestinian potential for further violent resistance had been broken.

◆

The new state of Israel was declared on 14 May. In the previous months the Haganah had evolved from an underground militia into a regular army and was now the core of the IDF (Israeli Defence Forces). As expected, it had to respond to an Arab invasion of its fledgling territory.

Who were the Arabs involved? A preliminary glance, in turn, at the Arab League, the Mufti Amin al-Husayni, and King Abdullah of Transjordan, will help to make sense of this, the second stage of the conflict.

Seven neighbouring Arab states were notionally bound together under the Arab League.[5] The British had helped to bring this group into being in Alexandria in 1945, seeking future stability for the region and maintenance of their own influence (and repair of some of the damage done to their standing from the time of the Arab Revolt). The League encompassed keen inter-state rivalries and was not to prove a coherent force. But it expressed general Arab support for the Palestinians and apprehension regarding the founding of a Jewish state in their midst. League members were in agreement that the British should implement their White Paper of 1939. Increasingly it claimed to speak for the Palestinian Arabs, whose own nationalist political movement continued to be weak, riven by new rivalries (such as between a revived Istiqlal and

David Ben-Gurion (1886–1973)
Proclaiming the Declaration of Independence, Tel Aviv, 14 May 1948. David Ben-Gurion was the inter-war leader of the Jewish community in Palestine; the head of Histadrut (the Zionist Labour Federation), 1921–1935; the head of the Jewish Agency from 1935; and the first Prime Minister of Israel.

a revived Palestine Arab Party under Jamal al-Husayni).

At the end of the Second World War, the Mufti was in France. The Allies considered trying him for collaborating with the Nazis – or, in the case of Britain, exiling him to the Seychelles – but he escaped, to Cairo. Even so, in the war's aftermath the Mufti found himself cold-shouldered by the British and lacking influence over the Arab League. In the 'civil war' stage of the first Arab-Israeli conflict he had his own Holy War Army, under Abd al-Qadir al-Husayni, the son of Musa Kazim, but this was not integrated into the Arab League's plans. It enjoyed some successes, but only in the period before the Haganah counter-offensive, during which Abd al-Qadir was killed. The Mufti's appeals to Palestine's Arabs not to flee from their land at this time were in vain: a further sign of the Mufti's declining influence.

King Abdullah was committed neither to the League nor to preventing a Jewish state in Palestine. Son of the Hashemite Sharif of Mecca, and brother of Faisal (King of first Syria, then Iraq), he wanted to acquire the East of Palestine (allocated to Palestine's Arabs) for his own kingdom of Transjordan. His British-officered army, the Arab Legion, was the one that most alarmed the Jewish leadership. It was the best prepared and the only one that was battle-hardened. But Israel had little to fear. Abdullah preferred a Jewish state as a neighbour to a state ruled by the Mufti. His Arab Legion (soon to become the Royal Jordanian Army) would be deployed in the interests of its own king – not those of the Palestinians or of the Arab cause generally.

Abdullah had long sought for himself a Greater Syria, or Transjordan with Palestine. This being his priority, years earlier he had accepted the projected Jewish national home: partly to please the British, and partly to attract some Zionist funding. His own proposed enlarged state would accommodate a homeland for the Jews. He outlined his plan in 1934: it would have recognised both the British mandate and Jewish rights. The Nashashibis accepted it, but it was rejected by Amin and the Husaynis and also by the Zionists. In 1937, Abdullah welcomed the Peel partition proposal. This was no surprise, as the Peel Report envisaged an Arab state 'consisting of Transjordan united with that part of Palestine' allocated to the Arabs. In the aftermath of the Second World War, in 1946, he held detailed discussions with a representative of the Jewish Agency, which led to a firm, albeit unwritten, understanding that he would recognise a Jewish state and this would in turn agree to his incorporation of much of Arab Palestine. In November 1947, Abdullah had talks with the *yishuv*'s Golda Meir (another future Prime Minister of Israel) which confirmed that in the event of war he would restrict his ambitions to the West Bank, and that a Jewish state would accept that outcome.

The role of the British here was of considerable significance. The Peel

Report, as we have just seen, incorporated Abdullah's ambitions. And from the same month as the Abdullah-Meir talks there is evidence that nothing in this respect had changed. It was the judgement of J.E. Cable of the Eastern Department of the British Foreign Office that 'the only alternative [to annexation by Abdullah] would be a puny Arab Palestine dominated by an unreliable Mufti'. The 'civil war' period threatened to unravel some key assumptions shared by Abdullah, the Zionists and the British; but in the event they survived.

But Abdullah did not speak for Palestinians. Indeed, Palestinian nationalists saw him as an outsider (his family being from the Hijaz) who was an enemy both of Palestinian statehood and of the Mufti, Amin al-Husayni.[6] Yet the understanding between Abdullah and the Zionists was only one illustration of the way in which the Palestinian Arabs were continuing to have their future decided for them by others. They were marginalised. They were regarded by the Arab League as worthy of no part in their plans. They were indeed politically weak and by May 1948 had no surviving military capability. They would have no part in determining the outcome of the ensuing conflict.

◆

The second, conventional, stage of the war began with the invasion of Israel on 15 May 1948 by the Arab League forces of Iraq, Egypt, Jordan, Syria and Lebanon. It ended, in early 1949, in victory for Israel. The military situation during those critical months resembled that of the Russian Civil War of 1918–21, when the Reds' survival owed as much to the lack of shared purpose and co-ordination of its many foes as to its own discipline, commitment and unity of command. As in the former instance, the forces summoned to crush a passionate, new and threatening presence lacked agreed war aims, unity of command and military-political co-ordination. Nor did the mass of Arab soldiers have a motivation to compare with any involved in the conflict that had raged across pre-partition Palestine in its final months. These men were not fighting for their own survival or homes.

The first phase of the war lasted until a four-week truce, beginning on 11 June. By that time, it was clear that the seasoned Israeli forces had fared better than their opponents. They had withstood a multi-pronged attack and inflicted heavy casualties; they had held most of their UN-allocated state (apart from much of the largely empty Negev to the south). In the armed struggle for Jerusalem, for a while Israeli forces confronted those of the Arab Legion which, as had been expected if not formally agreed, had occupied the core of the 'Arab state' on the West Bank. This episode ended in a draw: Abdullah's men held the East and the IDF retained control of the West of the city. But overall the balance had tipped. From now on, the IDF held the initiative; and in order fully to exploit that, during the truce they raised the number of their men under arms from 35,000 to 65,000.

The Arabs broke the truce on 8 July, and for ten days there was renewed, if inconclusive, military action. A second, longer-lasting truce held for the period from late July until mid-October, during which the IDF further boosted its forces, to 88,000, to give it a clear numerical superiority over the combined Arab forces it now faced. In late September, Ben-Gurion had proposed breaking the understanding with Abdullah by taking on the Arab Legion to acquire the West Bank and East Jerusalem, but he was narrowly overruled in cabinet. So, the main campaign of this final phase saw the IDF in action against the biggest Arab army, that of Egypt: to protect Jewish territory such as the coastal city of Tel Aviv, and to secure the Negev.

A series of armistices in early 1949 marked the ending of this first Arab-Israeli conflict. It was fitting, in the light of what had preceded this conclusion of the war, that each Arab state negotiated its own armistice, with no apparent concern for inter-Arab co-ordination, or for the future of the Palestinians.

◆

Though 6,000 of their fighters were dead, this was clearly a momentous victory for the Israelis. At the heart of the Arab/Muslim world, a Jewish state was established – enlarged by the war, with its people elated by success against the odds. Though only after the horror of the Holocaust, the dream of Theodor Herzl and Chaim Weizmann had thus, in part at least, become reality.

The Arab states had been beaten and demoralised. Though Jordan was able to annexe the West Bank, and Egypt occupied Gaza, both of these adjacent states were taking on land peopled by Palestinians suspicious or hostile towards their new masters.

And there was nothing for the Palestinian Arabs; quite the reverse. In 1937 (Peel) and again in 1947 (the UN), partition was intended to produce a two-state solution to the problems of Palestine. At the end of this war, a state for the Jews was a *fait accompli*. But there was no state at all for the Palestinians. Areas allocated to them in the plans of others had either been seized by the Haganah/IDF or been acquired by two of their neighbours.

And during these months of 1947 to 1949, 700,000 Palestinians – roughly two-thirds of the country's population – 'were driven from or fled from their homes'.[7] For decades, Zionists had been insisting that the forced 'exile' of the Jews from Palestine in the first century AD established a 'right of return'. The first Arab-Israeli War showed emphatically that they had 'returned'. Henceforth there was to be a different people in exile, wanting to return.

This was how the Zionism that the British had rescued from obscurity in 1917 had developed. The 1947–49 conflict and its aftermath carried stronger echoes of Ze'ev Jabotinsky in 1923 than of Yitzhak Epstein in 1905. The former had argued that only after Arab opposition to colonisation had been crushed could the Jews make peace with them. The latter, it will be recalled, had in 1905 labelled the infant Zionist movement irresponsible for having so far ignored the Arabs resident in Palestine. And he had issued a clear warning: 'We must not uproot people from land to which they and their forefathers dedicated their best efforts and toil... Powerful is the passion', he added, 'of those who suffer such an experience.'[8]

Conflict: 1949 to the present

The bonfire which David Lloyd George laid, Arthur Balfour ignited, and British imperial and mandate governments fanned thereafter until the heat forced them to abandon it, has continued to burn – mostly smouldering, periodically bursting into flame.

The developments that followed the First Arab-Israeli War may best be seen as twin continuities, from each stage of that conflict (and their interaction): the 'civil war' stage and the subsequent inter-state stage. We will begin by tracing the latter thread, since it provided a context for the former.

After the armistices of 1949, Arab states wanted to gain revenge on Israel, while some Israeli generals were eager to crush the Arab armies, especially Egypt's. Thus, the Suez Crisis of 1956[9] was the anticipated second round of the Arab-Israeli conflict. On this occasion, Israel was a junior partner of Britain and France in their confrontation with General Gamal Abdel Nasser of Egypt. But the new state benefited more from this episode than either European power, especially Britain, the humiliated former mandatory authority in Palestine. At first sight, Egypt appeared the winner, with Nasser hailed as an Arab hero; but he owed his success largely to US intervention, and euphoria was to lead to calamitous miscalculation in the years that followed. For its part, Israel proved the effectiveness of the IDF, emerged with a more secure southern border, and demonstrated its potential for the West as an ally, in the Middle East, during the era of Cold War. There was no liberation for Palestinians: after Israeli troops withdrew from Sinai and Gaza, Egypt resumed its occupation of the latter.

The 1967 Six Day War, or Third Arab-Israeli War, was again an inter-state conflict. This one was to have immense consequences for the Palestinians of the West Bank and of Gaza. It began after Israel won prior approval from America to launch a long-planned pre-emptive strike against her Arab neighbours, President Johnson's UN Ambassador having assured Arab officials that he was trying to restrain Israel.[10] In succession, the bombing of Egypt's air force while it was on the ground, invasion by IDF land forces of Gaza and Sinai, and counter-attacks against Jordanian and Syrian forces, brought Israel an astonishing military success and the admiration of much of the watching world. In less than a week, Israel had defeated her enemies and had seized Gaza and Sinai (from Egypt), the Golan Heights (from Syria), and the West Bank along with East Jerusalem (from Jordan).

Six years later, seeking to reverse the land losses – and humiliation – of the Six Day War, the forces of Egypt and Syria launched surprise attacks on Sinai and the Golan Heights, on 6 October 1973: Yom Kippur, one of the holiest days in the Jewish calendar. Initially suffering unprecedented losses, the IDF recovered in the two weeks or so before a ceasefire held. But something had changed: Egypt, buoyed by its initial success, appeared to gain the confidence to negotiate with Israel as an equal; Israel, in turn, saw sense in making peace with (and gaining recognition from) its most powerful neighbour, and thus returned Sinai to Egypt.

Yom Kippur illustrated again how highly the West regarded its alliance with Israel in the context of superpower rivalry. Massive Soviet and Czech arms supplies reached Egypt and Syria; and American supplies reinforced Israel. Furthermore, a decade on from the Cuba Missile Crisis, Yom Kippur resurrected the menace of a 'Cold War' nuclear exchange. Israel possessed missiles that could be fitted with nuclear warheads, and his country's plight led Defence Minister Moshe Dayan to consider using them. Meanwhile, President Brezhnev of the USSR was moving nuclear cargo towards Egypt, and the American President, Richard Nixon, raised the nuclear alert level of the US forces. Such was the perceived strategic importance of this Middle Eastern conflict. In this context, the Palestinians' struggle against America's protégé could be ignored.

By the end of 1973 the state of Israel was evidently established. Through its military triumphs of 1948–49 and 1967 it governed more

territory than the 55 per cent of mandate Palestine awarded it by the
UN in 1947. It had proved its worth to the West, where among people
as a whole it retained much admiration, and sympathy too in the light
of terrorist attacks by armed groups of Palestinians. Not least, peace had
been made with Egypt, its most powerful Arab neighbour.

◆

The outcome of the Six Day War proved a calamity for the Palestinians –
who had played no direct part in it – in two ways. First, the war created
another 300,000 Palestinian refugees who, as in the 1947–49 conflict,
were driven out or fled. It created Jewish refugees too, as Arab states,
responding in ways foreseen by Edwin Montagu in 1917, expelled
their Jewish communities, who then sought new homes in Israel or in
Europe. Second, Israel began to settle Jews on Arab land. In the first
decade, the settlement programme (primarily though not exclusively
in the West Bank and East Jerusalem) was gradual and targeted. But
after the Likud Party came to power in Israel in 1977, it accelerated.
At this time, to quote British historian Bernard Wasserstein, 'a revived
version of Revisionist Zionism coalesced with a religious Zionism':
areas of the West Bank, in particular around Hebron, were subjected
to 'wildcat occupations', though most new settlements were developed
by commercial entrepreneurs as extended suburbs of Tel Aviv and
Jerusalem.[11] In planting these settlements, Israeli governments alienated
not only Palestinians but in due course many former supporters in the
West. Critical observers could conclude that 'the IDF was transformed
from a first-rate regular army into an army of occupation or, to put it
more strongly, into an instrument of colonial repression.'[12]

The settlement policy ignored Israel's internationally recognised
1949 territorial limits. It was the subject of keen debate within Israel
between doves, who favoured a policy of handing back occupied land
in return for peace (though early offers thus to cede Sinai and the Golan
Heights were rejected by Egypt and Syria); and Zionist hawks who were

determined to create Greater Israel and regarded the West Bank as not occupied but liberated. And the settlements violated UN Resolution 242 of November 1967. This emphasised 'the inadmissibility of the acquisition of territory by war, and the need to work for a just and lasting peace in which every state in the area can live in security'. Specifically, the Resolution called on Israel to withdraw its armed forces from territories occupied in 'the recent conflict', the Six Day War, while each party should acknowledge 'the sovereignty, territorial integrity and political independence' of every state in the area. It also stated, 'the necessity for achieving a just settlement of the refugee problem'. Resolution 242 has continued to be a reference point in the on-going conflict, not least in regard to the question of Israel's borders (and thus the specific 'Israel' which its critics and opponents might reasonably be expected to 'accept'[13]). Moreover, it provides a lens through which to review the evolution of the Palestine Liberation Organisation (PLO).

◆

The PLO was established in 1964 by the Arab League as an umbrella organisation for a number of political groups. By the end of 1967 these included Fatah, the largest, founded by Palestinians in the diaspora in 1959, its chairman being Yasser Arafat; and the Popular Front for the Liberation of Palestine (PFLP), the second largest, a Marxist-Leninist group led by George Habash. The PLO's policy-making authority was the Palestinian National Council; its founding document was the Palestinian National Covenant.

For around twenty years the PLO was committed to the liberation of the whole of Palestine, through armed struggle. According to the Covenant, 'Palestine with the boundaries it had during the British mandate is an indivisible territorial unit.'

One aspect of armed struggle was incursion into Israel from Palestinian camps in neighbouring Arab countries. Numerous Palestinians had found refuge in Jordan. Tensions with the Jordanian government increased to the point at which, in September 1970, King Hussein ordered the destruction of their 'state-within-a-state'. Thousands of Palestinians were killed, and thousands exiled once more.

Two years later, a group calling itself Black September (in reference to that Jordanian assault) took hostage eleven members of the Israel team competing in the Munich Olympic Games. They demanded the release of over 200 Palestinian prisoners in Israel. Attacked by West German police, they killed all their hostages. Four years later, in July 1976, Palestinian militants who were a breakaway group of the PFLP hijacked an Air France plane and demanded the release of forty Palestinians imprisoned in Israel. The plane was diverted to Entebbe, Uganda. The crisis ended when, after a week of planning (and just ninety minutes of action on the ground), the Israeli forces of Operation Thunderbolt rescued the ninety-four Israeli hostages still held after the release of the other passengers and killed the hijackers.

Such actions not only failed to achieve their immediate objectives but inflicted damage on the instigators' cause. Though the militants regarded themselves as freedom fighters, in the eyes of Israel and many in the West they were terrorists. Reputational damage was enormous. By killing athletes and seizing air passengers at random they achieved publicity, but not sympathy; it was Israel that gained both sympathy (in the first instance) and respect (in the second). Even so, in 1974 the UN recognised the PLO as representative of the Palestinian people and it was given observer status, as an organisation.

Shortly afterwards, Israel's conflict with the PLO continued in another theatre. Hundreds of thousands of Palestinian refugees from the First Arab-Israeli War had crossed into Lebanon. Against this background, the IDF intervened in the Lebanese Civil War of 1975–90, prompted by PLO cross-border raids into Israel. An Israeli invasion of Southern Lebanon in 1978 was followed by a larger-scale invasion in 1982. On this occasion the Israeli forces drove the PLO out of Beirut (to Tunis, where the IDF bombed them in 1985).

Then, in November 1988, Yasser Arafat announced a historic change in PLO policy towards Israel. No longer was the whole of Palestine to be won, through the use of force. Rather, Israel was to be recognised as part of a two-state solution to the conflict, and negotiation would take the place of violence. The PLO now accepted all relevant UN Resolutions, from the November 1947 vote authorising partition and including Resolution 242. Israel had a right to exist. As for an Arab state, the PLO proclaimed the independence of a Palestine comprising Gaza, the West Bank and East Jerusalem. In 1993, secret negotiations in Norway gave rise to the Oslo Accords: a commitment by the PLO and Israel to renounce terrorism and violence, and to engage in a longer-term peace process, based on mutual recognition (and the imminent creation of a Palestinian Authority). In September the world was treated to photographs of the historic, sealing, handshake – on the White House lawn – of Yasser Arafat, for the PLO, and Prime Minister Yitzhak Rabin, for the government of Israel.

However, none of the main issues separating the two sides was resolved; and Rabin soon paid the price of pursuing compromise. On 4 November 1995, at the end of a peace rally in Tel Aviv, he was killed. This was the act of a lone ultra-nationalist, but it occurred in the context of a virulent campaign against Rabin waged by domestic political opponents such as Benjamin Netanyahu and right-wing pro-settler rabbis.

Nonetheless, by that time a Palestinian (National) Authority had come into being. From May 1994, it was intended to be an interim self-governing body for Gaza and also – on the withdrawal of most Israeli forces – of designated Arab regions of the West Bank. (These were known as Areas A and B; Area C, of Jewish settlements, remained under Israel, as did all of Jerusalem.) But from 2006 the PA held sway over the West Bank alone, for in that year elections in Gaza brought to power Hamas, the Palestinian Islamic nationalist party. Though the Americans had called for elections in Gaza, they did not accept this result: they deemed Hamas a terrorist organisation and withheld recognition and aid. The upshot was that Palestine's political representatives no longer spoke with one voice, as Hamas (Gaza) fell out with Fatah (in the West

Bank). Nonetheless, in 2012 'Palestine' was given non-member observer status at the UN, this time as a state.

◆

Distanced from such political initiatives and manoeuvrings – and in despair at their fruitlessness – grass-roots Palestinian protests had spontaneously broken out by this time in two sustained waves of *intifada*, the (attempted) 'shaking off' of Israeli subjection. The first may be dated 1987 to 1993; the second, 2000 to 2005.

The people of Gaza, many of whom were refugees from the First Arab-Israeli War, were impelled not so much by 'nationalism' as by destitution, the humiliation of occupation, repression and, if not fear of eviction, the prospect of annexation. Post-1967 Jewish settlements allocated 40 per cent of the arable land there to less than 1 per cent of the total population of Gaza. The first *intifada* was remarkable not only for being spontaneous (sparked by a collision between an IDF vehicle and a civilian car which resulted in the deaths of four Palestinians) but also for involving all classes – men, women and children – in town and country.

Years of resistance, civil disobedience, strikes and commercial boycotts, street demonstrations and barricades followed, and took their toll. Repression was harsh; many were killed. This phase of popular Palestinian protest ended in 1993, the year of the Oslo Accords.

The start of the second *intifada* owed something to the failure of the Oslo process to bring significant change, and to the subsequent failure of talks in 2000 at the US Presidential retreat of Camp David to resolve any of the abiding core issues. In addition, settlement in the occupied territories was expanding. The spark this time was the provocative visit, in September 2000, of Israel's combative Prime Minister Ariel Sharon to Temple Mount in Jerusalem (the city having been unilaterally merged, West and East, in 1980).

Demonstrations were met by forceful dispersion. Suicide bombings followed – strengthening Israel's determination to build a West Bank

Barrier. Initiated in 1994, this was for Israel a 'security fence'; for Palestinians, it was 'the wall of *apartheid*'. Given extra impetus by the second *intifada*, the first continuous stretch was completed in 2003. Its route ran in part along the 1949 armistice line with Jordan; and in part it encroached into the West Bank to incorporate post-1967 Jewish settlements (and East Jerusalem). By 2006, it stretched for 225 miles. Insofar as it was a response to suicide bombings, it was successful. But it resolved none of the issues. Instead, it dramatically displayed the extent to which Arabs and Israelis remained far apart. We may note in passing that this was not what Ze'ev Jabotinsky had advocated in the early days of the mandate. He wrote, metaphorically, in 1923 of 'an iron wall of Jewish military forces' to protect continuing Jewish colonisation. That is, he wanted an all-powerful militia to defeat the opponents of Zionism, not an actual physical barrier to separate a Jewish state from them.

Eventually, in February 2005, Mahmoud Abbas of the Palestinian National Authority met Sharon. They agreed to work for a reduction in the levels of violence – of repression and resistance – and the Israeli government agreed to the release of some Palestinian prisoners. Shortly afterwards, Israel cut its losses and withdrew its settlers from Gaza. But to contain perennial Palestinian resistance from that quarter, Israel has since exercised considerable external control over the territory and over the lives of those who live in it.

One hallmark of the *intifadas* has been the imbalance of forces deployed by occupier and occupied – each has utilised the weaponry at its disposal – and, partly arising from this, the unequal levels of casualties. Another has been the absence of foreign intervention. Israel has been free to respond to perceived threats to the security of its territory and people, however it has chosen to do so.

◆

Over this whole period since May 1948 there has, of course, been change as well as continuity. One of the main underlying changes has been demographic. While the immigration of Jews from the diaspora has slowed (after two dramatic airlifts of Ethiopian Jews to Israel, for example), the growing number of Palestinian Arabs in Israel and the occupied territories is striking. In 1967, after the war, there were still 1.2 million Arabs under occupation in the West Bank and Gaza. By 2003 this had grown to 3.3 million.[14] It may be that demographic trends prove at least as significant in the long run as the fluctuation of political relations.

But the essential point is that none of the main issues separating the protagonists in the Israel-Palestine conflict (insofar as this is distinct from the Arab-Israeli conflict) has been resolved: Palestinian state-hood (and the borders for any lasting 'two-state solution'); settlements in the West Bank; the status of Jerusalem; and the right of return. There has been little international enthusiasm for criticising Zionism, past or present, or for putting effective pressure on Israel to re-orientate its policy priorities.

Although the Cold War came to an end, Israel is still deemed to have considerable strategic significance for the West, not least as America's éminence grise in its relations with Iran. American support of the state of Israel was critical at the time of its foundation and has been unflinching since the presidency of Ronald Reagan. In brazen acts of partiality, Donald Trump went further than his predecessors by recognising Jerusalem as Israel's capital, the Golan heights as part of Israel, and Jewish settlements in the West Bank as consistent with international law. The 'Deal of the Century', publicised in January 2020, followed negotiations with West Bank settlers and Gulf States ... but not with one of the two main parties concerned, the Palestinians. The following month, in *The Guardian*, fifty former European Prime Ministers and Foreign Ministers compared the proposed outcomes with Apartheid. Jared Kushner, Trump's son-in-law, had been commissioned to seek a deal, but he had no previous experience of diplomacy and flaunted his ignorance of the history of the conflict. There is little prospect of any resolution. The rest of the world has other preoccupations and priorities.

9

HAS IT BEEN COLONIALISM?

'Israel has had the problem that it is a twentieth century version of a seventeenth through nineteenth century colonialism.' Noam Chomsky[1]

We have been well advised to question 'the easy equation of Zionism and colonialism'.[2] Zionism has been a distinctive ideology and movement, hard precisely to categorise. There is an enduring insistence among sympathetic students of Zionism that it presents a complex picture. To be sure, there has never been a single – or pure – type of colonialism.

Yet colonialism is, at heart, simply the domination of one (or more) people by another and/or the occupation of one (or more) people's land by another. From the outset this was, if not the primary purpose, a necessary outcome of Zionism. Twenty years after the foundation of the state of Israel, its Minister of Defence, Moshe Dayan, acknowledged that 'there is not one place built in this country that did not have a former Arab population'.[3]

Nonetheless, Hillel Cohen (Associate Professor of Islamic and Middle Eastern Studies at the Hebrew University of Jerusalem) has asked, of Zionism: 'Has it been colonialism?'[4] This question requires an answer. While the question implies continuation, our focus here remains on the past.

First, a note on chronology and context. In the 1890s, there was little exceptional, or to prevailing opinion exceptionable, about the Zionist project to colonise Palestine. It was launched at the high watermark

Cease-fire
lines 1974

Israeli occupied
Golan Heights

Israel-Lebanon border,
known as the Blue Line.
Not a formal international
border but accepted by
both sides

LEBANON

SYRIA

Haifa

Sea of
Galilee

Mediterranean Sea

Nablus

WEST
BANK

Jordan

Tel Aviv

Ramallah

Amman

Jerusalem

Bethlehem

Dead
Sea

GAZA   Gaza City

Hebron

Rafah
Crossing

ISRAEL

NEGEV
DESERT

JORDAN

EGYPT

SINAI DESERT

N

Gulf of
Aqaba

| 0 | 10 | 20 | 30 | 40 | 50 | 60 miles |
| 0 | 20 | 40 | 60 | 80 | 100 kilometres |

— · — 1949 Armistice Line

· · · · · · Israeli occupied
Golan Heights

· · · · · · The Occupied territories

**ISRAEL AND PALESTINE TODAY
SHOWING THE OCCUPIED TERRITORIES**

of European colonialism. Indeed, these were Europeans, albeit Jewish Europeans, who were advocating it. They were imitating the peoples of the Great Powers in promoting emigration, land acquisition and long-term settlement. To this extent, Palestine was to be a new home for Jews, just as, for example, the East Africa Protectorate (Kenya) and Southern Rhodesia were to be new homes for (mainly) British white settlers of that time. Even Karl Marx had depicted colonialism as necessary and progressive. Few felt the need to apologise for it. After all, those lower in the perceived racial hierarchy of the time – such as 'the African' or 'the Arab' – would be beneficiaries in the end.

◆

An argument that runs through pro-Zionist historiography is that Zionism was distinct from other contemporary European movements. Thus, for example, if it was colonialism, it uniquely entailed a return to the colonisers' own country; and it was relatively benign insofar as it was non-violent. The counter argument is that while it was, in a number of respects, different in motivation and character, it was nonetheless broadly similar in outcome, but harsher. This latter view focuses on the passionate intensity of a movement that was indifferent, if not remorseless, towards native people and did not intend to include them in the benefits of a new political order.

As the Conservative American rabbi Arthur Hertzberg put it, 'all of the other nineteenth century nationalisms based their struggle for political sovereignty on an already existing national land or language (generally there were both). Zionism alone proposed to acquire both of these usual preconditions of national identity by the *élan* of its nationalist will.'[5] This was a unique case of a people migrating towards, and not away from, what they regarded as their home; and – again unlike other contemporary European migrants – they regarded it as a home to which they had an ancient national, as well as a religious, claim. Zionism was powered by a sense of destiny and historic right.

Dwelling on the distinctiveness of Zionism in Palestine, Hillel Cohen presents the claim that 'the Jews were not in fact foreigners in the country but natives whose ancestors had been sent into exile generations previously'.[6] However, Jewish settlers did 'in fact' arrive as 'foreigners', from the late nineteenth century onwards, largely from Russia and elsewhere in Eastern Europe; and they were regarded as foreigners by the majority of Palestine's residents.

Zionists envisaged that, in this colonial project, land would not be seized by the power of the gun, but strategically purchased with the power of money. Nonetheless, land purchase tended to be followed by dispossession; and from the early 1930s the territory would threaten to come effectively under the sway of the immigrant Jewish settlers – 'homeland' turning towards 'state' – through the power of ever-increasing numbers. Force was used, too, from the early days, to protect settlements and communities. And it was to be used to devastating effect later, in 1948 and 1967, against the reality or anticipation of invading Arab armies. Was this self-defence? It was – though only in the sense originally that, elsewhere in the British Empire, Fort Salisbury and Fort Victoria were built in the 1890s for self-defence during the occupation and pacification of Southern Rhodesia. That is, they were built by colonisers to defend themselves against the resistance of the colonised.

Edward Said was born into a Christian Palestinian family. He saw Zionism as less benign than comparable contemporary movements. 'Zionism was a colonial vision unlike that of most other nineteenth-century Europe powers, for whom the natives of outlying territories were included in the redemptive civilising mission.' European colonisation in Africa, while using force initially, where needed, to acquire land and 'pacify' peoples, sought not to remove but to incorporate native peoples: at worst, as labourers and tax-payers; at best as subjects to 'protect', to 'civilise' and (in due course) to advance towards self-government.

Some early Zionist settlers were socialists, and they could envisage a place for Arabs in their enterprise. But there was little left of this aspiration by the 1920s when Ze'ev Jabotinsky rose to prominence. Furthermore, most early Zionists sought not so much to *exploit* the indigenous people as to *exclude* them by not employing them at all. Overall, the Jews' own 'national self-determination' could only be accomplished in Palestine at the expense of another people in the process of discovering its own national consciousness and aspirations.

Zionists argued that Arabs who were dwelling in their Promised Land could, without great hardship, be transferred to neighbouring areas of the wider Arab world. But this belief was self-serving and heartless. Said's overall judgement is severe. 'The whole scheme for displacing the native population of Palestine,' he wrote, 'far outstripped any of the then current plans for taking over vast reaches of Africa.'[7]

◆

Zionism was driven by a rare zeal. The Basel Programme appears quite bland, but the Zionist project was widely advertised as a necessary means of survival: not for *ad hoc* clusters of enterprising individuals but for an entire and desperate people. The *'fatal* source of weakness in the Jewish struggle for existence,' wrote Chaim Weizmann, was the lack of a stable home. His biographer adds that Weizmann was profoundly influenced by Nietzsche; and that the 'conception of the will to power as the basic drive of human behaviour' might well have appealed to this most prominent of Zionists.[8] Not all Jewish settlers in Palestine were so motivated, of course; rather, like their European counterparts migrating elsewhere, many were families just seeking a better (and safer) life. But they were part of a movement of do-or-die messianism.

In this light, there is a case for comparing Zionism not with, say, the British or the French in Africa, but with westward migration across the American continent during the nineteenth century. White Protestant North Americans, one-time settlers, saw themselves as God's Chosen People and, inspired by the Bible, regarded their expansion across the entire continent as a matter of Divine Providence.

Their destiny, like the Zionists', related to a specific territory, which they were to occupy irrespective of the will and interests of those who already resided there. In July 1845, an article in the *Democratic Review*, one of America's most popular magazines, referred to 'our manifest destiny to overspread the continent allotted by Providence for the free development of our yearly multiplying millions'. This newly minted concept of 'manifest destiny' 'postulated a vacant continent, ignoring the prior claims of Native Americans and Mexicans'.[9] Americans were happy to be described as imperialists, and they assumed a sense of cultural if not racial superiority which entitled them to ignore all others.

There was also, in the notion of American 'martial manhood', a parallel with the Zionist goal of Jewish regeneration; and the spread of participatory democracy in new lands corresponded, to a degree, with Zionist settler socialism. Finally, at a foundational stage at least, advocates of the American movement claimed – like first generation 'spiritual' Zionists – that it would produce an exemplary new society. As a senior US government official put it, 'a higher than earthly power still guards and directs our destiny, impels us onward, and has selected our great and happy country as a model ... for all nations of the world'.[10]

Manifest Destiny, like political Zionism, had its critics. The preacher and theologian William Ellery Channing, for example, opposed the annexation of Texas. 'The United States ought to provide its less fortunate sister republics with support [and] assume the role of sublime moral empire, with a mission to diffuse freedom by manifesting its fruits, not to plunder, crush and destroy.'[11] This critique may be compared to that applied to political Zionism by Yitzhak Epstein or Ahad Ha'am.

Manifest Destiny encompassed migration across America, settlement by displacement of native Americans, and regeneration of pioneering white Americans through the frontier experience. And there was another parallel with the Zionism which followed: the unambiguous assumption that liberty for the settlers would not be shared with indigenous peoples who stood in history's way. As another contemporary American, one-time attorney-general Caleb Cushing, put it in 1857: 'In our conquest of nature with our stalwart arms and with our dauntless hearts to back them, it happens that men ... will perish before us. That is inevitable. There can be no change for the better, save at the expense of that which is.'[12]

The promised land of America was not to be shared; Manifest Destiny was to be fulfilled, where necessary, at the expense of those who obstructed it. There was a strong, if often submerged, strand in Zionist thinking that mirrored this: that Jewish Palestine would be separate from Arab Palestine; and that in time the Arabs of Palestine would have to move, or be moved, to another place. In the words of Palestinian writer and academic Nur Masalha, 'The fostering of Arab-Jewish separation was not merely an ideological decision. It advanced in pragmatic terms Zionist goals of colonisation and could be said to lay the groundwork for the transfer solution.'[13] As we have seen, Theodor Herzl himself was committed (albeit in secret) to the removal of 'the penniless population' from Palestine. Other contemporary Zionists were outspoken, making their intentions clear long before the First World War. So, for example, Nahman Syrkin, in a pamphlet of 1898: 'Palestine ... must be evacuated for the Jews'; or Leo Motzkin, co-author with Herzl of the Basel Programme, in a speech of 1912: 'The fact is that around Palestine there are extensive areas. It will be easy for the Arabs to settle there with the money that they will receive from the Jews.'[14]

More remarkable, perhaps, are the words of Theodor Herzl's associate Israel Zangwill who, while preferring migration (and assimilation) elsewhere, urged Zionists to face the facts. In 1905, he gave a talk in Manchester in which he said that Zionists 'must be prepared either to drive out by the sword the [Arab] tribes in possession, as our forefathers did, or to grapple with the problem of a large alien population'. Thereafter committed to territorialism – the search for a location other than Palestine – he stated in 1916 that it would be 'utter foolishness' to allow Palestine to be the country of two peoples. 'A different place must be found either for the Jews or for their neighbours.'[15]

During the mandate, the Zionist commitment to transfer became more openly articulated. In the same year, 1930, as Weizmann received a sympathetic hearing from British policy-makers for his plans, the Russian-born Zionist Menachem Ussishkin said: 'We must continually raise the demand that our land be returned to our possession... If there are other inhabitants there, they must be transferred to some other place.'[16]

This was not quite in line with public assurances that Herzl had given. In 1899 he was in correspondence with Yusuf Zia Khalidi, Palestinian scholar, Member of the Ottoman Parliament and Mayor of Jerusalem. 'You see another difficulty,' Herzl wrote, 'in the existence of the non-Jewish population in Palestine. But who would think of sending them away? It is their well-being, their individual wealth which we will increase by bringing in our own.'[17]

It is striking that an ideology committed to a 'homeland' for *one* people allowed no space for sympathetic recognition that innumerable members of *another* people had a strong sense of belonging to where they lived: to their homes. Instead, 'transfer', once an aspiration, became something of a self-fulfilling prophecy. The Peel Report sadly concluded in 1937 that, because separation and conflict between the peoples had already reached such a level, partition – which would involve transfers of population, especially Arab – was the only feasible solution.

Zionism in Palestine was initially based, as we have seen, not on physical conflict but on land purchase and force of numbers; violence came later, in defending settlements during the British mandate, and subsequently in 1948 and 1967. Even so there seems to be something anticipatory as well as backward-looking in the words of a South Carolina poet, in 1846: 'We do but follow our destiny, as did the ancient Israelites.'[18]

◆

The historic character of Zionism appears complicated when the relationship between Jewish immigrants and indigenous Palestinians is presented as a tragic clash of two competing nationalisms. Avi Shlaim, for example, has written that 'in origin and in essence, the Arab-Israeli conflict is a clash between two national movements: the Palestinian national movement and the Jewish national movement, or Zionism'.[19] Or, in the words of Shlomo Ben-Ami, historian and former Israeli politician, 'the encounter between Zionism and the Palestinian Arabs started as an experiment in mutual ignorance, an obsessive determination by each to overlook the powerful, genuine national sentiments and the spirit of communal identity that motivated the other'. 'In a way,' he adds, 'Zionism and Palestinian nationalism developed as twin movements.'[20]

Good journalists in the best of the British press continue to describe the situation in similar ways. Thus, David Aaronovitch recently wrote: 'Two rights, then. First, the right of the persecuted Jewish people to a homeland. Where would that be but in some part of the historic land of the Jews: yearned for, learnt about in scriptures and synagogues over the centuries? Second, the right of the Palestinian people who, due to no fault of theirs, were forced to leave their homes and become citizens of nowhere.'[21]

While there is, of course, considerable substance in such statements as they stand, they cast shadow rather than light. The *origin* and the *start* lay not in rival nationalisms but in a colonising project. In its essentials, Zionism was quite uncomplicated in theory and in practice. From its articulation in the Basel Programme in 1897, it sought to colonise Palestine and, as Herzl had earlier acknowledged, create a Jewish state there. To be sure, the simplicity of this ambitious aspiration was something which leading Zionists – Herzl, Weizmann, Ben-Gurion – sometimes sought to disguise.

Since their time, discussion of the origins of the Palestine-Israel conflict has been weighed down by its apparent complexity. As a result, many have failed to see the wood for the trees. Noam Chomsky puts it this way: 'The tale of Palestine ... is a simple story of colonisation and dispossession' and yet 'the world treats it as a multifaceted and complex story.'[22] Zionists could at times be quite open on this point. David Ben-Gurion once acknowledged that, as far as the Arabs were concerned,

Zionism meant land loss, and went on to ask, 'what Arab cannot do his math and understand that immigration at the rate of 60,000 a year means a Jewish state in all Palestine?'[23] Sequence matters: colonialism begets nationalism.

In an assessment that underlines complexity, Hillel Cohen writes: 'The Jews experience it [Zionism] primarily as a realisation of their goal as a nation, while the Palestinian Arabs experience it as colonialist.'[24] Presented thus are two contrasting 'experiences' of questionable equivalence: one ideological (how the Zionists justified to themselves what they were doing); and the other empirical (how immigration and dispossession impacted on the indigenous people). Yet, in acknowledging what Palestinians have indeed experienced, Cohen has incidentally answered the question he initially posed. In its core ingredients, this settler-colonialism was no more 'complex' than a number of nineteenth-century parallels: whether classic British, French and even German initiatives in the Dark Continent, or America's conquest of its continental west. Here was a posited (Jewish) national movement for survival, hitched to conventional (British) imperialism. Zionism may have been *sui generis*. But if we pare away the particulars, it emerges as colonialism in one of its more unyielding forms.

◆

It is little surprise, given the circumstances of Israel's gestation and birth, that several of its first Prime Ministers brought to that office previous experience in Haganah, Irgun or the IDF.[25] In 2001, the UK-based journalist and author Anton La Guardia wrote that in modern Israel 'the army remains the single most important institution in Israeli life. It seeps into every corner of society. It is, in many ways, a state within a state, a body entrusted not only with the nation's defence but also with nation-building itself.' And he quoted a former Israeli chief of staff who liked to say that 'every Israeli citizen is a soldier on eleven month's annual leave'.[26]

The army 'remains' so important largely because the creation of Israel was, as Arthur Hertzberg put it in 1959, 'a singular accommodation to peculiar circumstances at a juncture of the moment'. It came into being in a Palestine where it was evidently not welcome and, moreover, 'on the edge of the Western sphere of influence, in the midst of a region which channelizes much of its growing revolt against Western power and culture into hatred of its new neighbour'.[27]

There is a deeply sad, albeit widely predicted, irony here. To the beleaguered and persecuted Jews of Central and Eastern Europe, the homeland-state was supposed to bring peace and security. Zionism was meant to answer the Jewish Question, not to have it reformulated and kept open.

CONCLUSION

'In order that the Jewish immigration may be diverted to colonisation of undeveloped countries, it is ... necessary that the immigration to the previous centres become more difficult. This, as a matter of fact, is taking place.' Ber Borochov[1]

The Holocaust was the most terrible event of the twentieth century. The genocide unleashed by Adolf Hitler across Nazi-occupied Europe exceeded in horror even the mass famines inflicted on their own people by Stalin and Mao. In *If This Is a Man*, Primo Levi, a survivor of Auschwitz, explained why:

Then for the first time we became aware that our language lacks words to express this offence, the demolition of man. In a moment, with almost perfect intuition, the reality was revealed to us: we had reached the bottom. It is not possible to sink lower than this; no human condition is more miserable than this, nor could it conceivably be so.

No normal human being will ever be able to identify with Hitler, Himmler, Goebbels, Eichmann and endless others. This dismays us, and at the same time gives us some sense of relief, because perhaps it is desirable that their words (and also, unfortunately, their deeds) cannot be comprehensible to us. They are non-human words and deeds, really counter-human.

'The demolition of man'; 'non-human deeds': what happened to the

Jews involved all mankind. The sufferings of the inhabitants of Palestine before, during and after 1948 are not equivalent. Echoing Edward Said's advice that it would be foolish morally to equate mass dispossession with mass extermination, the Lebanese-born professor Gilbert Achcar argues persuasively that 'the Palestinians cannot ... advisedly and legitimately apply to their own case the superlatives appropriate to the Jewish genocide'.[2]

A different lens is required. The Palestinian experience is to be compared, rather, to the more mundane phenomena of nineteenth- and twentieth-century colonialism. In this context, Israel may be seen as the only European colonial settler state in which the political aspirations of the native population for independence have not been met.

◆

But our concern is with origins. 'As the pogroms in Russia in the 1880s had launched modern Zionism, so the largest pogrom of all, the Holocaust, was to propel the movement, almost instantly, into statehood.'[3] Benny Morris offers, here, more than a haunting parallel. That original launch, along with Zionism's subsequent and increasingly assertive association with British imperial rule over three decades in Palestine, provides the key to understanding the shape, character and fault-lines of the state that the Second World War 'propelled' into being in May 1948.

By this time, the peoples of all the other mandated regions of the former Ottoman Empire had achieved independence, their territories intact. It could be argued that in those cases Article 22 of the League of Nations Covenant – requiring that the 'well-being and development' of the peoples should be furthered, 'until such time as they are able to stand alone' – had been honoured. By contrast, over half of the land of Palestine henceforth defined a Jewish state, even though the resident Arab population retained a majority in the land as a whole, and their leaders had consistently rejected partition.

Thereafter, the events and aftermath of the First Arab-Israeli War finally reversed the demographic balance. Zionist colonisation by patronage and purchase gave way to colonisation by conquest and expulsion, occasioned by considerations of self-defence. Thus by 1952 the remaining Arab population in former mandatory Palestine, approximately 1.2 million, was surpassed by Israel's Jewish population of 1.4 million.[4] Even so, at this time, in continuing proof of the stronger appeal of the USA over Palestine to European victims of anti-Semitic persecution for many decades, there were still more Jews living in New York than in Israel.

As for the British, their commitment to the Zionist cause, first undertaken in the Balfour Declaration thirty years earlier, ended in May 1948 as an enforced retreat from a territory where it lacked all authority and whose peoples it could no longer govern.

◆

Yet, as we have seen, core elements which would determine the future were in place before the Second World War. Who was responsible for the situation in Palestine by the late 1930s? In particular, who was to blame for what the Peel commissioners termed 'the gulf between the races' in that deeply troubled land?

The Nazis, of course, played the critical part. The rapid rise in the number of immigrants into Palestine dates, as we have seen, from 1933; and by 1939 over half of all legal Jewish immigrants into Palestine were Jews from Germany.

Many years earlier, Zionists had the primary role. From the late nineteenth century, Zionist settlement made inroads into Palestine: modest, yet sufficient to arouse an Arab resistance which was never to end. Indeed, Zionism's most significant characteristic was its commitment to Palestine, prioritising this over any alternative place or places where threatened Jews might find a refuge and secure a future. Always obsessive, this commitment became increasingly ruthless. Thus, in the wake of *Kristallnacht* in 1938, David Ben-Gurion interpreted the possibility of various countries admitting Jewish child refugees from Germany as a threat to Zionism. 'If I knew that it was possible to save all the children in Germany by transporting them to England, but only half of them by transporting them to Palestine, I would choose the second.'[5] The observation of historian and former Israeli politician Shlomo Ben-Ami, that 'Jewish catastrophe was the propellant of the Zionist idea and a boost to its prospects,' is sobering.[6] The association of *catastrophe* and *homeland* was not a necessary one; but modern Zionism insisted, from its origins in the 1890s, that it was. Bizarrely served by anti-Semitism in Germany, Zionists in Palestine welcomed Jews fleeing the Nazis. A *yishuv* of over 400,000 people by the mid- to late 1930s was, in the light of the Basel Programme of forty years before, a quite remarkable achievement.

How different it had looked at the Eighteenth World Zionist Congress, when it convened in Prague in August 1933. Hitler had come to power seven months earlier. This was a moment of truth for Zionists. Evidence of weakness abounded: of 4 million American Jews, a mere 80,000 had voted in the elections for this congress; and membership of the American Zionist Federation had declined since the late 1920s. The movement was (still) small and (still) divided. It seems that, even now, with the Nazis installed in Germany – and on the verge of conducting 'the largest pogrom of all' – world Jewry as a whole continued to be less committed to the project for a Jewish national home in Palestine than the British imperial government was.

The key player was indeed Britain. Before 1917, Zionism's prospects were meagre. Only then did it find a Great Power to sponsor it. In adopting the Zionist project, Britain was to give roots to the division, dysfunction and disorder that ensued.

Traditionally, the British Empire had been reluctant to take on poor and undeveloped lands. In the case of Palestine, however, Lloyd George and his colleagues were enthusiastically expansive, confident that Zionist-inspired Jewish immigration would minimise any financial strain and even, in time, come to be welcomed by the Arabs. Yet in Palestine British rule was crippled by a unique political burden. Contradictory promises, first made to two communities in Balfour's Declaration of 1917, had disastrous repercussions.

Before 1914, Jews and Arabs in Palestine had for the most part lived peacefully side by side. Zionism changed that. In 1945, the Arab states encapsulated their assessment of what had occurred since. They were 'second to none in regretting the woes which have been inflicted on the Jews of Europe... But the question of these Jews should not be confused with Zionism, for there can be no greater injustice and aggression than solving the problem of the Jews of Europe by ... inflicting injustice on the Palestine Arabs.'[7] The mandate replaced harmony with rivalry, and condemned Palestine to increasing Arab opposition to Jewish colonisation and eventually revolt against Zionism's British sponsor. By its own agency, the British administration was doomed from the outset. And this is not the wisdom of hindsight. As usual, the truth can be found in contemporary documentary evidence: in, for example, the verdicts of Henry King and Charles Crane, of Major-General Sir Philip Palin and Thomas Haycraft, of Walter Shaw and John Hope Simpson, and of the Peel commissioners. As for the British government itself, expressions of failure may have been partial in the 1939 White Paper; but admission of defeat in Ernest Bevin's announcement of imminent abdication in February 1947 was total.

Zionism had proved a uniquely forceful partner. The relationship between Zionists and the British changed considerably in our period. In 1917, Zionism became the adopted child of British policy-makers who, subsequently victorious in war, had the world at their feet. After twenty years of uneasy liaison, the development of the Jewish national home was unstoppable, with the British no longer in control of events. After ten more years, it was ironic that the forces of armed Zionism, not those of Arab resistance, put pressure on Britain to abandon its administration of Palestine after the Second World War.

Arthur Koestler's often quoted aphorism – that 'one nation solemnly promised to a second nation the country of a third' – points to an exceptional, hybrid, form of British colonial rule. This proved exceptionally unsustainable and also distinctive in its outcome. Whereas in Africa British settlers eventually had to accept indigenous majority rule (in Kenya after Mau Mau, and in Rhodesia after years of liberation war), in Palestine it was Zionists acting in the name of the settlers – Koestler's 'second nation' – who in the end persuaded the British to leave and inherited the land they had colonised.

◆

Britain's responsibility has a further, disturbing, dimension. The British played a decisive part in focusing – on Palestine – the attention of other governments that were looking for an answer to the Jewish Question beyond their own shores. In effect, her own nimbyism legitimised that of many countries who thereby contributed, if for the most part passively, to the situation in Palestine before and after the Second World War.

The US decision to cut immigration via the Johnson-Reed Act of 1924 gave legislative expression to widespread American xenophobia. Its co-sponsor, Representative Albert Johnson, declared 'it has become necessary that the US cease to become an asylum'.[8] The Act came into being two years after the British had written the Balfour Declaration into their mandate for governing Palestine. Theodor Herzl had observed in *The Jewish State* that, whenever Jews moved from places of persecution to other lands, their presence produced an anti-Semitic reaction. This had been borne out in the USA, to which so many Jews had migrated in search of a better, safer, life. A little before Johnson-Reed, the powerful industrialist Henry Ford had published a four-volume set of anti-Semitic booklets, the first titled *The International Jew: The World's Foremost Problem*.

The consequences of 1924, intended or unintended, were to be disastrous for European Jews fleeing persecution or the fear of persecution between the wars. This closing door did more than hinder further Jewish immigration into the USA. It powerfully signalled to numerous other countries that there was no moral objection to their acting in a similar way. From having been a Promised Land for millions of Jews, the USA became inaccessible for all but a relative few – just when refuge was an increasingly urgent necessity.

The Evian Conference of 1938 illustrated an enduring, general, anti-Semitic nimbyism. Jews in any number were not wanted anywhere. The following year, in June 1939, came an illustration of how far US attitudes, in particular, had hardened. The German captain of an ocean liner, MS *St Louis*, tried to find a harbour in Florida for over 900 Jewish refugees from Nazi Germany. US officials withheld landing rights (as did Canadian officials, subsequently). They were all turned away.

In key respects, Edwin Montagu had been right about Zionism. Zionism, he wrote, 'will prove a rallying ground for anti-Semites in every country of the world … When the Jews are told that Palestine is their national home, every country will immediately desire to get rid of its Jewish citizens'. To be sure, as Herzl had done, Montagu overstated his case. America and Britain, for example, did not in fact take steps to rid themselves of their Jewish citizens; but they would block new arrivals. The Zionist project could provide justification for governments 'in every country' to keep their own doors closed, for fear of popular objection, to immigrants who would have augmented their existing Jewish populations – and instead to redirect desperate refugees to Palestine, where Arab objections to their arrival could be collectively disparaged or ignored. Montagu had called Zionism 'a mischievous creed'; one might in turn regard Britain's calculating embrace of Palestine as a mischievous mandate.

In November 1947, the UN partition plan proved the rule about colonialism. Just when Europe's imperial powers came under multiple pressures to prepare their overseas possessions speedily for self-government, the on-going colonisation of Palestine initiated by Zionists in the late nineteenth century was given near universal approval. There are two main explanations for this exceptionalism: one noble, one less so. It occurred, in part, in genuine sympathetic response to the enormity of the suffering of the Jewish people throughout the previous decade. Yet it occurred, too, because 'supporting the creation of the state of Israel was the way that North America, Europe and the Soviet Union solved, on the cheap, the embarrassing problem represented by this multitude of unfortunates whom neither the Americans nor the Europeans nor the USSR wished to take in' – the judgement of Gilbert Achcar.[9] In short, British 1917 nimbyism on a global scale.

Reference has already been made to the British House of Lords debate in July 2017. During its proceedings, one lord, Lord Mendelsohn, placed Britain's pro-Zionist initiative of 1917 in a wider context. 'The Balfour Declaration', he argued, 'should properly be seen as one of the steps in the development of an international consensus, with the leading democracies and powers of the day converging in their support for the establishment of a Jewish state.' A nice example of being right for the wrong reasons. Earlier in the debate, Lord Turnberg had declared: 'Despite their history of anti-Semitism, the French had already given their written approval for a Jewish home in Palestine'. One may query this: 'despite', or 'because of'? The contradiction is more apparent than real.

The eventual birth of Israel was 'facilitated' – made possible, indeed – only through the pro-Zionist response of Britain to earlier, lesser, acts of anti-Semitism, and its own former (and continuing) nimbyism.[10] In answering the Jewish Question as it did in 1917, the Balfour Declaration set a precedent. Zionism was an enduring convenience. It went some way to justify, subsequently, the reluctance of Britain, the US and other governments to offer Jews a home among their own peoples. The modern state of Israel was Arthur Balfour's and David Lloyd George's legacy, as well Herzl's and Hitler's.

◆

It is ironic, if not tragic, that Ireland should offer so many parallels. Historic settler colonialism in Britain's own back yard was itself in turmoil at the very time of the creation of the British mandate for Palestine. Here were two cultures, two identities, two competing claims to the same land, and two 'histories'. Colonialism, here, had bred nationalism. Yet even against the background of Irish uprisings, Lloyd George's government failed to register the probability that Palestine would in time prove, for comparable reasons, ungovernable and unviable as a unitary state.

When studies such as Walter Laqueur's *A History of Zionism* (1972) referred to 'The Arab Problem', they were imitating traditional English school history text books that reserved a late chapter for 'The Irish Problem'. It is a truism that history is written by the victors, but these terms made much more sense the other way round. The Irish had a *British* Problem; and the Arabs in Palestine had a *Zionist* Problem.

For a pertinent Irish nationalist perspective, we may turn to Erskine Childers, the Irish journalist and senior UN civil servant. Having in mind the prevailing attitude of not only the Israeli government but Western governments generally he wrote in 1965, more than fifty years ago, before even the Six Day War, that 'to demand that the victims make peace, while telling the rest of the world – in their hearing – that what was actually done to them simply never happened, is not normally recognised as sound peace-making'.[11]

◆

There was no inevitability about what occurred in November 1917. The Balfour Declaration owed much to a remarkable convergence: the fall of Asquith; a military opportunity in the war against the Ottomans; the association in London of Chaim Weizmann with the British governing establishment; a presumed strategic case for acquiring Palestine among the spoils of war and the readiness of the French to accede to this British priority; a Christian Zionist predisposition among key decision-makers to embrace the national home project (from a mixture of anti-Semitic and philo-Semitic motivations, on top of material calculation); and, not least, the absence of any effective countervailing Arab voice.

In *War and Peace*, Leo Tolstoy famously scoffed at the notion of significant human agency – even Napoleon's – in 'the swarm life of mankind', and he concluded that history is too complex for us to understand. This remains a challenging insight. But it is not persuasive in all cases. The British endorsement of Zionism was not brought about by unstoppable impersonal forces. Rather, we are free to speculate. What if Lloyd George had shed what his biographer Roy Hattersley calls the 'affectionate acquaintance with the Tribes of Israel, which his Baptist boyhood had provided'?[12] What if he had said 'no' to Weizmann?

By contrast, what *followed* the mandate in Palestine was inevitable. After 1922–23 there were only consequences. The mandate, by adopting the Balfour Declaration in full, consolidated pledges which were impossible to fulfil. This is what Sir John Chancellor concluded, impotently witnessing the results of inherited British policy unfold. It is also what the Peel Commission concluded, and this conclusion led them in 1937 – before the onset of the Second World War – to their historic proposal to partition Palestine.

◆

There is a pressing need for knowledge of all perspectives. Edward Said observed: 'Very little is said about what Zionism entailed, for non-Jews who happened to have encountered it.' Yet, for the Palestinian, 'Zionism was somebody else's idea imported into Palestine and for which in a very concrete way he or she was made to pay and suffer.'[13]

Arthur Koestler was Jewish and a Zionist. But he could see what Zionism meant to those who paid the price for its mission, and he could articulate it forcefully. In one of his novels, *Thieves in the Night*, he imagined a formal luncheon in Jerusalem given by a high-ranking British official for local Palestinian dignitaries. When discussion turns to Zionism and Jewish immigration, the editor of a moderate Arab newspaper suddenly addresses his host, thus:

I care not for their hospitals and their schools. This is our country, you understand? We want no foreign benefactors. We want not to be patronised. We want to be left alone, you understand? We want to live our own way, and we want no foreign teachers and no foreign money and no foreign habits and no smiles of condescension and no pat on the shoulder and no arrogance and no shameless women with wriggling buttocks in our holy places... This you can tell them. If they are thrown out in other countries – very bad, very sorry. Very, very sorry – but not our business. If they want to come here – a few of them, maybe a thousand, maybe two thousand – *t'faddal*, welcome. But then know you are guests and know how to behave. Otherwise – to the devil. Into the sea – and *hallass*, finished. This is plain language. You tell them.[14]

The newspaper correspondent Joseph Jeffries hinted at what is needed when, in a passage quoted already, he commented on Herbert Samuel's offer to the Arabs in 1923 of an Arab Agency. 'To this offer,' he wrote in 1939, 'the Arabs gave the reception which we should give to an offer of a "British Agency" in Britain. They dismissed it without thanks.' In effect, Jeffries asks us, whoever we are and whichever country we inhabit, to consider an important counterfactual question. What if it had happened *here*, and to *us*? What if a foreign power had 'facilitated' the settlement, in parts of England, say, of a foreign people whose political leaders were intent on securing it all? How would the English have responded?

Earlier, reference was made to Herzl's diary entry of 4 June 1902. The Jewish Question, he wrote, was 'a matter which only blockheads cannot find crystal clear'. Clarity is in the eye of the critic. There are several grounds, now, as there were in his own day, for challenging some of Herzl's judgements. In response to his frustration and disdain, one might argue that 'only blockheads' fail to see what is 'crystal clear' today. The observation of Palestinian-born historian Walid Khalidi is pertinent here. The Western public's attitude to the Palestine conflict, he wrote in 1971, seems to be characterised by 'a certain aversion to the task of identifying the roles of the protagonists, and an almost grateful acceptance of the topsy-turvy versions put about'.[15]

This is not a zero-sum game: recognition of one people's 'history' does not exclude recognition of another's. The opposite is the case. A prerequisite for moving towards reconciliation is sympathetic imagination, applied on behalf of all involved. These include not only the colonisers – many, of the first generation, traumatised survivors of the Holocaust – but also the colonised and dispossessed.

On a track laid down by the British a century ago, antagonism between Arabs and Jews in Palestine developed with 'a certainty like fate'. Though much has changed in the meantime, there is continuity in the form of the Arab-Israeli conflict. In researching for *The Iron Cage* (2006), Rashid Khalidi studied the memoirs and reports of many British officials in mandatory Palestine. He was repeatedly struck by their 'tone of innocent wonderment at a bizarre and often tragic sequence of events for which these officials rarely if ever acknowledged the slightest responsibility'.[16] It is time, now, for the British (including members of the House of Lords) to properly recognise the seminal part played by their own country, from when it was near the height of its imperial power.

If this is the last colonial problem to survive from an earlier age, it is a uniquely difficult one. Only the central players, Jewish and Arab, can bring about resolution. It would help if Israel shed the poisonous claim that anti-Zionism – or criticism of Israel – is necessarily anti-Semitic; and if the Palestinians found a way of negotiating with one voice. But among external agencies, none is better qualified by history than Britain to help put the Balfour Declaration to rest. While it would be hard for the USA to offer itself as an honest broker, the British government could acknowledge historic responsibility, shed stale partisanship and initiate a renewed search for justice and peace.

AFTERWORD

ON DAVID LLOYD GEORGE,
ANTI-SEMITISM AND ANTI-ZIONISM

Three-quarters of a century after his death, David Lloyd George's reputation is largely positive. The National Library of Wales, Aberystwyth, held an exhibition of his life and work in 2013–14. There was perhaps something equivocal in the title they chose – 'Lloyd George: The Wizard, the Goat, and the Man Who Won the War' – but the emphasis was clear, and the message too: this was a (Welsh) Prime Minister to celebrate, not to criticise. But there is something in addition to his philandering which should be taken as a negative into an overall assessment of the man: Lloyd George's anti-Semitism. His was very much the prejudice of the period, but in the heart and mind of a powerful national leader it had special significance.

His biographers have not dwelt on it, but the evidence lies in their work. As we have seen, Lloyd George was not the first British Prime Minister to try to keep Jews out of Britain: Arthur Balfour did what he could in 1906. Before him, in 1892, Lord Salisbury asked his Ambassador to St. Petersburg – privately, since this was, as he described it, a 'delicate' matter – to ask Russia to prevent Russian Jews from emigrating to Britain.[1] And we may note that in 1903, Colonial Secretary Joseph Chamberlain offered the Zionist movement a refuge in East Africa, not in Britain.

Meanwhile, the Boer War revealed something of the young Lloyd George's anti-Semitism. According to John Grigg – liberal Tory and author of a generally sympathetic multi-volume biography – the Boer War revealed 'a distinct, even a venomous, prejudice against Jewry'. As

Lloyd George put it himself at the time: 'The people we are fighting for, those Uitlanders, are German Jews – 15,000 to 20,000 of them... Pah! Fighting for men of that type!' Most of them, he added, ran away when the trouble started.[2]

In 1911, as a radical Chancellor of the Exchequer in Asquith's government, Lloyd George campaigned for a National Insurance Bill which would provide workers with invalidity and unemployment benefits. Some of his ministers had concerns. These included Edwin Montagu, who expressed his to Lloyd George in person. His doubts were dismissed out of hand and, after he had left, the Chancellor exhibited the anti-Semitism which was 'a usually submerged' feature of his character: 'Dirty coward. Men of that race usually are'.[3]

But the most damning evidence comes from the 1930s, long after his prime ministership. In 1936, Lloyd George visited the 'new' Germany and met Hitler. During the previous year, the Nuremberg Laws had deprived Germans Jews of their citizenship and banned marriage between Germans and Jews. They cannot have escaped Lloyd George's notice. However, there is no reference to them in the *Daily Express* newspaper article he wrote on 17 September 1936. It was as though these harshly discriminatory laws had not been issued. The former British Prime Minister, who had steered through the Balfour Declaration twenty years earlier, wrote instead of 'a general sense of security' and 'a happier Germany. I saw it everywhere'. 'A magnetic and dynamic personality' had accomplished 'this miracle'. 'Catholic and Protestant, Prussian and Bavarian, employer and workman, rich and poor, have been consolidated into one people'.[4] No mention of the Nazis' obsessive racism. Here was the prevalent contemporary indifference to the fate of the Jews – that casual anti-Semitism which proclaimed sympathy but, refusing welcome, advocated participation in the Zionist colonisation of the Palestinians. And here again was Lloyd George's uncritical adulation of the charismatic leader – one comparable with himself? – noted above regarding Venizelos and Weizmann.

A final illustration of Lloyd George's lack of judgement. As we have seen he, along with Balfour, insisted on acquiring Palestine despite numerous warnings that here was a mandate which could not be fulfilled. A comparable lesson ignored – that Arabs in the Middle East did not generally welcome subjection to British hegemony – lay in Palestine/ Transjordan's easterly neighbour, Iraq. The de Bunsen Report of 1915 had highlighted this region, Mesopotamia, as the proper focus of post-war British imperial interest; but during the war it became evident that pre-mandated British imperialism was not welcome. Just as the British were committing themselves to governing Palestine, between July 1920 and February 1921 a great Iraqi Arab uprising 'came perilously close to inflicting a shattering defeat upon the British Empire'.[5]

◆

Since the Second World War, many have mistakenly assumed, or asserted for political purposes, that anti-Zionism – *criticising* Israel or its policies – is somehow anti-Semitic. What is not at all widely recognised is the reverse, at first sight perverse, phenomenon, as illustrated by David Lloyd George: that *before* the Second World War, *supporting* the Zionist project for the creation of Israel was anti-Semitic.

Clarification of the essential distinction between anti-Semitism, on the one hand, and anti-Zionism, on the other, is hard to come by. If you turn to the BBC online, for example, you will be frustrated.[6]

The introduction to the BBC Israel Country Profile carries a single passing reference to Zionism (without explaining what it is).[7] Thereafter, its 'chronology of key events' comprises 84 entries covering the period since Israel was created in 1948, and just 6 before 1948. None of these mentions Zionism at all, let alone the 'key event' in the history of Zionism: the movement's adoption of the Basel Programme in 1897 which advocated 'the promotion on suitable lines of the colonisation of Palestine'.

Another BBC web page, 'Israel-Gaza Violence: The Conflict Explained', is also disappointing.[8] It does not offer any explanations and is most sloppily phrased. For example, after mention of a post-First World War Jewish minority and Arab majority in Palestine, it declares that 'the international community gave Britain the task of establishing a "national home" for Jewish people. For Jews it was their ancestral home, but Palestinian Arabs also claimed the land and opposed the move'. In fact, in 1920 the 'international community' – an anachronistic rendering of the League of Nations – formerly authorised the British to act. This was years after Britain's own declaration of 1917 and the occupation of Palestine in that same year. As for the two peoples mainly concerned, Palestine was indeed for *some* Jews the 'ancestral' home; Palestinian Arabs – around 90 per cent of the population – 'opposed the move' because it was their actual home and had been for centuries.

A third BBC news web page explicitly offers to distinguish anti-Semitism and anti-Zionism.[9] But it does not do so. The article is undermined by its preoccupation with recent Labour Party history; and rather than offer its own grounded definitions, it quotes – without scrutiny, presumably in the search for 'balance' – the differing views of a range of contemporary commentators. Muddle remains.[10] Zionism, it states, 'refers to the movement to create a Jewish state in the Middle East, roughly corresponding to the historical land of Israel, and thus support for the modern state of Israel. Anti-Zionism opposes that.' But it does not explain *why* anti-Zionists are, or were, anti-Zionist. It fails to distinguish between anti-Zionists in the period before the state of Israel was declared, and those who criticise its policies and/or continue to challenge its right to exist today. Regarding the former, it does not mention the historic Zionist commitment to the colonisation of Palestine; nor that Britain supported that project in 1917 initially to consolidate support during the First World War, and thereafter to divert Jewish victims of persecution in Europe away from its own shores; nor that a majority of the world's Jews were opposed to Zionism before the 1930s, and many thereafter; nor, finally, that many of the fiercest critics of Israel today are Jewish.

The distinction may in fact be clearly stated. Semites (in this case, Jews) are *people* who have been born Jewish. To be anti-Semitic is thus outrageous.

By contrast, to be anti-Zionist is to be critical of a *political ideology* that a small minority of Jews chose to adopt around the dawn of the twentieth century, which led to the creation of Israel and which, by association with Israeli policies since, many people (not all of them Jewish) continue to choose to support. To be anti-Zionist is neither inherently reprehensible nor, by definition, anti-Semitic.

Israel is a self-proclaimed Jewish state, founded on a colonising project. It is not surprising, though deplorable, that ignorant people in the West have assumed that it acts for all Jews everywhere. Those who fail to recognise the difference between anti-Zionism (or criticising Israel) and anti-Semitism do so because they do not understand how Israel came into being.

They need to know the history.

ACKNOWLEDGEMENTS

As soon as I turned to this new field, I was driven – initially in a number of directions – by an interest that was self-propelled. However, for the encouragement and guidance that I required to turn this somewhat amorphous fascination into a book with a single, central theme I have a number of people to thank.

First in time and significance, my companions at St Antony's, Oxford, on 15 June 2016. An old friend, Nick Stadlen QC, a Visiting Fellow, had arranged for us to share lunch and conversation with resident Professors Eugene Rogan and Avi Shlaim. That was the stimulus I needed: I started to write. Many thanks, to each of them. Later, Robin Tudge, Hester Vaizey and Ed Thompson were the first who gamely read a full draft and gave priceless commentaries on it. Foremost among others who read parts of even earlier, introductory, text, providing formative feedback at a crucial time are Tom Farrell, Celia Randall, Adam Rothwell, David Smart, Daniel Wolf and Charles Wrangham. Later, Kenneth Wolfe kindly reviewed Chapters 1 and 2. The commitment of Peter Rogers to this project in its early stages was generous and is appreciated.

For encouragement, timely advice and guidance I thank Carne Ross, Karl Sabbagh, Rory Stewart, Norman Stone and Bernard Wasserstein.

Not least, I would like to acknowledge my debt to family members, along with innumerable friends and acquaintances, who convinced me that there remains among the general, non-specialist, reading public not only ignorance of the background to this controversial and still contemporary topic but also a considerable appetite for learning about it. In other words, all those I have encountered who are where I was myself, three or four years ago, in relation to the origins of the Arab-Israeli conflict.

They provide the collective link between the two people to whom this project owes most: Avi Shlaim, who initially suggested I write a book and subsequently insisted that I get it published; and Lynn Gaspard, publisher at Saqi Books, who received my draft book with disarming enthusiasm before, in the nicest possible way, telling me what changes and additions she would like.

To all the above – and, surely, others whom I have failed to acknowledge – my warmest thanks for participating, knowingly or not, momentarily or over the long haul, in this adventure.

BIBLIOGRAPHY

Most of these events occurred not in the Dark Ages but in the late nineteenth and early twentieth centuries. There is no shortage of material. But this is a multi-dimensional subject: contested, controversial ground. E.H. Carr distinguished between facts of history and historical facts: it was the latter that shed light on our past. But who is to say which is which? It is largely a matter of selection.

I have turned to a number of primary sources, many readily accessible online: would that just half a dozen of these were much more widely known! I am of course much indebted to the secondary literature and have sought at times to engage with it.

Note. In recent decades, there has been a bitter and at times personal row among (Jewish) historians of modern Israel, following the emergence of a number of revisionist 'new historians': among them, Benny Morris, Avi Shlaim and Ilan Pappé. These and others challenged a narrative which they regarded as unduly sympathetic to Zionism and to positions adopted by Israel's leaders since the birth of the new state. Efraim Karsh led a fierce counter-attack, accusing the 'new historians' of partisanship, rewriting Israel's history 'in the image of their own choosing' – and doing so by shedding historical professionalism and indulging in a shameful methodology that included 'falsification of documentation'. My academic specialism lying elsewhere, in the history of British colonialism in Africa, for the most part I leave this historiographical fray to others. In any case, the issues most fiercely contested relate to Israel's *birth*, after the Second World War ('transfer' of populations; Hashemite-Zionist collusion; the role of Ernest Bevin), not to the *origins* of Israel, before the Second World War, which has been my main focus. I have mined the works of a number of the historians who come under Karsh's fire, largely for factual content and contemporary quotation. Interpretations are my own.

Primary

1896 *The Jewish State*, Theodor Herzl [https://www.gutenberg.org/files

August 1897 *The Basel Programme* [https://www.jewishvirtuallibrary.org]

1905 *The Hidden Question*, Yitzhak Epstein [https://www.balfourproject.org]

January 1915 *The Future of Palestine*, Sir Herbert Samuel [https://en.wikisource.org]

June 1915 *Report* of the de Bunsen Committee of Imperial Defence: Asiatic Turkey, National Archives CAB 42/3/12

24 October 1915 *Letter* from Sir Henry McMahon to Sharif Hussein [https://www.jewishvirtuallibrary.org]

May 1916 *The Sykes-Picot Agreement* [http://avalon.law.yale.edu]

August 1917 *Memorandum on the Anti-Semitism of the Present (British) Government*, Edwin Montagu [https://www.jewishvirtuallibrary.org]

2 November 1917 *The Balfour Declaration* [https://www.jewishvirtuallibrary.org]

8 January 1918 *Fourteen Points*, Woodrow Wilson

1918 *What is Zionism?*, Chaim Weizmann [London: Zionist Organisation, 1918]

April 1919 *Covenant* of the League of Nations

August 1919 *Report* of the King-Crane Commission [https://wwi.lib.byu.edu]

April 1920 *Report* of the Court of Enquiry (Nabi Musa), General Palin [https://en.wikisource.org]

August 1921 *Reports* of the Commission of Inquiry into Disturbances in May 1921, Thomas Haycraft [https://ecf.org.il]

4 July 1922 *British Mandate for Palestine* [https://www.jewishvirtuallibrary.org]

1922 *The Handbook of Palestine* [London: Macmillan, 1922]

June 1922 *Palestine, Correspondence with the Arab Delegation and the Zionist Organisation*, Statement of Policy by HMG [White Paper, Winston Churchill] [https://israeled.org; http://avalon.law.yale.edu]

4 November 1923 *The Iron Wall*, Vladimir Ze'ev Jabotinsky https://www.jewishvirtuallibrary.org]

October 1930 *Palestine*, Statement of Policy by HMG [White Paper, Lord Passfield], [https://www.jewishvirtuallibrary.org]

1928–1931 *Papers* of Sir John Chancellor [Bodleian Library, Oxford]

13 February 1931 *Letter* from Ramsay MacDonald to Chaim Weizmann, aka 'The Black Letter' [https://www.jewishvirtuallibrary.org]

July 1937 *Mandates Palestine Report* of the Palestine Royal Commission, Earl Peel [https://www.jewishvirtuallibrary.org]

21 May 1939 Palestine, Statement of Policy by HMG [White Paper, Malcolm MacDonald] [https://www.jewishvirtuallibrary.org]

11 May 1942 Biltmore Programme [https://www.jewishvirtuallibrary.org]

3 September 1947 *Report* of the United Nations Special Committee on Palestine (UNSCOP), [https://www.jewishvirtuallibrary.org]

14 May 1948 *The Declaration of the Establishment of the State of Israel*, Israel Ministry of Foreign Affairs [https://www.knesset.gov.il/docs]

Secondary Sources

Achcar, Gilbert, *The Arabs and the Holocaust: The Arab-Israeli War of Narratives*, London, Saqi Books, 2010

Avineri, Shlomo, *Herzl: Theodor Herzl and the Founding of the Jewish State*, London, Weidenfeld & Nicolson, 2013

Baddiel, David, *Jews Don't Count*, London, TLS Books, 2021

Barbour, Nevill, *Nisi Dominus: A Survey of the Palestine Controversy*, London, George Harrap, 1946

Barr, James (ed.), *A Line in the Sand: Britain, France and the Struggle that shaped the Middle East*, London, New York; Simon & Schuster, 2011

Ben-Ami, Shlomo, *Scars of War, Wounds of Peace: The Israel-Arab Tragedy*, London, Weidenfeld & Nicolson/Phoenix, 2005

Berg, A. Scott, *Wilson*, London, New York; Simon & Schuster, 2013

Blum, John M., *The National Experience: A History of the United States of America*, Belmont CA, Wadsworth, 1993

Cesarani, David, *Final Solution: The Fate of the Jews 1933–49*, London, Pan, 2017

Chomsky, Noam and Pappé, Ilan, *On Palestine*, London, Penguin, 2015

Cohen, Hillel, *Army of Shadows: Palestinian Collaboration with Zionism, 1917–1948*, Berkeley, Los Angeles, London; University of California, 2008

Cohen, Hillel, *Year Zero of the Arab-Israeli Conflict: 1929*, Waltham MA, Brandeis University Press, 2015

Cohen, Michael J., *The Origins and Evolution of the Arab-Zionist Conflict*, Berkeley, Los Angeles, London; University of California, 1987

Cohn-Sherbok, Dan & El-Alami, Dawoud, *The Palestine-Israeli Conflict*, Oxford, Oneworld, 2001

Dalyell, Tam, *Dick Crossman: A Portrait*, London, Weidenfeld & Nicolson, 1989

Dugdale, Blanche, *Arthur James Balfour* (vol.1), London, Hutchinson, 1936

Flapan, Simha, *The Birth of Israel: Myths and Realities*, New York, Pantheon Books, 1987

Flapan, Simha, *Zionism and the Palestinians*, London, Croom Helm, 1979

Geifman, Anna (ed.), *Russia under the Last Tsar*, Malden MA, Oxford; Blackwell, 1999

Gelvin, James L., *The Israel-Palestine Conflict: One Hundred Years of War*, Cambridge, Cambridge University Press, 2006

Gilbert, Martin (ed.), *Lloyd George*, New Jersey, Prentice-Hall, 1968

Gilbert, Martin, *Never Again: A History of the Holocaust*, London, HarperCollins, 2000

Gorodetsky, Gabriel (ed.), *The Maisky Diaries*, Newhaven, Yale University Press, 2016

Grigg, John, *The Young Lloyd George*, London, Eyre Methuen, 1973

Halper, Jeff, *Decolonising Israel, Liberating Palestine*, London, Pluto Press, 2021

Hattersley, Roy, *David Lloyd George: The Great Outsider*, London, Abacus, 2010

Hertzberg, Arthur (ed.), *The Zionist Idea: A Historical Analysis and Reader*, New York, Temple/Atheneum, [1959] 1982

Hobsbawm, Eric, *Interesting Times: A Twentieth-Century Life*, London, Penguin/Allen Lane, 2002

Hourani, Albert, *A History of the Arab Peoples*, London, Faber and Faber, 1991

Howe, Daniel Walker, *What Hath God Wrought: The Transformation of America, 1815–1848*, Oxford, Oxford University Press, 2007

Howell, Georgina, *Queen of the Desert: The Extraordinary Life of Gertrude Bell*, London, Pan/Macmillan, 2006

Hughes, Matthew, 'Lawlessness was the Law: British Armed Forces, the Legal System and the Repression of the Arab Revolt in Palestine, 1936–1939', in Rory Miller (ed.), *Britain, Palestine and Empire: The Mandate Years*, Farnham, England; Burlington VT, USA; Ashgate, 2010

Isaacson, Walter, *Einstein: His Life and Universe*, London, New York; Pocket Books, 2007

Jeffries, Joseph, *Palestine: The Reality. The Inside Story of the Balfour Declaration, 1917–1938*, Northampton MA, USA, Olive Branch Press; Bloxham, Oxford, Skyscraper, [1939] 2017

Karsh, Efraim, *Fabricating Israeli History: The 'New Historians'*, London, Portland; Frank Cass, 2000

Khalidi, Rashid, *The Hundred Years' War on Palestine*, London, Profile Books, 2020

Khalidi, Rashid, *The Iron Cage: The Story of the Palestinian Struggle for Statehood*, Oxford, Oneworld, 2006

Khalidi, Walid (ed.), *From Haven to Conquest: Readings in Zionism and the Palestine Problem until 1948*, Beirut, Washington DC; Institute of Palestine Studies, 1971

Khoury, Philip S., *Syria and the French Mandate: The Politics of Arab Nationalism, 1920–1945*, London, I.B. Tauris, 1987

Klein, Menachem, *Lives in Common: Arabs and Jews in Jerusalem, Jaffa and Hebron*, London, Hurst, 2014

Klier, John D., 'The Jews', in Edward Acton (ed.), *Critical Companion to the Russian Revolution 1914–1921*, London, Arnold, 1997

Klug, Brian, *Being Jewish and Doing Justice: Bringing Argument to Life*, London, Vallentine Mitchell, 2011 [https://www.balfourproject.org/the-other-arthur-balfour]

Koestler, Arthur, *Bricks to Babel: Selected Writings*, London, Picador, 1980

Krämer, Gudrun, *A History of Palestine: From the Ottoman Conquest to the Founding of the State of Israel*, Princeton, Princeton University Press, 2011

La Guardia, Anton, *Holy Land, Unholy War: Israelis and Palestinians*, London, John Murray, 2001

Laqueur, Walter, *A History of Zionism*, London, Weidenfeld & Nicolson, 1972

Lebrecht, Norman, *Genius and Anxiety: How Jews Changed the World 1847–1947*, London, Oneworld, 2019

Lipstadt, Deborah, *Antisemitism: Here and Now*, London, Scribe, 2019

Lockman, Zachary, 'Railway Workers and Relational History: Arabs and Jews in British-ruled Palestine', in Ilan Pappé (ed.), *The Israel/Palestine Question:*

Rewriting Histories, London, New York; Routledge, 1999

Lloyd George, David, *Memoirs of the Peace Conference*, Vol. II, Newhaven, Yale University Press, 1939

Lokshin, Aleksandr, 'The Bund in the Russian-Jewish Historical Landscape', in Anna Geifman (ed.), *Russia under the Last Tsar: Opposition and Subversion, 1894–1917*, Oxford, Malden MA; Blackwell, 1999

Luke, Harry Charles and Keith-Roach, Edward (eds), *The Handbook of Palestine*, London, Macmillan, 1922

MacMillan, Margaret, *Peacemakers: Six Months that Changed the World*, London, John Murray, 2002

Mann, John (ed.), *Anti-Semitism: The Oldest Hatred*, London, Oxford, New York; Bloomsbury, 2015

Masalha, Nur, *Expulsion of the Palestinians: The Concept of 'Transfer' in Zionist Political Thought, 1882–1948*, Beirut: Institute for Palestine Studies, 1992

Mattar, Philip, *The Mufti of Jerusalem: Al-Hajj Amin Al-Husayni and the Palestinian National Movement*, New York, Columbia University Press, 1988

McHugo, John, *A Concise History of the Arabs*, London, Saqi Books, 2014

Mearsheimer, John J. and Walt, Stephen M., *The Israel Lobby and US Foreign Policy*, London, New York; Penguin, 2007

Miller, Rory, 'Lawlessness was the Law: British Armed Forces, the Legal System and the Repression of the Arab Revolt in Palestine, 1936–1939', in Miller (ed.) *Britain, Palestine and Empire*

Miller, Rory (ed.), *Britain, Palestine and Empire: The Mandate Years*, Farnham, England; Burlington VT, USA; Ashgate, 2010

Monroe, Elizabeth, *Britain's Moment in the Middle East, 1914–1956*, London, Methuen, 1963

Montgomery, Field Marshall Bernard, *Memoirs*, London, Collins, 1958

Morgan, Kenneth O., *David Lloyd George*, Cardiff, University of Wales Press, 1981

Morris, Benny, *Righteous Victims: A History of the Zionist-Arab Conflict, 1881–1999*, New York, Alfred A. Knopf, 1999

Nafi, Basheer M., *Arabism, Islamism and the Palestine Question 1908–1941: A Political History*, Reading, England, Ithaca Press, 1998

O. Morgan, Kenneth, *Lloyd George*, London, Weidenfeld and Nicolson, 1974

Oz, Amos, *A Tale of Love and Darkness*, London, Vintage, 2005

Pappé, Ilan (ed.), *The Israel/Palestine Question: Rewriting Histories*, London, New York; Routledge, 1999

Pappé, Ilan, *The Making of the Arab-Israeli Conflict, 1947–1951*, London, New York; I.B. Tauris, 2015

Pappé, Ilan, *Ten Myths about Israel*, London, Verso, 2017

Pedersen, Susan, 'The Impact of League Oversight on British Policy in Palestine', in Rory Miller, (ed.), *Britain, Palestine and Empire: The Mandate Years*, Farnham, England; Burlington VT, USA; Ashgate, 2010

Peres, Shimon, *Ben-Gurion: A Political Life*, New York, Nextbook/Random House, 2011

Regan, Bernard, *The Balfour Declaration: Empire, the Mandate and Resistance in Palestine*, London, New York; Verso, 2017

Robson, Laura, *Colonialism and Christianity in Mandate Palestine*, Austin, University of Texas Press, 2012

Rogan, Eugene, *The Arabs: A History*, London, Penguin, 2010

Rogan, Eugene and Shlaim, Avi (eds), *The War for Palestine: Rewriting the History of 1948*, Cambridge, Cambridge University Press, 2001

Rose, John, *The Myths of Zionism*, London, New York; Pluto, 2004

Rose, Norman, *Chaim Weizmann*, New York, Viking/Penguin, 1986

Rutledge, Ian, *Enemy on the Euphrates: The Battle for Iraq 1914–1921*, London, Saqi Books, 2014

Said, Edward W., *The Question of Palestine*, New York, Vintage, 1992

Sand, Shlomo, *The Invention of the Jewish People*, London, New York; Verso, 2009

Schneer, Jonathan, *The Balfour Declaration: The Origins of the Arab-Israeli Conflict*, London, New York, Berlin, Sydney; Bloomsbury, 2010

Segev, Tom, *One Palestine, Complete: Jews and Arabs under the British Mandate*, London, Abacus, 2001

Shavit, Ari, *My Promised Land: The Triumph and Tragedy of Israel*, Melbourne, London; Scribe, 2014

Shlaim, Avi, *War and Peace in the Middle East: A Concise History*, London, Penguin, 1995

Shlaim, Avi, *The Iron Wall: Israel and the Arab World*, London, Penguin, 2014

Shlaim, Avi, *Israel and Palestine: Reappraisals, Revisions, Refutations*, London, New York; Verso, 2009

Sizer, Stephen, *Christian Zionism*, Leicester, Intervarsity Press, 2004

Stanislawski, Michael, *Zionism: A Very Short Introduction*, Oxford, Oxford University Press, 2017

Stein, Kenneth W., *The Land Question in Palestine, 1917–1939*, Chapel Hill, London; University of North Carolina, 1984

Stone, Norman, *Turkey: A Short History*, London, Thames & Hudson, 2012

Sykes, Christopher Simon, *The Man who Created the Middle East: A Story of Empire, Conflict and the Sykes-Picot Agreement*, London, William Collins, 2016

Taylor, A.J.P., *English History 1914–1945*, Oxford, Oxford University Press, 1965

Vermes, Géza, *Jesus the Jew*, London, SCM, 1983

Vital, David, *A People Apart: A Political History of the Jews in Europe, 1789–1939*, Oxford, Oxford University Press, 1999

Wasserstein, Bernard, *Britain and the Jews of Europe 1939–1945*, London and New York, Leicester University Press, 1979

Wasserstein, Bernard, *The British in Palestine: The Mandatory Government and the Arab-Jewish Conflict 1917–1929*, Oxford, Blackwell, 1991

Wasserstein, Bernard, *Israel and Palestine: Why They Fight and Can They Stop?*, London, Profile, 2003

Weinstock, Nathan, *Zionism: False Messiah*, London, Pluto, 1989

Weisbord, Robert G., *African Zion*, Philadelphia, The Jewish Publication Society of America, 1968

Weizmann, Chaim, *What is Zionism?*, London, The Zionist Organisation, 1918

NOTES

Introduction

1. *The Times*, 30–31 August 2021.
2. Chaim Herzog, Israel's Ambassador to the United Nations: address to the General Assembly of the United Nations, 10 November 1975.
3. David Cesarani, *Final Solution: The Fate of the Jews 1933–49*, London. Pan, 2017, p. 777.
4. From the King-Crane Commission Report, 1919: see Chapter 4.
5. House of Lords Debates, 5 July 2017, vol. 783, cols. 948–72. I am grateful to David Natzler for providing me with a transcript.

Chapter One

1. Yitzhak Epstein, *The Hidden Question*, 1905: https://www. balfourproject.org 24/2/19.
2. Ahad Ha'am, formerly Asher Ginsberg, quoted in Walter Laqueur, *A History of Zionism*, London, Weidenfeld & Nicolson, 1972, p. 107.
3. Theodor Herzl, *The Jewish State,* pp. 16, 19: https://www.gutenberg. org/files 25/2/19.
4. Quoted in Michael J. Cohen, *The Origins and Evolution of the Arab-Zionist Conflict*, Berkeley, Los Angeles, London; University of California, 1987, p. 39.
5. Herzl's pamphlet did not mark the birth of Zionism itself. Moses Hess was among earlier theoreticians of Zionism: his *Rome and Jerusalem,* 1862, 'contains the seed of the entire Zionist enterprise' (Weinstock, p. 37). Nonetheless, Herzl was so dynamic in following up his own publication, and his congress, that it is conventional to acknowledge his lead role in the story of modern political Zionism.
6. This, first, World Zionist Congress in Basel founded the World Zionist Organisation, of which Chaim Weizmann was to be President, 1921–31 and 1935–46. Following 1897, annual or biennial congresses were held.
7. https://www.jewishvirtuallibrary.org 24/2/19.

8. In adopting the term 'Zionism', its founders focused on Palestine, and especially on Jerusalem, Judaism's holiest city. Here according to the Hebrew Bible stood the First Temple, built by King Solomon, and also the Second Temple, destroyed by the Romans in 70 ad. Depending on context, 'Zion' itself could refer to Jerusalem, or to the holiest mountain of Jerusalem, or even to the land of Israel.

9. Herzl, p. 12.

10. Ari Shavit, *My Promised Land: The Triumph and Tragedy of Israel*, Melbourne, London; Scribe, 2014, p. 4. One-and-a-half million lived in the USA, and up to 1 million in North Africa, the Mediterranean and Asia.

11. In 1894, Captain Alfred Dreyfus, a young officer in the French army, was falsely accused of passing military secrets to the Germans. Convicted of treason, he was sentenced to life imprisonment. Within two years, it was clear that another officer was the real culprit; but the military continued with the framing of (the Jewish) Dreyfus until, after several years of campaigning by powerful figures in politics, journalism and the arts (including Emile Zola), Dreyfus was fully exonerated in 1906. The Dreyfus Affair both revealed and caused deep and lasting division in France, between the pro-army, mostly Catholic, anti-Semitic right and the anticlerical, republican left.

12. Laqueur, p. 17.

13. David Vital, *A People Apart: A Political History of the Jews in Europe, 1789–1939*, Oxford, Oxford University Press, 1999, pp. 125–26.

14. I am indebted to Dr Kenneth Wolfe, whose grandparents were deported from Berlin to Estonia in September 1942, for this observation from his unpublished manuscript *A Holocaust Legacy*.

15. The title of his pamphlet, *Auto-Emancipation*, implied Pinsker's deep scepticism regarding assistance from sympathetic gentiles.

16. Herzl, p. 3.

17. Chaim Weizmann, *What is Zionism?*, London: The Zionist Organisation, 1918, pp. 9–11.

18. Weizmann, p. 3. Italics added.

19. Quoted in Norman Rose, *Chaim Weizmann*, New York, Viking/Penguin, 1986, pp. 33, 77, 85.

20. Amos Oz, *A Tale of Love and Darkness*, London, Vintage, 2005, p. 186.

21. Shavit, p. 5. Italics added.

22. The Italian *Risorgimento* had provided one inspiration for Zionism.

23. Herzl, pp. 16, 19, 52. Italics added.

24. Quoted in Gilbert Achcar, *The Arabs and the Holocaust: The Arab-Israeli War of Narratives*, London, Saqi, 2010, p. 22.

25. Norman Stone, *Turkey, A Short History*, London, Thames & Hudson, 2012, p. 128.

26. Quoted in Laqueur, p. 51. Such an approach was actually adopted, but the Sultan did not take the bait.

27. Arthur Hertzberg (ed), *The Zionist Idea: A Historical Analysis and Reader*, New York, Temple/Atheneum, [1959] 1982, pp. 16, 17. In Judeo-Christian teachings, messianism entails awaiting salvation through the coming of a messiah, anointed by God. More generally it may describe any sense of special destiny: of future participation in an anticipated, beneficial and transformational change.

28. Hertzberg, p. 21.

29. Hertzberg, p. 46. Italics original.

30. *Aliyah* = a wave of Jewish immigration into Palestine. These are conventionally divided according to timing and character: first, 1882; second, 1904–14; third, 1918–23; fourth, 1924–28; fifth, 1929–39.

31. *The Hidden Question* is the source of the extracts which follow.

32. Shavit, pp. 12, 13.

33. Norman Rose, p. 39.

34. Quoted in Vital, p. 623.

35. Quoted in John Rose, *The Myths of Zionism*, London, New York; Pluto, 2004, p. 106.

36. See Aleksandr Lokshin, 'The Bund in the Russian-Jewish Historical Landscape', in Anna Geifman (ed), *Russia under the Last Tsar: Opposition and Subversion, 1894–1917*, Oxford, Malden MA: Blackwell, 1999. This adoption of Yiddish compares with the adoption of Hebrew as the national language for Zionism in Palestine.

37. Quoted in Norman Rose, p. 60.

38. Klier, p. 700.

39. Quoted in Anton La Guardia, *Holy Land, Unholy War: Israelis and Palestinians*, London, John Murray, 2001, p. 74.

40. Laqueur, p. 213.

41. Benny Morris, *Righteous Victims: A History of the Zionist-Arab Conflict, 1881–1999*, New York, Alfred A. Knopf, 1999, pp. 17, 18.

42. Quoted in Shimon Peres, *Ben-Gurion: A Political Life*, New York: Nextbook/Random House, 2011, pp. 20, 21.

43. Ilan Pappe, *The Making of the Arab-Israeli Conflict, 1947–1951*, London, New York; I.B. Tauris, 2015, p. 1.

44. Quoted in Morris, p. 61.

45. Kenneth W. Stein, *The Land Question in Palestine, 1917–1939*, Chapel Hill, London; University of North Carolina, 1984, p. 85.

46. Quoted in Norman Rose, p. 106.

47. *The Hidden Question.*

48. Borochov himself chose to emigrate not to Palestine but to the USA.

49. 'Our Platform', 1906, quoted in Herzberg, p. 361.

50. Morris, p. 53.

51. Peres, p. 15.

52. Quoted in Peres, p. 25.

53. Quoted in Shlomo Sand, *The Invention of the Jewish People*, London, New York; Verso, 2009, p. 259.

54. Margaret MacMillan, *Peacemakers: Six Months that Changed the World*, London, John Murray, 2002, p. 423.

55. Laqueur, p. 213.

56. Quoted in Bernard Wasserstein, *Israel and Palestine: Why They Fight and Can They Stop?*, London, Profile, 2003, p. 32.

57. Quoted in Laqueur, p. 211.

58. Morris, p. 47.

59. Herzl, p. 18. Italics added.

60. Quoted in Norman Rose, p. 108.

61. Quoted in La Guardia, p. 78.

62. Laqueur, p. 212.

63. Morris, pp. 59, 60.

64. Quoted in La Guardia, p. 101.

65. Quoted in Laura Robson, *Colonialism and Christianity in Mandate Palestine*, Austin, University of Texas Press, 2012, p. 32.

66. Quoted in 'Najib Nassar', https://www.paljourneys.org 22/11/18.

67. Quoted in Morris, p. 28.

68. Quoted in Morris, p. 57.

69. Rashid Khalidi, *The Iron Cage: The Story of the Palestinian Struggle for Statehood*, Oxford: Oneworld, 2006, p. 102.

70. Quoted in Morris, p. 64.

71. Nathan Weinstock, *Zionism: False Messiah*, London, Pluto, 1969, p. 84.

72. Basheer M. Nafi, *Arabism, Islamism and the Palestine Question 1908–*

1941: A Political History, Reading, England, Ithaca Press, 1998, pp. 61, 62. These elections followed those of 1908 and 1912; under the Ottomans, Syrians/Palestinians had a representative voice.

73. Shlaim, *The Iron Wall: Israel and the Arab World*, London: Penguin, 2014, p. 5.

74. Herzl sought a charter comparable with the charters awarded by the British at around this time to Cecil Rhodes, for the exploitation of Southern Africa, and George Goldie, for the exploitation of West Africa. He was not to succeed. Nonetheless, the Balfour Declaration of 1917 was a kind of a charter, and has been described as Zionism's 'Magna Carta'.

75. Weinstock, p. 38.

76. Michael Cohen, p. 35.

77. Quoted in Laqueur, p. 115.

78. Quoted in Laqueur, p. 108.

79. Quoted in Norman Rose, p. 103.

80. Quoted in Norman Rose, p. 71.

81. Quoted in Edward Said, *The Question of Palestine*, New York, Vintage, 1992, p. 13.

82. Quoted in Peres, p. 19.

Chapter Two

1. Hertzberg, p. 15.

2. Michael Cohen, p. 32.

3. Gudrun Krämer, *A History of Palestine: From Ottoman Conquest to the Founding of Israel*, Princeton, Princeton University Press, 2011, p. 138.

4. Bernard Wasserstein, *The British in Palestine: The Mandatory Government and the Arab-Jewish Conflict, 1917–1929*, Oxford, Blackwell, 1991, p. 4 f.n.

5. Quoted in Morris, p. 64.

6. Note Avi Shlaim's necessary and persuasive condemnation, a century later, of 'the propagandist ploy of equating anti-Zionism with anti-Semitism' in discourse regarding Israel: *Israel and Palestine*, p. 371.

7. Quoted in Joseph Jeffries, *Palestine: The Reality. The Inside Story of the Balfour Declaration, 1917–1938*, Northampton MA, USA, Olive Branch Press; Bloxham, Oxford, Skyscraper, [1939], 2017, p. 155.

8. 'Memorandum on the anti-Semitism of the (present) British

Government', August 1917 [jewishvirtuallibrary.org]

9. Quoted in Jeffries, p. 155.

10. Oz, pp. 2, 11.

11. 'Memorandum'. Italics added.

12. Quoted in James Gelvin, *The Israeli-Palestine Conflict: One Hundred Years of War*, Cambridge, Cambridge University Press, 2006, pp. 59, 60. Italics added.

13. Weizmann, p. 4.

14. Sand, p. 252.

15. 'The children of Israel' were to give 'every man a ransom for his soul unto the Lord'. As for Moses, 'thou shalt take the atonement money ... and shalt appoint it for the service of the tabernacle of the congregation: that it may be a memorial unto the children of Israel before the Lord, to make an atonement for your souls'.

16. Laqueur, p. 512.

17. Weizmann, p. 16.

18. Sand, p. 188.

19. https://www.knesset.gov.il/docs 24/2/19.

20. Sand, pp. 145, 146. The Parthian Empire covered, roughly, today's Iran and Iraq.

21. Shlomo Sand devotes a sixty-page chapter of *The Invention of the Jewish People* to 'The Invention of the Exile'.

22. Sand, p. 135.

23. Quoted in Laqueur, p. 414.

24. Herzl, p. 3.

25. Shavit, pp. 4, 5.

26. John Rose, p. 114.

27. Eric Hobsbawm, *Interesting Times: A Twentieth Century Life*, London, Penguin/Allen Lane, 2002, p. 418.

28. Quoted in Gelvin, p. 44.

29. Quoted in Tom Segev, *One Palestine, Complete: Jews and Arabs under the British Mandate*, London, Abacus, 2001, p. 92.

30. Palestine Arab Delegation to Secretary of State, 17 June 1922, pp. 21–28 [israeled.org]

31. Sand, p. 71.

32. Herzl, p. 43.

33. Hertzberg, p. 74.

34. Quoted in La Guardia, p. 74.

35. Quoted in Hertzberg, p. 35.

36. Peres, p. 49.

37. Quoted in John Mearsheimer and Stephen Walt, *The Israel Lobby and US Foreign Policy*, London, New York; Penguin, 2007, p. 96. Italics added.

38. In this light, late-nineteenth-century Zionism was advocating a *re-colonisation* of Palestine.

39. Quoted in Norman Rose, p. 85.

40. Peres, pp. 51, 59.

41. The fusion has continued. In 1962, the Supreme Court of Israel ruled that a Jewish individual's decision to adopt a different religion was not just an act of taking on another religion but of placing oneself outside the bounds of Jewish nationhood.

42. Like assimilation, 'the right of return' spreads across a spectrum: from, say, Rastafarians on the one hand (seeing themselves as a chosen people of God, in exile from their African homeland) to, say, the entire population of Diego Garcia (forcibly removed by the UK and the USA between 1968 and 1973 to accommodate an American military base in the Indian Ocean). We may also note here that not every religious community – or 'nation' – has a homeland, or has felt the need for one: for example, up to 20 million Ismailis thrive today in over twenty-five different countries.

43. Quoted in Stephen Sizer, *Christian Zionism*, Leicester, Intervarsity Press, 2004, p. 59.

44. Jewish characters were not usually so positively portrayed in nineteenth-century English novels. *Daniel Deronda* came out forty years after Fagin appeared in Charles Dickens's *Oliver Twist*, though only one year after Augustus Melmotte figured prominently in Anthony Trollope's *The Way We Live Now*.

Chapter Three

1. Edwin Montagu: Memorandum, August 1917.

2. Nevill Barbour, *Nisi Dominus: A Survey of the Palestine Controversy*, London, George Harrap, 1946, p. 5.

3. The Future of Palestine: CAB 37/123/43, National Archive, Kew https://en.wikisource.org 25/2/19.

4. Norman Rose, p. 162.

5. The National Archives: CAB 42/3/12.

6. Italics added.

7. Jonathan Schneer, *The Balfour Declaration: The Origins of the Arab-Israeli Conflict*, London, New York, Berlin, Sydney; Bloomsbury, 2010, p. 371.

8. The Sharif was steward of the holy cities of Mecca and Medina and the surrounding Hejaz (the western region of today's Saudi Arabia). He claimed to speak for the Arab nation; his son Faisal was to lead the Arab Revolt against the Turks, supported by the British; and Faisal was briefly King of Greater Syria, in 1920, before being ousted by the French and installed by the British as ruler of Iraq.

9. Eugene Rogan, *The Arabs: A History*, London, Penguin, 2010, p. 187. The others were the Sykes-Picot Agreement (1916) and the Balfour Declaration (1917).

10. Britain would 'guarantee the Holy Places' of Jerusalem.

11. Jeffries, pp. 80–81, 91.

12. Although the post-war settlement did incorporate a comparable 'line in the sand' which separated the French mandated territories of Syria and Lebanon from Britain's Palestine and Iraq, there were important differences by the time the same two powers, by now victorious, had negotiated again, at length and in detail, in 1919 and 1920.

13. The area did not extend far enough south to include Hebron (south of Jerusalem), in today's West Bank: a place of important burial sites, closely associated with the story of Abraham, and regarded as Judaism's second holiest city.

14. De Bunsen, paragraph 7. Italics added.

15. Quoted in Morris, p. 72.

16. Barr, p. 2.

17. Schneer, p. 368.

18. Quoted in Norman Rose, p. 159.

19. https://www.jewishvirtuallibrary.org 24/2/19.

20. Quoted in Monroe, p. 34.

21. Quoted in Morris, p. 74.

22. Michael Stanislawski, *Zionism: A Very Short Introduction*, Oxford, Oxford University Press, 2017, pp. 40, 41.

23. Norman Rose, p. 139.

24. A.J.P. Taylor, *English History 1914–1945*, Oxford, Oxford University Press, 1965, p. 5.

25. Quoted in Norman Rose, p. 169.

26. Quoted in Monroe, p. 38.

27. David Lloyd George, *Memoirs of the Peace Conference*, Vol II, Newhaven, Yale University Press, 1939. pp. 721–26. There are generic reasons for scepticism towards political memoirs as evidence. There are particular reasons in this case. They were published long – twenty years – after the events described; and they are what Lloyd George, as the key actor, chose to present then in justification of what he had done. Yet his rambling passages reveal something of value, the more so perhaps as they come across as a stream of consciousness – 'improvised' – rather than as a laboriously worked and reworked text.

28. Quoted in Sizer, p. 62.

29. Laqueur, pp. 182, 193.

30. Lloyd George, p. 723.

31. Quoted in Barbour, p. 136.

32. Quoted in Monroe, pp. 37, 38.

33. Barr, p. 35.

34. Quoted in Roy Hattersley, *David Lloyd George: The Great Outsider*, London, Abacus, 2010, p. 455.

35. Quoted in Morris, p. 74.

36. Lloyd George, *Memoirs*. We cannot know if either power would actually have made a comparable pledge; nor if, having won the war, chosen to honour and implement it. Thus there are insufficient grounds for arguing that the British decision was inevitable from the point of view of imperial rivalry.

37. MacMillan, pp. 357, 362.

38. Kenneth Morgan, *David Lloyd George*, Cardiff, University of Wales Press, 1981, p. 87.

39. MacMillan, p. 363.

40. Quoted in Norman Rose, p. 327.

41. Lloyd George, *Memoirs*.

42. Quoted in Norman Rose, p. 145. Weizmann is indeed commemorated at Rehovot, south of Tel Aviv, by the Institute of Science that bears his name; and also at his former home, which houses a Weizmann Archive.

43. Lloyd George asked Weizmann to accept an honour from the King. Weizmann declined. Pressed by the Prime Minister, Weizmann replied that he would like support for the cause of Zionism. Lloyd George wrote in his memoirs: 'That was the fount and origin of the famous

declaration about the National Home for the Jews in Palestine.' But we may demur. Not even Lloyd George at his most mercurial was likely to have made such a decision – and carried his Cabinet – on so flimsy a ground.

44. Tam Dalyell, *Dick Crossman: A Portrait*, London, Weidenfeld & Nicolson, 1989, pp. 68–70.
45. Quoted in Norman Rose, p. 161.
46. Quoted in Norman Rose, p. 144.
47. Quoted in Macmillan, p. 424.
48. Schneer, p. 366.
49. Blanche Dugdale, *Arthur James Balfour* (vol. 1), London, Hutchinson, 1936, p. 433.
50. MacMillan, p. 424. Balfour failed to hold his seat, Manchester East, in the Liberal landslide.
51. Jeffries, p. 161.
52. Walid Khalidi (ed), *From Haven to Conquest: Readings in Zionism and the Palestine Problem until 1948*, Beirut, Washington DC; Institute of Palestine Studies, 1971, p. 112.
53. Quoted in W. Khalidi, p. 196.
54. Quoted in Monroe, p. 65.
55. Quoted in Michael Cohen, p. 49.
56. Sykes, pp. 267, 83.
57. Sykes, p. 268.
58. Published in the *Illustrated Sunday Herald*, 8 February 1920: quoted in John Mann (ed), *Anti-Semitism: The Oldest Hatred*, London, Oxford, New York; Bloomsbury, 2015, p. 178.
59. It has recently been argued that 'anti-Semitism is a worldview, a conspiracy theory'. The use of the present tense, in 2019, is deliberate and sobering, though these views are rightly regarded as 'delusional and absurd': Deborah Lipstadt, *Antisemitism: Here and Now*, London: Scribe, 2019, pp. x, 7.
60. Herzl, pp. 17, 67.
61. Quoted in Sizer, p. 57.
62. *Memorandum on the Anti-Semitism of the Present (British) Government*, August 1917. https://www.jewishvirtuallibrary.org 24/2/19
63. Quoted in Norman Rose, p. 181.
64. Lloyd George, *Memoirs*.
65. Quoted in MacMillan, p. 391. Events of the last two decades suggest

that neither Britain nor the USA recognised the fallacious vacuity of Balfour's lofty assertion. Underlying the questionable strategic goals of the allied invasions of Afghanistan and Iraq was the continuing assumption that the West could 'tell the Muslim what he ought to think'. In view of the outcomes, it is hard – even for President Joe Biden – to see how western interests have been served.

66. Schneer, p. 340.
67. Quoted in Morris, p. 74.
68. Quoted in Shlaim, *Israel and Palestine*, p. 12.
69. Quoted in Michael Cohen, p. 51.
70. Quoted in Sizer, p. 56.
71. Michael Cohen, p. 49.
72. Quoted in MacMillan, p. 427.
73. Ilan Pappé, *Ten Myths about Israel*, London, Verso, 2017, p. 19.
74. Quoted in Michael Cohen, p. 63.
75. C.R. Ashbee, quoted in Segev, p. 5.
76. Jeffries, pp. 148, 149.
77. Quoted in Monroe, p. 39.
78. Quoted in Jeffries, p. 157.
79. Michael Cohen, p. 53.
80. MacMillan, p. 428.
81. Quoted in Norman Rose, p. 197.
82. Quoted in Morris, p. 75.
83. Segev, p. 194.
84. Quoted in Morris, pp. 75, 76.
85. Quoted in W. Khalidi, p. 225.
86. Quoted in Norman Rose, p. 183.
87. Quoted in Barbour, p. 65.
88. Said, pp. 15, 16. Italics original.
89. Jeffries, p. 210.
90. Quoted in Barbour, p. 107.
91. Monroe, p. 43.
92. Jeffries, p. 228.

Chapter Four

1. Yitzhak Epstein, 'The Hidden Question', https://www.balfourproject.org.

2. Notably, as it was interpreted among the Arabs, the earlier, 1915, pledge in McMahon's correspondence with Faisal. Also, terms of the Sykes-Picot Agreement with France.

3. Quoted in Gelvin, p. 87.

4. Quoted in Wasserstein, *The British in Palestine*, p. 32.

5. Quoted in Georgina Howell, *Queen of the Desert: The Extraordinary Life of Gertrude Bell*, London, Pan/Macmillan, 2006, p. 382.

6. Quoted in Wasserstein, *The British in Palestine*, p. 23.

7. Nafi, p. 96.

8. Quoted in Monroe, p. 49.

9. Quoted in Morris, p. 89.

10. Quoted in Kramer, p. 158.

11. Quoted in Morris, p. 91.

12. Letter to Lloyd George, quoted in Barr, p. 81.

13. https://wwi.lib.byu.edu 24/2/19.

14. http://www.atour.com/government/un/20040210f.html 25/2/19.

15. Jeffries, p. 317. J.M.N Jeffries (1880–1960) was an Irish-born journalist who became Middle East correspondent for *The Daily Mail*. His great work – 748 pages of text – incorporates a treasure-house of primary source material as well as the writer's consistently elegant if acerbic commentary on the British administration. However, its publication in the spring of 1939, by Longman's, was untimely and it remained largely neglected. Worse, the publisher's warehouse was bombed in the Blitz, in 1941, and copies of *Palestine: The Reality* were destroyed. For several decades, it remained scarcely known. It is estimated that fewer than twenty copies could be found in British public libraries by the end of the twentieth century. Olive Branch Press decided to reprint it to mark the centenary of the Balfour Declaration, the 'sham character and deceptive phraseology' – and doleful consequences – of which are its core subject matter.

16. Palin Report, April 1920, https://en.wikisource.org 25/2/19.

17. Jeffries, p. 439.

18. Quoted in Jeffries, p. 45.

19. Quoted in Norman Rose, p. 202.

20. Quoted in Michael Cohen, p. 68.

21. Quoted in Barbour, pp. 96, 97. The Zionist Commission began as a six-man delegation to Palestine, in early 1918 and evolved into an agency for managing the affairs of all Jews in Palestine under the British mandate.

22. Quoted in Segev, p. 63.

23. Quoted in Segev, p. 147.

24. Haycraft Commission Report, October 1921, https://ecf.org.il 25/2/19.

25. Quoted in Wasserstein, *The British in Palestine*, p. 110.

26. Quoted in Morris, p. 104.

27. Quoted in Wasserstein, *The British in Palestine*, p. 135. Italics added.

28. Quoted in Wasserstein, *The British in Palestine*, p. 136.

29. *Ibid.*

30. *Ibid.*

31. The British decision to execute the leaders of the short-lived rising was an enormous blunder. It turned them from unrepresentative adventurers into national martyrs. British imperial arrogance, short-sightedness and incompetence were not wholly confined in this period to their dealings with the Middle East.

32. MacMillan, p. 45.

33. Quoted in Rory Miller, '"An Oriental Ireland": Thinking about Palestine in Terms of the Irish Question during the Mandatory Era' in Rory Miller (ed.), *Britain, Palestine and Empire: The Mandate Years*, Farnham, England; Burlington VT, USA; Ashgate, 2010, p. 161.

34. Quoted in Wasserstein, *The British in Palestine*, pp. 106, 107.

35. Quoted in Wasserstein, *The British in Palestine*, p. 17.

36. Jeffries, p. 1.

37. *Palestine, Correspondence with the Arab Delegation and the Zionist Organisation*, Statement of Policy by HMG: Winston Churchill, White Paper https://israeled.org 25/2/19.

38. Dan Cohn-Sherbok and Dawoud El-Alami, *The Palestine-Israeli Conflict*, Oxford, Oneworld, 2001, p. 24.

39. British Mandate for Palestine, https://www.jewishvirtuallibrary.org 25/2/19.

40. Quoted in Jeffries, p. 597.

41. Italics added.

42. Quoted in Norman Rose, p. 217.

43. Quoted in Norman Rose, p. 219.

44. Quoted in Morris, p. 99.

45. Quoted in Michael Cohen, p. 62. 'Postponement' arose from American and French objections.

46. 14 July 1921. Quoted in Michael Cohen, p. 59.

47. Quoted in Nur Masalha, *Expulsion of the Palestinians: The Concept of*

'Transfer' in Zionist Political Thought, 1882–1948, Beirut, Institute for Palestine Studies, 1992, p. 15.

48. Quoted in Wasserstein, *The British in Palestine*, p. 114.

49. Krämer, p. 157.

50. 'The Importance of the Territorial Army', Major John K. Dunlop, 1933. Printed by J. Salmon, Sevenoaks. Copy in possession of author.

51. Segev, p. 92.

52. Reported in Segev, pp. 198, 201.

53. Wasserstein, *The British in Palestine*, p. 9.

54. Britain's pursuit of mandatory control over Iraq, despite a huge Arab revolt against its occupation at the close of the First World War, had always been driven by an appetite for whatever oil Iraq might yield. Oil was at last struck in Northern Iraq in 1927. Wrangling with the French ended with agreement in 1930 that Haifa (by now in Mandated Palestine) would be the Mediterranean terminus for the oil pipeline 'and the railway that was supposed to accompany it'. Barr, pp. 158, 163.

55. Sykes, p. 269.

56. Quoted in Said, pp. 27, 28.

57. Reported in Segev, p. 109.

58. Shavit, p. 18.

59. Quoted in Avi Shlaim, *War and Peace in the Middle East: A Concise History*, London, Penguin, 1995, p. 15. No date is given for 'one of the few honest remarks on the subject'.

60. Sykes, p. 280.

61. Jeffries, p. 446.

62. Shavit, p. 413.

63. Barbour, p. 159.

64. J.C. Scott, Seeing Like a State, Yale University Press, 1998. Scott studies the tendency of twentieth-century states to make policy, and pursue it, in defiance of local realities. British rule in Palestine appears to be a case of what he terms 'tragic episodes of state-initiated social engineering' (p. 4).

65. Quoted in Segev, p. 94.

66. Quoted in Norman Rose, p. 193.

67. Quoted in Scott Berg, *Wilson*, London, New York; Simon & Schuster, 2013, p. 528.

68. Quoted in Norman Rose, p. 201.

69. By this time, Congress had overruled Wilson regarding American

membership of the League of Nations.

70. Quoted in Segev, pp. 194, 195.

71. Quoted in Segev, p. 175.

72. Jeffries, p. 31.

73. Quoted in MacMillan, pp. 425, 427.

74. Quoted in MacMillan, pp. 421, 423.

75. Barbour, pp. 152, 159.

76. Barbour, p. 150.

Chapter Five

1. Herbert Samuel, 1921, quoted in Harry Luke and Edward Keith-Roach (eds), *The Handbook of Palestine*, London, Macmillan, 1922, p. 27.

2. Palestine was indeed 'small', being roughly the size of Wales, or New Jersey, and much of it, up to half, was all but uninhabitable. NB The 'Wales' comparison was already being used in the 1920s (for example by the *Encyclopaedia Britannica*).

3. A Kentucky businessman, Colonel Clifford Nadaud, exported barrels of Jordan river water (authenticated by the American consulate in Jerusalem) for use in Christian baptisms.

4. Krämer, p. 135.

5. Shlomo Ben-Ami, *Scars of War, Wounds of Peace: The Israel-Arab Tragedy*, London, Weidenfeld & Nicolson/Phoenix, 2005, p. 2. David Ben-Gurion: 1886, born in Poland; 1906, visited Palestine, engaged in agricultural labour and activism; 1919, head of Labour Zionist movement; 1921–35, General Secretary of *Histadrut* (Zionist Labour Federation); 1936, head of Jewish Agency; 1937, accepted 'partition'; 1948, first Prime Minister of Israel.

6. Notice once more the British colonial formula. For reasons covered elsewhere, no such legislative council came into being during the mandate years.

Chapter Six

1. Albert Einstein, 1929, quoted in Walter Isaacson, *Einstein: His Life and Universe*, London, New York, Pocket Books, 2007, p. 381.

2. Quoted in Wasserstein, *The British in Palestine*, p. 88.

3. Quoted in Wasserstein, *The British in Palestine*, pp. 78, 79.

4. Quoted in Segev, p. 192.
5. Stein, p. 213. Italics added.
6. Jeffries, p. 605.
7. Quoted in Wasserstein, *The British in Palestine*, p. 124.
8. 1937 Peel Report.
9. Quoted in Jeffries, p. 611. Italics added.
10. Jeffries, p. 610.
11. Quoted in Wasserstein, *The British in Palestine*, p. 128.
12. Klein, pp. 115, 116.
13. https://www.jewishvirtuallibrary.org 24/2/19.
14. Shlaim, *The Iron Wall*, p. 17.
15. 'Indirect' rule had many variants, in theory and practice, throughout the British Empire. Some were more 'indirect' than others. In a number of locations, British imperial officials recognised – where they found them, and found them willing to accept British overrule – not only existing authorities but also complete indigenous social and political systems. 'Indirect rule' was relatively cheap and minimised (costly) confrontation. In Palestine the British used long-established Arab families and individuals as intermediaries, while, in the districts, *mukhtars* (village headmen, inherited from the Ottoman period) had responsibility for order, revenue collection and registration. But British rule remained more 'direct' over the Arab majority – especially in the absence of a legislative council or Arab Agency – than over an increasingly autonomous Jewish *yishuv*.
16. Quoted in Morris, p. 105.
17. Nafi, p. 92.
18. Krämer, p. 221.
19. Quoted in Zachary Lockman, 'Railway Workers and Relational History: Arabs and Jews in British-ruled Palestine', in Ilan Pappé (ed), *The Israel/Palestine Question* (Rewriting Histories), London, New York; Routledge, 1999, p. 109.
20. Stein, p. 215.
21. The 1858 Land Code was an Ottoman reform that had long-lasting and unintended consequences. It recognised for the first-time *private* ownership of former state or communal land. Individuals could *register as their own* the lands they cultivated, and thereby assume the tax burden (which was the point of the reform). In practice, village chiefs were well placed to register land in their own names, while

urban notables (responsible for implementing the reform) managed to acquire much property as absentee landlords. For them, land was a financial investment, not an economic or even emotional attachment. Given eager buyers, they would sell.

22. Hillel Cohen, *Army of Shadows: Palestinian Collaboration with Zionism, 1917–1948*, Berkeley, Los Angeles, London; University of California, 2008, pp. 3, 4.

23. Stein, p. 66.

24. The Western ('Wailing') Wall, revered by Jews as the only remnant of Herod's Temple destroyed in 70 ad, adjoins the location where the Prophet Muhammad is believed by Muslims to have tied the animal (*Buraq*) which he rode on the night of his ascension.

25. Chancellor Papers, box 13.

26. Quoted in Segev, p. 307.

27. Chancellor Papers, box 13.

28. Quoted in Morris, p. 116.

29. Masalha, p. 32.

30. Quoted in Stein, p. 105.

31. Michael Cohen, p. 86.

32. Lord Passfield (Sidney Webb): Colonial Secretary in Ramsay MacDonald's Labour Government of 1929–31.

33. Palestine, Statement of Policy by HMG [Passfield, White Paper] https://www.jewishvirtuallibrary.org 24/2/19.

34. Chancellor, note of the interview, 17/7/30.

35. https://www.jewishvirtuallibrary.org 24/2/19.

36. Quoted in Norman Rose, p. 282.

37. Quoted in Norman Rose, p. 285.

38. Michael Cohen, p. 89; Norman Rose, p. 285.

39. Quoted in Morris, p. 122.

40. Chancellor Papers: 12/03/1931.

41. Quoted in Segev, p. 381.

42. Letter to son, Chancellor Papers: 13/1/30.

43. Telegram to Secretary of State, Chancellor Papers: 30/8/29.

44. Telegram to Secretary of State, Chancellor Papers: 14/10/29.

45. Notes of interview with PM, Chancellor Papers: 17/7/30.

46. Italics added.

47. However, Chancellor's proposals echo those of Wyndham Deedes in 1921.

48. Letter to his son, Chancellor Papers: 6/10/29.

49. Notes of interview with PM, Chancellor Papers: 17/7/30.

50. Speech, Chancellor Papers: 29/8/31.

51. Telegram to Secretary of State, Chancellor Papers: 14/10/29.

52. Chancellor Papers: 17/2/30.

53. Letter, Chancellor Papers: 25/10/29.

54. Notes of interview with PM, Chancellor Papers: 17/7/30.

55. Letter to son, Chancellor Papers: 14/10/29.

56. Letter, Chancellor Papers: 21/2/30.

57. Chancellor Papers: 26/8/31.

58. Letter to son, Chancellor Papers: 18/10/29.

59. Himadeh, Sa'id B. (ed) (1938) *Economic Organisation of Palestine* p.24; reproduced in Kramer, p. 241.

60. Quoted in Wasserstein, *The British in Palestine*, p. 18.

61. W. Khalidi, Appendix I, pp. 841, 842.

62. In an attempt to preserve an ideal of US homogeneity, the Act limited the number of immigrants *per annum* to 2 per cent of the total number of individuals of each respective nationality according to the census of 1890, a quarter of a century earlier. The quota for Germany was set at 51,000; but for Poland it was 6,000 and for Russia just 2,000. The favoured nationalities, regarded as racially most acceptable, were those of Western and Northern Europe.

63. W. Khalidi, pp. 853–55.

64. Michael Cohen, p. 80.

65. Michael Cohen, p. 90.

66. Quoted in Barbour, p. 150.

67. Quoted in Barr, p. 167.

68. Gelvin, p. 106.

69. Stein, pp. 214, 215.

70. Klein, p. 122.

71. Stein, p. 221.

72. Sir John Chancellor, notes of interview with the PM, 17/7/30.

73. Nafi, p. 121.

74. Philip Mattar, *The Mufti of Jerusalem: Al-Haj Amin Al-Husayni and the Palestinian National Movement*, New York. Columbia University Press, 1988, p. 67. Al-Qassam came to be regarded as a martyr by many. And, half a century later, the military wing of Hamas was to adopt his name as the al-Qassam brigade.

75. Rashid Khalidi, p. 80.
76. Mattar, p. 31.
77. Mattar, p. 71.
78. Quoted in Mattar, p. 71.
79. Quoted in Nafi, p. 197.
80. Field Marshal Sir Cyril Deverell, quoted in Barr, p. 173.
81. Quoted in Matthew Hughes, 'Lawlessness was the Law: British Armed Forces, the Legal System and the Repression of the Arab Revolt in Palestine, 1936–1939', in Rory Miller, *Britain, Palestine and Empire*, p. 149.
82. Members brought considerable relevant experience to the commission. As British high commissioner to Constantinople, its vice-chairman, Sir Horace Rumbold, had signed the Lausanne Treaty which finally brought peace with Turkey in July 1923. Thereafter he had served as Ambassador to Madrid and then to Berlin where he produced a penetrating early assessment of Hitler as Chancellor. Sir Morris Carter had been Chief Justice in Uganda and had chaired investigations into land issues both in that protectorate and also in the colonies of Southern Rhodesia and Kenya (in each case sympathising with the interests of white settlers rather than those of indigenous Africans). Sir Harold Morris had considerable experience of managing conflict, as chairman of the industrial court in Britain. Sir Laurie Hammond had been a provincial governor in India. Lastly, Reginald Coupland, Fellow of All Souls, and Beit Professor of Colonial History at Oxford, had unparalleled expertise in colonial administration.
83. *Mandates Palestine Report* of the Palestine Royal Commission, Earl Peel, 7 July 1937. https://www.jewishvirtuallibrary.org 24/2/19.
84. Iraq became independent in 1932; the French and Syrians negotiated an independence treaty in 1936.
85. There were comparable Catholic, nationalist minorities within the Six Counties of Northern Ireland after partition there in 1921. They were not 'transferred' to the new Irish Free State.
86. The commissioners had in mind a recent case of a successful exchange, between the Greek and Turkish populations following the war of 1922. A convention had been signed by the two governments; and the task had been supervised by the League of Nations. The numbers involved had been far higher than those in Palestine in 1937.
87. Quoted in Morris, p. 142.

88. Italics added.

89. 'Lawlessness was the law' – Hughes, p. 141.

90. Quoted in Hughes, pp. 143, 144.

91. Estimates range from 6,000 men (Nafi, p. 264) to 14,000 (Hughes, p. 155).

92. Quoted in Segev, p. 416.

93. Rashid Khalidi, p. 108. Some leaders of the Arab Revolt were interned in the Seychelles. This distant, isolated, imperial outpost – in the Indian Ocean, 900 miles off the coast of Africa – had already accommodated recalcitrant local agents of British 'indirect rule' and was to do so again. For example, the British had exiled African kings to the islands at the turn of the century: Mwanga II of Buganda was sent in 1899; and Prempeh I of the Ashanti arrived the following year. Archbishop Makarios of Cyprus, another would-be intermediary/liberator of his country, was removed to the Seychelles decades later in 1956.

94. F.L. Lucas, letter to *The Daily Telegraph*, 25 July 1935.

95. Quoted in Walid Khalidi, pp. 367, 368.

96. *Palestine*, Statement of Policy by HMG [Malcolm MacDonald, White Paper] https://www.jewishvirtuallibrary.org 24/2/19.

97. Note the conditional tense, and that 'good government' remained the elusive aspiration.

98. Michael Cohen, p. 93.

99. Italics added.

100. Italics added.

101. These and following figures, from the US Holocaust Memorial Museum website: https://encyclopaedia.ushmm.org

102. Quoted in Segev, p. 440.

103. Susan Pedersen, 'The Impact of League Oversight on British Policy in Palestine', in Rory Miller, *Britain, Palestine and Empire*, p. 41.

Chapter Seven

1. Albert Einstein, 1946, quoted in Isaacson, p. 520.

2. Mattar, p. 104.

3. Vital, p. 881.

4. 'Evian Conference', *This Month in Holocaust History: July*, Yad Vashem, Jerusalem: www. yadvashem.org/about_holocaust/month_in_holocaust/july/july_lexicon/evian_conference.html

5. Quoted in Vital, p. 886.

6. Quoted in Vital, p. 895.

7. Quoted in Vital, p. 888. Italics added.

8. Quoted in Vital, p. 889.

9. Gabriel Gorodetsky (ed.), *The Maisky Diaries*, Newhaven, Yale University Press, 2016, pp. 329–31.

10. https://www.jewishvirtuallibrary.org 24/2/19.

11. Quoted in Laqueur, p. 404. The ACJ still exists.

12. Segev, p. 465.

13. Quoted in Segev, p. 460. MacDonald had introduced and so attached his name to the White Paper of 1939. He was the first in a sequence of seven Colonial Secretaries (with responsibility for Palestine) in as many years.

14. Quoted in Segev, p. 495.

15. Hansard, Palestine Conference, House of Commons Debate, 18 February 1947. Balfour had died in 1930. Lloyd George lived almost long enough to witness the debacle but died in March 1945.

Chapter Eight

1. Nathan Weinstock, *Zionism: False Messiah*, London: Pluto, 1989, p. 89.

2. Report of the United Nations Special Committee on Palestine, 3 September 1947 https://www.jewishvirtuallibrary.org 25/2/19.

3. Quoted in Morris, p. 79.

4. During this time, the strategically important but otherwise insignificant Arab village of Deir Yassin was destroyed. Many of its residents, including whole families, were slaughtered by Irgun and 'Stern Gang' forces (subsequently condemned by the Haganah leadership and the Jewish Agency). This event, of 9 April, stirred much controversy, then and later. What is certain is that it had an immediate, profound and demoralising effect on Palestinian Arabs. Just four days later, Arabs attacked a Jewish convoy carrying mainly medical personnel and killed more than seventy. This was revenge, but it did nothing to diminish Arab apprehensions.

5. Egypt, Syria, Iraq, Lebanon, Saudi Arabia, Transjordan, Yemen.

6. Historically there is little room for doubt here. In May 1941, Winston Churchill, the British Prime Minister, approved an Irgun plan to

assassinate the Mufti, but only after Abdullah had proposed a similar step.

7. Morris, p. 214. 'Were driven from or fled from' touches on a major and continuing issue of debate.

8. 'The Hidden Question'.

9. The 1956 Suez Crisis arose from the invasion of Egypt by Israel, after Egypt's ruler General Gamal Abdel Nasser nationalised the Suez Canal. Britain and France demanded a ceasefire. This ultimatum being ignored, their own forces invaded (by prior, secret, arrangement with the government of Israel). Egyptians blocked the canal, but their armed forces were defeated. Political pressure from the USA (and USSR) forced the withdrawal of the allied invasion forces.

10. See Rashid Khalidi, *The Hundred Years' War on Palestine*, London, 2020, p. 104.

11. Wasserstein, *Israel and Palestine*, pp. 125, 126.

12. Shlaim, *Israel and Palestine*, p. 32.

13. Even so, 242 was not even-handed. Representing a 'new tolerance for Israeli territorial gains', it 'distilled the views of the United States and Israel' and reflected the weakened position of the Arab states. Khalidi, *Hundred Years*, pp. 104, 105.

14. Wasserstein, *Israel and Palestine*, p. 25.

Chapter Nine

1. Chomsky, p. 57.

2. Bernard Wasserstein, book review, *The Spectator*, 7 October 2017.

3. Quoted in Eugene Rogan and Avi Shlaim, *The War for Palestine: Rewriting the History of 1948*, Cambridge, Cambridge University Press, 2001, p. 207.

4. Hillel Cohen, *Year Zero*, p. 18.

5. Hertzberg, p. 15.

6. Hillel Cohen, *Year Zero*, p. 18.

7. Said, p. 71.

8. Norman Rose, p. 64. Italics added.

9. Daniel Walker Howe, *What Hath God Wrought: The Transformation of America, 1815–1848*, Oxford, Oxford University Press, 2007, p. 705.

10. Robert Walker, President Polk's Secretary of the Treasury, 1847, quoted in Howe p. 704.

11. Quoted in Howe, p. 706.
12. Quoted in John M. Blum, *The National Experience: A History of the United States of America*, Belmont CA, Wadsworth, 1993, pp. 284, 285.
13. Masalha, p.25.
14. Quoted in Masalha, pp. 11, 12.
15. Quoted in Masalha, p. 10.
16. Quoted in Masalha, p. 37.
17. Quoted in Walid Khalidi, p. 92.
18. William Gilmore Simms, quoted in Howe, p. 704.
19. Shlaim, *Israel and Palestine*, p. 25.
20. Ben-Ami, pp. xii, 1, 6. Ben-Ami describes himself as an ardent Zionist.
21. *The Times*, 17 May 2018.
22. Chomsky and Pappé, p. 13.
23. Quoted in Morris, p. 122.
24. Hillel Cohen, *Year Zero*, p. 19.
25. Ben-Gurion, the first Prime Minister, had created the IDF; four of the next six prime ministers had been active in Haganah or Irgun; the four most recent include a chief of general staff and a former major-general.
26. La Guardia, pp. 106, 107.
27. Hertzberg, p. 96.

Conclusion

1. Ber Borochov, Ukrainian, one of the founders of Zionism, 1906. Quoted in Hertzberg, p. 364.
2. Achcar, pp. 31–32.
3. Morris, p. 161.
4. Wasserstein, Israel and Palestine, p. 24.
5. Quoted in Segev, p. 394.
6. Ben-Ami, p. 591. Also sobering is that 'catastrophe' is the term used by Palestinians to describe their experience of 1947–49.
7. Quoted in Morris, p. 172. From the Alexandria Protocol of the foundation meeting of the Arab League.
8. History Art and Archives, US House of Representatives website: https://history.house.gov
9. Achcar, p. 26.
10. It should be noted that there have been exceptions to nimbyism as a political tool. In 1972, for example, Prime Minister Edward Heath

announced (in the face of some popular opposition) that Britain would accept any East African Asians fleeing Idi Amin's Uganda who could not find refuge elsewhere.

11. Erskine B. Childers, 'Palestine: The Broken Triangle', in Journal of International Affairs, Vol. XIX, No 1, 1965.

12. Hattersley, p. 455.

13. Said, p. 57.

14. Arthur Koestler, *Bricks to Babel: Selected Writings*, London, Picador, 1980, pp. 41, 42.

15. Walid Khalidi, p. xxiii.

16. Rashid Khalidi, p. 51.

Afterword

1. Andrew Roberts, *Salisbury: Victorian Titan*, London, 1999, p. 71.

2. *The Young Lloyd George*, London, 1973, p. 260.

3. Roy Hattersley, *David Lloyd George: The Great Outsider*, London, 2010, p.300.

4. www.nationalists.org/library/daily-express/lloydgeorge-hitler.html (Accessed 6 September 2021.)

5. Ian Rutledge, *Enemy on the Euphrates: The Battle for Iraq 1914–1921*, London, 2014, p. xxiii.

6. Following extracts taken from respective websites on 4 September 2021.

7. bbc.co.uk/news/world-middle-east - 14628835

8. bbc.co.uk/news/newssheet – 44124396

9. bbc.co.uk/news/magazine – 36160928

10. Thus, Ken Livingstone is presented as anti-Semitic for claiming that the Nazis supported Zionism before the Second World War. The accusation was as flawed as Livingstone's response was inarticulate. They did. In 1933, the Ha'avara ('Transfer') agreement was made. German Zionists, along with Zionists in Palestine, arranged with the Nazi Government for the emigration – with their assets – of Jews from Germany to Palestine. 60,000 Jews (approximately 10 per cent of all Germany's Jews) are estimated to have benefited from a deal which suited both parties: the Nazis did not want the Jews, the Zionists in Palestine did. In 1940, further deals over exit permits suited both the Reich Central Bureau for Jewish Emigration, headed by Adolf Eichmann, and the

Jewish Agency based in Palestine. See David Vital, *A People Apart: A Political History of the Jews in Europe 1789–1939*, Oxford, Oxford University Press, 1999, pp 864–866; Bernard Wasserstein, *Britain and the Jews of Europe 1939–1945*, London and New York, 1999, p. 38.

INDEX

Page numbers in bold refer to tables; page numbers in italics refer to illustrations; 'n' after a page number indicates the endnote number.